TT Topics & Tales

Other Books by David Wright

Travelling Marshals at the TT & MGP
TT Mixture
Vincents, HRDs and the Isle of Man
Vincent - The Complete Story
Vincent and HRD Motorcycles

TT Topics & Tales

David Wright

Amulree Publications of Laxey

TT Topics & Tales

ISBN: 1 901508 09 9

Published by Amulree Publications
Lossan y Twoaie
Glen Road
Laxey
Isle of Man
IM4 7AN

www.amulree.com

CONTENTS

Introduction

In the 100 years that motorcycles have competed over Manx roads for the Tourist Trophy, the racing has provided high adventure for riders, given ultra-close-up excitement to generations of spectators, been a source of fascination to those who have been forced to follow the event from afar, and generated many, many, stories.

With the centenary of the races upon us, **'TT Topics & Tales'** takes 100 TT-related topics and recounts the light-hearted, the serious and, in some cases, the unbelievable events that have occurred during that century of racing. Written to entertain the reader, amongst the items covered are: 'Bending the Rules', 'Brushes with the Law', 'Learning the Course', 'Near Misses', 'Oversize Engines', 'Scrutineering', 'Speeds', 'Triumph and Tragedy', 'TT Tipples', and many others covering the experiences of riders, spectators and organisers from 1907 to date.

Because the TT races are unique in so many ways, a read of **'TT Topics & Tales'** is guaranteed to bring a flood of memories for established fans of Manx racing, whilst showing those who are new to the event just how and why it has been considered the supreme road race for 100 years - yielding great races, great riders and great stories.

With the Manx Grand Prix race for amateurs being run over the same Isle of Man Mountain Course as the TT for over 80 years, a few of the 'too good to miss' stories generated by MGP riders are also included.

Acknowledgments

I have been fortunate to call upon the TT memories of many people and I thank them all for their assistance. Direct help has been sought and received from Alan Brodrick, Geoff Cannell, Ralph Crellin, Wyn Evans, Peter Murray, Bill Snelling, Dr David Stevens, MBE, and Paul Wright.

Some 350 illustrations are provided to supplement and enhance the text of 'TT Topics & Tales' and that would not have been possible without the help of Vic Bates, Ron Clarke of Manx Racing Photography, FoTTofinders, Steve Colvin, Mannin Collections, Ken Smith, John Watterson, and the work of unknown photographers of long ago.

Ruth Sutherland designed the cover, whilst the layout of the contents and preparation of the book for printing was carried out by Bill Snelling of Amulree Publications.

David Wright
Peel, Isle of Man

CHAPTER 1

TALES OF . . .

ACHIEVING AMBITIONS

The first Tourist Trophy (TT) race for motorcycles in 1907 was in itself the fulfilment of an ambition by a band of enthusiasts to create a competitive event for touring machines. They were concerned at the way in which racing motorcycles were developing in the early 1900s, where out-and-out speed seemed to be the sole objective, and ever larger and more powerful engines were fitted into spindly frames to be raced on special tracks. That approach was at odds with what those TT pioneers wanted, for although in their event the competing motorcycles would certainly have sporting pretensions, they would be fitted with reasonable-sized engines, proper mudguards, silencers, have respectable fuel consumption, and be capable of running over the ordinary roads of the day in competition for a Tourist Trophy.

After the first TT in 1907 the message went around the world of motorcycling that here was an event that was something special, and riders and manufacturers made big efforts to take part. Indian sent bikes from America in 1908 and later shocked the European manufacturers by taking the first three places in the 1911 Senior with their advanced chain-driven, two-speeders. Reflecting the TT's growth in popularity, entries grew from 25 in 1907 to 160 in 1914, after which the event was at a standstill for 5 years due to the First World War. When the races returned in 1920 they continued to be organised by the Auto-Cycle Union (ACU), who controlled most motorcycle sport in Britain. Along with the Manx authorities, the ACU recognised the wider publicity to be gained from having foreign riders competing, and in the 1920s it encouraged those from abroad who wished to race at the TT, even providing modest financial support by about 1930.

The original Tourist Trophy, donated by the Marquis de Mouzilly St Mars, now presented to the winner of the Senior TT

Although foreign competitors had become fairly common by the late 1920s, it still required a special effort by Kenzo Tada to realise his dream and travel from Japan to ride a Velocette into thirteenth place in the Junior race of 1930. He rode in company with competitors from Austria, Belgium, Egypt, Hungary, Iraq, South Africa and Sweden, as well as from all parts of Britain.

It was not just foreign racers who wanted to get to the TT, for the wish to visit the races was shared by far-flung members of the motorcycle trade and by ordinary spectators.

Distinguished Australian motorcycle engineer Phil Irving came to Britain overland on the back of a sidecar outfit, and was later involved with Velocette, Vincent, AJS, Brabham cars, etc. He recorded his first Island visit in 1931 in his autobiography, writing: *'All too often the fulfilment of a cherished dream falls far short of its anticipation, but in this instance arrival on the Island more than lived up to my expectations'.* He was impressed with the freedom with which spectators could get close to the action and, in particular, mentioned that: *'at the popular Highlander Hotel, there was nothing between the riders and the customers but the glasses of Manx ale held in their hands'.*

Another overseas visitor was Jock Leyden, a talented South African artist who was a fan of motorcycle racing in his home country and was keen to see what he called *'the cream of the world's road racing men pitted against each other in the International TT Races'.* In 1933 he got the opportunity to do so, paying part of the cost of his visit to the Island by providing sketches from the event for the press.

Jock Leyden's vivid sketch of Ginger Wood descending Bray Hill on his Jawa during the 1933 Senior TT.

In language of the time, Jock described his TT visit and experiences: *'The Isle of Man is sighted, and there starts the most enjoyable fortnight any motorcyclist could wish to pass . . . up at 4.00 am to watch the practising from various vantage points, seeing the new and untried machines, hearing stable gossip, and, in the refreshment tents, tales of blown-up motors, scraps and escapades on mist enshrouded Snaefell. Mornings spent in the camps examining the TT motors under the eagle eyes of ever-watchful mechanics; questions asked and evasively answered; lap times discussed; the weighing-in ceremonies watched with interest; all this in an atmosphere peculiar to the IOM TT'.* Jock Leyden immersed himself in the many behind-the-scenes activities that few spectators bother to seek out, and found it immensely interesting, saying: *'The practising period preceding the races meant more to me than the actual races. If I had gone on a day excursion to see the Senior Race it is certain that I would have come away unsatisfied'.* He went on: *'Brilliant riding, marvellous organisation, exceptional surfaces, stupendous crowds. The TT . . . A life-long dream realised!'*

The TT and the 'amateur' Manx Grand Prix (MGP) meetings have allowed riders to fulfil their racing dreams for a relatively uninterrupted 100 years. Major global conflicts have stopped the events and interfered with racing plans, but riders were usually determined enough to hold on to their racing dreams. A young clubman named Nigel Seymour Smith was typical of those who had to put his Island racing career on hold. Fitting in just a couple of mainland races before war broke out in 1939, Nigel had to wait 7 long years before he was able to fulfil his ambition to race on the Island, in his case in the MGP. Mounted on his 1936 Vincent Series A 'TT Replica' and wearing riding kit that he described as: *'a Cromwell helmet, bought in 1939 for thirty shillings from Lewis's of Carburton Street, racing leather jacket and breeches from Marble Arch Supplies, price two pounds ten shillings, and army despatch rider lace-up boots',* Nigel finally got his MGP ride in 1946 and was a regular for several years thereafter.

Kenzo Tada, the first Japanese rider to compete in a TT. Tada was later to be Japanese delegate in the FIM and was instrumental in Honda's entrance in TT and GP racing.

With its International appeal long-established, the TT has always been a magnet to riders from the former British colonies, and a typical example was Australian Eric 'Mouse' McPherson. In 1948 he travelled 13,000 miles for the pleasure of competing. Spending four weeks on a steamer to Marseilles, he then travelled overland to the Island, arriving almost a week before practice started in order to familiarise himself with the Course. Names that he and other antipodean racers had only read about came to life as Braddan Bridge, Ballacraine, Ballaugh Bridge and Parliament Square passed under his wheels on learning laps of the challenging Mountain Course. Come the first official practice session and 'Mouse' put in a steady opening lap, but on the second he took a simple fall at the ultra-slow Governor's Bridge, damaging his pelvis and putting himself out of the race. His long-cherished dream of a TT ride was not to be fulfilled in 1948 but, undaunted, he made similar journeys in 1949 & 50 to ride and record creditable performances in both Junior and Senior races.

Today's TT and MGP organisers look carefully at past race experience before deciding whether to accept rider entries, but they were not always quite so strict. John Davies was a Newcomer to the MGP in 1972 (at the age of 36) and although he had previously raced sidecars, he had not raced solos. However, his entry on a rather long-in-the-tooth 1956 Manx Norton was accepted for the Junior race. Not only was John short of solo racing experience he was also short of riding practice. In his words: *'For various reasons I did not have the opportunity to ride or even start the machine before the morning practice and, to be honest, I had not ridden even a road machine for 18 months and then only for a weekend trip'*. But by the end of practice he had completed 17 laps and had also: *'achieved part of my life's ambition - 114 mph past The Highlander - qualified'*. During one of his practice sessions he had a float-chamber mounting break, so he stopped at Hilberry, borrowed some wool from a lady who sat knitting on the bank, made a temporary repair and continued. It was rather like the occasion in the 1947 Clubman's TT when Triumph-mounted Jack Cannell used his bootlaces to tie the carburettors in place after the Triumph works mechanics had *'looked over'* the bike for him and forgotten to tighten the carbs.

The ambition of solo riders to compete in the TT is matched by many sidecar drivers and passengers. After a hesitant and poorly supported debut by three-wheelers in the 1920s it was another 30 years before they returned to establish themselves as part of the TT meeting. From the time of their return (1954) the long-running publication 'The TT Special' usually found room to report in detail on three-wheelers matters. That was particularly so in the 70s and 80s when the Editor was Fred Hanks, a former Sidecar racer (and scion of the Hanks clan of charioteers). The 1976 issue told of one particular sidecar man who waited a long time for his dream of TT success to come true, saying: *'Having ridden in fifteen TT races, Mick Burns, who on this occasion was passenger to Mac Hobson, had almost despaired of ever finishing in a race yet alone collecting a silver replica. But on Monday his fortunes changed when he finished third in the 500cc Sidecar race and on Wednesday he achieved what must surely be the ambition of every passenger - a win in the 1000cc'.*

Mac Hobson (right) and passenger Mick Burns collect the victors spoils after the 1976 Sidecar TT.

Another sidecar exponent who had to wait a long time for a win was driver Mick Boddice. After 14 years of trying, and many near misses, he powered his way to victory in 1983 - the first of many. Some people felt that the name of Boddice was overdue being inscribed on the Sidecar Trophy, for

Mick's father, Bill, achieved podium places with Norton outfits in the 1950s, but never quite a win. (Mick's son, Mick Boddice Jnr, has also raced an outfit at the TT.)

Whatever their dreams, most people have to resign themselves to the fact that they are never going to put in a racing lap of the TT Course, and amongst them was a member of long-time TT sidecar racer Kenny Howles support team. His greatest wish over a number of years was to accompany Kenny for a lap in the chair - something that, for several reasons, he was unlikely to achieve. But, surprisingly, his dream did come true in 2003, even though he died in 2002! With special permission from the organisers, Kenny took his team-mate's ashes on a high-speed run during practice, so giving him the elusive lap that he had wished for.

A mid-race wheelie for Nick Jefferies as he powers his Castrol Honda away from Sulby Bridge.

After the initial fulfilment of their dreams to ride and finish in the TT, the aspirations of most riders turn to the winning of a Silver Replica, whilst those with major talent set their sights on a race win. No one doubted the pedigree or ability of Nick Jefferies as he raced through the 1980s and early 90s but, although a regular leader board finisher, a TT win eluded him. He had already made his name in Manxland by winning the famous off-road Two-Day Trial and had shown his tarmac ability with victory in the Senior MGP, but even though he claimed that he only rode for the enjoyment, what seemingly easy-going Nick really wanted was a TT win. It was the notoriously focused ex-TT winner Phil Read who once told him: *'If you are still enjoying yourself as much as you say you are, then you're probably not going fast enough'.* Perhaps Read's words hit the spot, because Nick, good enough to get 'works' bikes from Honda, eventually fulfilled his wish for TT victory with success in the opening Formula 1 race of the 1993 meeting.

Multiple TT winners and lap record breakers like Steve Hislop and Philip McCallen would appear to have had little left in terms of TT aspirations before they ended their Island racing careers. But both shared an unfulfilled dream, and that was to win a TT on a 250cc machine. Both came near, but both missed out.

In contrast to the likes of Hislop and McCallen who each rode hundreds of laps of the Mountain Course and took eleven victories apiece, often in fully supported 'works' rider roles, there are many who are prepared to commit all their resources to get just one TT ride. In 2000, two Argentinians, Walter Cordoba and David Paredes realised boyhood dreams to race on the Island. Walter explained: *'When I was a kid, I watched videos and magazines telling incredible stories of the TT and I always dreamed to be there one day'.*

Walter Cordoba and David Paredes were regular TT competitors when this photograph was taken in 2004.

From the countless thousands of motorcyclists who dream of taking part in a TT race over the famous Isle of Man Mountain Course, or in its 'amateur' version the MGP, only a select few get to fulfil their ambitions. Long gone are the relatively casual days when, if you had a motorcycle and wanted to race, you submitted an entry and you were in. Nowadays, a racer has to be immensely keen to overcome all the obstacles on the road to TT competition. Licensing, medical clearance, proven race experience, expensive machinery, ability to lap within prescribed qualifying times, plus a race-transporter, back-up team, substantial finance (or a sponsor with very deep pockets), months of planning, etc, are just a few of the problems to be overcome. But overcome them they do, for road-racers are not the sort of people to be denied their ambitions.

ADVERTISING

The racing of motorcycles has attracted strong interest from motorcyclists down the years, even though the majority are forced to accept that the skill, endeavour and finance required to race is beyond what they can muster. Certainly the dash and bravery of racers like the Collier brothers, Stanley Woods, Howard Davies, Jimmy Guthrie, Freddie Frith, Geoff Duke, Mike Hailwood, Joey Dunlop, Steve Hislop, David Jefferies and John McGuinness have made lasting impressions on the ordinary motorcyclist, and fans of every era have held the stars of their day in high regard. Motorcycle manufacturers and the suppliers of associated components quickly realised that the ordinary road-going riders' appreciation of the stars could easily be extended to appreciation (and purchase) of their products, if they could arrange for timely advertising linked to racing successes.

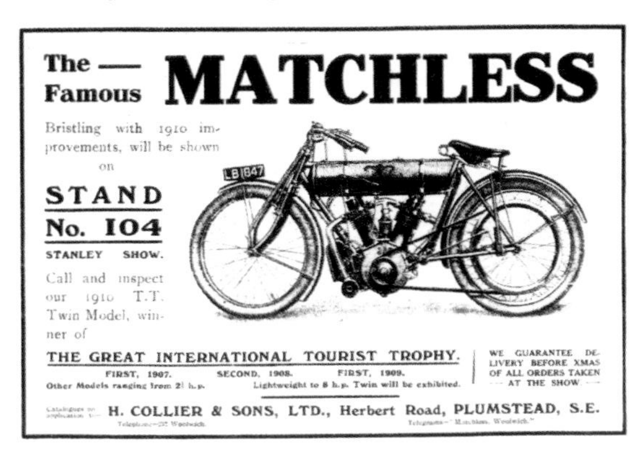

How the Matchless concern used TT success in their advertising for 1910.

Dunlop were associated with the very first motorcycle TT in 1907, when they gave out hundreds of coloured balloons and provided a finishing arch decorated with a Dunlop banner. Since then they have found it worthwhile to maintain their association with the races for most of the last 100 years. The TT races have also been supported by many motorcycle dealers, who provide much of the expensive race machinery that competitors would not otherwise be able to afford.

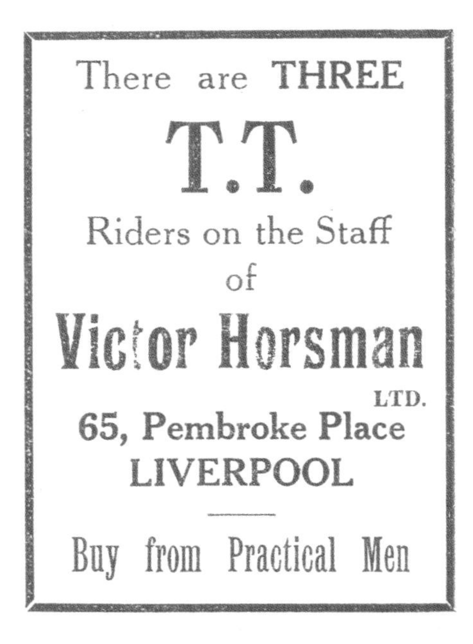

Liverpool dealer Victor Horsman sought to associate themselves with the TT in a slightly unusual way. They also advertised that their staff would buy and sell bikes on the Island at TT time - so combining a little business with a lot of pleasure.

Successful racing firms like Norton and Velocette advertised their TT wins because they were justifiably proud of them, but they also received publicity from the advertising of their many component suppliers. Items like sparking plugs, magnetos, tyres, carburettors, brake linings, chains, plus the petrol and oil used by winning machines received full page advertising in the motorcycle press. Also, and coming on a scale that money just could not buy, there was a huge amount of free publicity for makers from the detailed race reports and results published in newspapers world-wide. Such reports and results are still published, but not on the scale of earlier days, when it was said that the man in the street was as keen to hear the result of the Senior TT as he was that of the Cup Final.

Race periods have always seen the Mountain Course bedecked with advertising banners, and the providers are prepared to pay to have them located in the choicest positions. They know that photographs taken at Quarter Bridge, Ballacraine, etc, will include the carefully placed banners carrying their company names and that, as a result, they will also receive massive off-Island exposure. Such exposure has been much heightened by the extensive growth in TV and video coverage that now sees images of the races beamed around the world to an even greater audience than before.

Fibrax advertised that Freddie Dixon used their brake linings in his 1927 Junior win.

Riders were quick to realise that they too could capitalise on their race successes and top runners did very well out of money that they earned from the Trade, signing contracts with suppliers of all major components and earning 'bonus' payments for a win or a good finishing position.

Despite the apparent public appreciation of advertising, race machines of the early days carried no more than the maker's name on the tank and all riders wore plain leathers. Today both a rider's machine and leathers will be largely covered in adverts. Wanting a share of that space will be the many sponsors whose financial support does so much to keep the wheels turning on modern-day racing motorcycles.

Even the many Course Marshals sometimes wear advertising on their tabards, and Travelling Marshals are a form of advertising for the

Dunlop Tyres and a flying Brian Reid combine to provide a strong advertising image at Ballaugh Bridge.

machines that they ride. Where else can Honda have their sports bikes repeatedly demonstrated at speed for a fortnight in front of 40,000 potential buyers?

For enthusiasts the TT is principally about the racing, but the commercial aspect cannot be ignored, because it has been there since the very first meeting. Today the TT offers a huge advertising opportunity that helps to spread the names of makers, suppliers, sponsors, riders and the Isle of Man to all parts of the world.

In plain black leathers the three class winners of the 1967 Production TT chat after the race. From the left: Neil Kelly, John Hartle and Bill Smith.

ALIASES

In the world at large there has always been an undercurrent of opposition to motorcycling, but it was much stronger through the 1920s to the 1950s than it is today. Riding on the road might just have been socially acceptable but, to those to whom social niceties were important, the racing of motorcycles could barely be contemplated. Despite such opposition, racing was, and is, a way of life that attracts people from all levels of society.

The first three men in the 2004 Formula One TT. 2nd Adrian Archibald (left), winner John McGuinness (centre) and 3rd place Bruce Anstey (right), show off their multi-coloured leathers bedecked with advertising that also extends to helmets, boots, gloves and even their knee-sliders.

Many riders of those earlier years entered the TT and MGP in the face of opposition from their families and employers. Others, knowing that they would face such opposition, entered in secret. However, in their attempts to conceal their Island racing they reckoned without the publicity machine associated with the races, for it has long been the custom of the organisers to advise local newspapers if a rider from their area of circulation entered the TT or MGP and most papers would run a story during the race period, complete with a picture and name of rider. The result was that our racer would get home to find that family and employer knew all about his fortnight of racing. It is easy to smile about such things nowadays, but 60 and 70 years ago it could be a much more serious matter. It is well documented that some riders arrived home, went back to work and were immediately called into the office of their boss and told to choose between racing and their job.

To overcome this very real problem some riders took to entering under an alias. They were required to declare their real names on their entry forms but the organisers would co-operate by ensuring that it was a rider's chosen alias that appeared in the Programme and results. Going back to the Amateur races of 1926 (predecessor to the MGP) there were entries from 'A. Menace', 'A. Shortus', and 'A. Reserve', the latter being Rex Adams who rode well enough to win the Senior race, a fact that he had hoped to conceal from his parents by use of his alias.

At the 1928 TT a 'W.T. Carlisle' entered in the Senior race on a Scott, whilst the 1930 Junior and Senior MGP had entries from 'A. Macintosh', the 1932 Senior Manx from 'Q. Ack', and the newspaper 'The TT Special' tells that a Robert Ellis used two different aliases: 'R. Nixon' and 'C. Roberts'.

Harry J Bacon (usually known as Bert) started his Island racing career in the 1928 Amateur race, where he rode under his own name. He graduated to the TT in 1929 and rode until 1931. With the approach of the 1935 TT Bert felt the urge to compete again, but as he was under wifely pressure not to do, he entered under the alias 'B. Shaw'. It was the time when many competitors still rode their race bikes to the Island and, telling his wife he was off for a holiday he departed with his Velocette. His race was spoilt by a broken primary chain and his return home was spoilt by the fact that his wife had discovered that he had been racing!

J. Alexander Edwards was a fairly successful rider who used the alias 'J. Alexander' through the late 1940s and 50s, hoping, as a Local Government officer from North Wales, to conceal his racing activities from his employers. Although riding under an alias could be taken as suggesting that a rider was seeking to avoid publicity, competitor 'Anno Domini' could not avoid it at the 1948 Senior MGP when he finished second. It was not until later that his identity was revealed as Norman Culpan, together with the fact that he had made his Manx debut as far back as 1928.

Even foreign riders resorted to the use of aliases.

Rex Adams (AJS) who won the Senior class of the 1926 Amateur race riding under the alias of 'A. Reserve'.

'Bert' Bacon with his 350cc Velocette at the 1935 TT. Is that worried look in case his wife should discover what he had been up to?

In the Senior TT of 1936 the entry of 'J. Richardson' was actually that of Frenchman Richard de Garade. It is said that he sought to conceal his identity *'to avoid his father's ire'*. However, Monsieur Garade (Junior) was spared that ire when he failed to get a machine to ride. Better known in TT racing is the name of 'John Grace'. He was bestowed with a far more Spanish name by his parents but, riding with a racing licence from Gibraltar, he anglicised his name and was a good TT runner between 1952 and 62, concentrating on 125 Bultacos in his later rides.

Graham Downes rode the MGP from 1955 to 59 and then moved on to the TT. Finding time to do a Travelling Marshal's job at the 1961 MGP, Graham did not know that his racing days were numbered due to his employer's anti-racing attitude. Not permitted to ride in the 1962 TT or even act as a Travelling Marshal at the MGP, Graham was forced to employ an alias to get his next ride. Come the 1963 Sidecar TT and the entry of 'V.E.R. Boten' was, in reality, Graham Downes. On an outfit that cost him £80, Graham rode to nineteenth place in what was his last Island race. Another entry in the 1963 Sidecar TT who used an alias was the passenger to Swiss Claude Lambert, who was named only as 'Fiston'.

One former TT winner, Geoff Davison, used an alias to both protect his identity and to have a bit of fun at the expense of some of the other top competitors. It was at the 1925 TT, at the time that Italian machines and riders were beginning to make their mark, that Geoff persuaded the organisers to give him a reserve entry under the alias 'Ferodo Vaselini'. By then working for the magazine 'Motor Cycling', his idea was to test a Lightweight New Imperial, Junior Sunbeam and Senior Scott over the TT Course during practice and report his findings by way of articles in the magazine. Entering fully into the part, on his first appearance he smeared his face with burnt cork to gain a darker complexion and stuck an immense black moustache to his upper lip. The 'tache only lasted a couple of miles and the Scott failed to complete a lap but respectable times were set on the other bikes, thus setting the Paddock buzzing with concerned chatter about the apparent threat from the Italian sounding 'Ferodo Vaselini'.

Digressing slightly from the matter of aliases, mention has been made of riders who risked their jobs by engaging in the socially unacceptable (to some employers) pursuit of motorcycle racing during their holidays. But there were many other racers who would love to have ridden the TT or MGP but were prevented from doing so by the fact that they could not pick and choose when they would take their holidays. It was their misfortune to be restricted by their employers to the 'works fortnight', when a firm would shut-down for two weeks and all employees took their holidays at the same time. (Fifty years ago the average working man only received two weeks holiday a year.) In 'History of the Manx Grand Prix 1923-1998' by Peter Kneale and Bill Snelling, a tale is told of Colin Watson from Scunthorpe. Colin was employed in the steel industry at Scunthorpe and all the steelworks closed for annual holidays in August. This did not coincide with the dates that Colin wanted to take his holidays to compete in the MGP, so he took time off to ride in the 1954 MGP without permission. On his return to work he was sacked. Finding employment with another steel firm he did the same thing in 1955, and was sacked, he found another firm, rode in 1956 - and was sacked!

4	W. G. Boddice (J. W. Tanner) ...	499 Norton	00
5	F. Scheidegger (Switzerland) (J. Robinson)	492 B.M.W.	00
6	O. Kolle (W. Germany) (K. D. Hess)	492 B.M.W.	00
7	C. Lambert (Switzerland)("Fiston")	492 B.M.W.	00
* 8	M. Deubel (W. Germany) (E. Horner)	492 B.M.W.	00
* 9	C. Vincent (K. Scott)	498 B.S.A.	00
10	C. Seeley (W. Rawlings)	496 Matchless	00
†11	...		00
12	C. Freeman (B. Nelson)	499 Norton	00

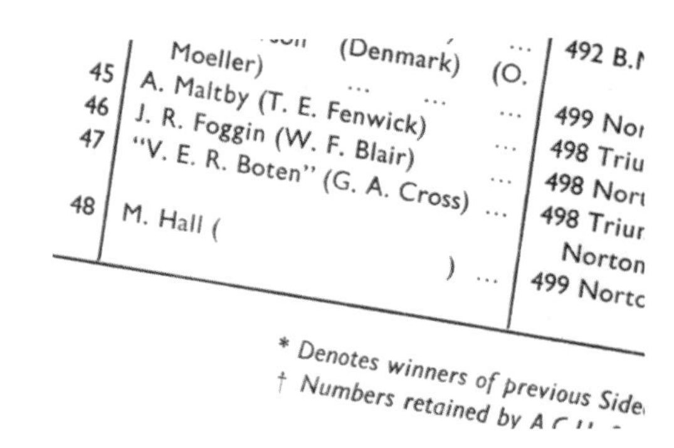
	Moeller) (Denmark) ... (O.	492 B.M
45	A. Maltby (T. E. Fenwick) ...	499 Nor
46	J. R. Foggin (W. F. Blair) ...	498 Triu
47	"V. E. R. Boten" (G. A. Cross) ...	498 Nor
48	M. Hall ( ) ...	498 Triu
		Norton
		499 Norto

* Denotes winners of previous Side
† Numbers retained by A.C.U.

How the entries of 'Fiston' (no.7) and 'V.E.R. Boten' (no.47) appeared in the 1963 TT Programme.

ALTERNATIVE COURSES

The first TT for motorcycles was held in 1907 on a course of just over 15 miles in length in the west of the Island. The start was at Tynwald Hill at St Johns, from where it travelled to Ballacraine, turned left on to the current TT Course and continued to Kirk Michael. At Douglas Road Corner in Kirk Michael it turned sharp left and followed the coast-road south to Peel. Dropping through the narrow streets of Peel, it then headed east and back to St Johns. The race was over 10 laps of this narrow, dusty and unsurfaced route, with riders being allowed a 10 minute rest and refuelling stop at half-distance.

Keen to push the development of touring motorcycles, the organisers soon looked for a hillier and more demanding route. For 1911 they they chose the much longer Snaefell Mountain Course, and the first three places in the Senior race were taken by two-speed, chain-driven Indians.

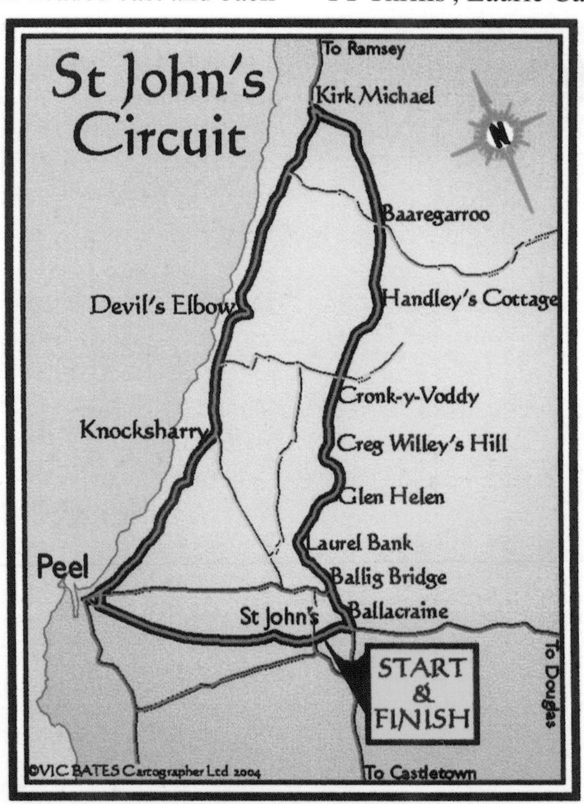

The St Johns course used from 1907-1910.

The Mountain Course used from 1911-14 was almost the same as todays (see inside front cover) except that towards the end of the lap riders turned right at Cronk ny Mona and cut across to the top of Bray Hill. It was only when the TT races returned after the first World War (in 1920) that riders went straight on from Cronk ny Mona to Signpost Corner, Governor's Bridge and Glencrutchery Road to create the route we now know. The main reason for that change was to take advantage of the increased space for Start/Finish and Pits facilities that were offered at Nobles Park on the Glencrutchery Road.

The TT races are so closely linked to the famous Mountain Course that it is difficult to believe that there have been occasions when the use of those famous 37¾ miles has been threatened, but in the early 1920s the ACU (race organisers) gave serious consideration to taking the TT races to Belgium or Ireland if the Manx authorities did not provide financial assistance towards their running costs. Then, as a result of several races being run in very poor weather and the postponement of the 1935 Senior TT (the first ever race postponement), questions were asked about the possibility of finding an alternative course on the Island. In his book 'TT Thrills', Laurie Cade mentions that in the mid-1930s *'The Manx Highways Board did in fact survey and produce an entirely new course, measuring twenty miles; this was claimed to have an enormous advantage in that it did not traverse the mountains, and so was not subject to the Mantle of Mona, that quickly-arising mist which sometimes enveloped the high roads'.* There was no change for 1936 but that year's race Programme said:

'Although considerable controversy arose following the 1935 races, The ACU, for various reasons, has decided for this year at least, to utilise again the course that has been used for every post-war race - known throughout the world as the Mountain Course'. The ACU appointed a sub-committee to consider the matter and they recommended that the organisation: *'should carefully explore the possibilities of a new course for 1937'.* Whatever the debate, the Mountain Course was used again in 1937 and has been ever since.

The biggest problem with the Snaefell Mountain Course is the effect of 'Mist on the Mountain', an expression that covers low cloud, fog, heavy rain (even snow). Sometimes these weather elements seem to occur together, and although prior to 1935 every race was run to schedule, since then there have been an ever-increasing number of postponements to race and practice sessions due to 'Mist on the Mountain'.

It's a clinging Mountain mist this morning"

A light-hearted view of the serious problem of misty conditions that can affect the Mountain Course.

Other weather factors affecting the Mountain Course include frequent strong winds and, when the weather is good, dazzling low sunlight on the stretch after Kirk Michael in the mornings (no longer a problem with the abandonment of early morning practice) and on the run to Ballacraine in the evenings.

In 1954 the Clypse Course was introduced for Lightweight 125s and Sidecars, whilst the remaining classes continued to race over the Mountain. The new Course was 10.79 miles long and used the existing Start and Finish areas, but riders turned right at the top of Bray Hill and went on for a couple of miles to join the main TT Course at Cronk ny Mona. From there they travelled in the reverse direction to Creg ny Baa, turned right and made their way over narrow roads to Onchan, before rejoining the TT Course at Signpost Corner and running in the normal direction (but excluding the Governor's Bridge dip) to finish at the Grandstand. The Lightweight 250s and Clubman's races later joined the 125s and Sidecars on the Clypse, but the Course was dropped after the 1959 TT.

Although the TT is synonymous with the Mountain Course, well-meaning attempts have been made down the years to find a site for a short circuit to GP standards on the Island. Some saw a short-circuit as a replacement for the Mountain Course, while others envisaged the world stars who were shy of the Mountain, competing on the short circuit during TT fortnight whilst the real road racers raced on the traditional Course in the same two weeks. The Island's Tourist Board even created a Short Circuit Sub-Committee and in 1982 and 1983 it received several proposals. Well known racers such as Geoff Duke lent their names to schemes, but despite agreeing that *'further investigations should take place into the feasibility, desirability and viability of such a project'*, it went no further, and when the new and expensive Grandstand was built in 1985/6 it was clear that an alternative Course was a non-starter.

Despite the attempts to find alternative courses, to most motorcyclists the TT remains firmly linked to the Mountain Course and for true enthusiasts attendance takes the form of an annual pilgrimage, meaning that they are prepared to go through any hardship to achieve it. One enthusiast wrote of this annual migratory need: *'To lack this urge . . . to go to the TT races . . . is, I suggest, to lack an essential quality as a motorcycle enthusiast'*.

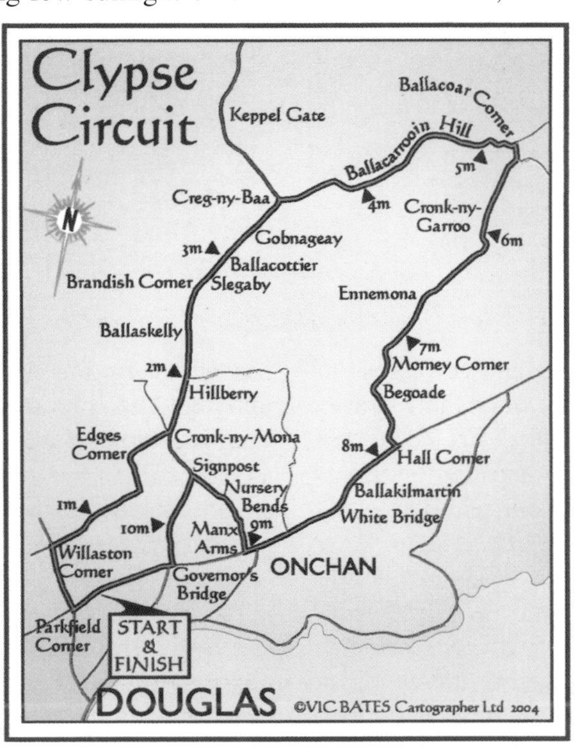

The 10.79 mile Clypse Course.

AS THINGS WERE

Having adopted several different formats in its earliest years, by 1914 the TT meeting was run as two separate races comprising a six lap Senior (for up to 500cc) machines and a five lap Junior (up to 350cc). The event attracted a record entry of 160, comprised of 111 Senior and 49 Junior, with 14 different makes represented in the Junior and a remarkable 35 different makes in the Senior.

Harry Stevens was one of the brothers who ran the original AJS concern (named after eldest brother, Albert John Stevens). The Company competed in the TT in 1911 and 1913 with modest results and it was following a late decision to compete in 1914 that Harry wrote a fascinating account of their efforts. It is one that really provides a snapshot of how things were in the early days of the event.

A.J. 'Jack' Stevens and J.D. Corke with the two-speed AJS machines that they rode in the 1911 TT.

Although it had an engine designed for speed work on the drawing board, the late decision of AJS to compete in 1914 forced it to use relatively standard side-valve engines with a bore and stroke of 74 x 81 mm for the Junior race. In Harry's words: *'They were fitted with loose heads with large valve ports. This part of the engine was very carefully machined, and you would be surprised if you knew the time these heads took to prepare. They were polished like silver inside, the cylinder barrels were machined from practically a solid chunk of cast iron . . . the flywheels were slightly lighter than standard, the con rods were our standard rod lightened when necessary, and when finished were a beautiful piece of work. They weighed 10 ozs each, two rings were fitted to the top of the piston, which were of cast steel, and weighed 12 ozs each complete'.* Plain bearings were used throughout because at the TT *'absolute reliability must take its place even in front of efficiency . . . it is not always the fastest machine that wins the race'.* This policy was extended to the frame that was standard even to a carrier (which strengthened the rear end). Fitted with one internal expanding brake at the rear, the wheels were shod with 26x2¼" Avon tyres.

Billy Jones finished 4th in the 1914 Junior TT on this AJS.

From past experience, Harry Stevens knew that correct gearing was vital on the Mountain Course. AJS fitted a two-speed countershaft gearbox as standard but he devised a system of double sprockets and chains that provided four gears, and thus a wider choice of ratios *'to get every ounce of power to the road wheels'.* He stressed, however, that whilst he wanted all possible speed, particularly down the Mountain, he also wanted to avoid over-revving. Going on with his description, he explained: *'I may say that building these special machines cost us a good deal of money, as from start to finish they had to be very carefully watched, and only the best men were allowed to do anything on them'*. The Company initially intended building two machines but ended up building four and supporting a fifth, that of Billy Jones, which was the only one to have a three-speed arrangement. Normal output of road machines from the Wolverhampton factory dropped by half in the weeks approaching the TT and the whole work-force was bitten by the TT bug. When the race bikes were complete they were road-tested and *'although all these machines were built to the micrometer in every part, you would be astonished at the varied results we got when we took them on the road'*.

Eldest brother John, known as Jack, took the bikes to Liverpool by train and thence by boat to the Island, where they were ridden to their TT base at The Hawthorn Inn, Greeba.

First practice showed that the compression ratio of 6:1 was too high and it was reduced to about 5:1 by the fitting of what was described as *'cooperite washers underneath the foot of the cylinders'*. Second practice saw several seizures on the Mountain climb with one bike running its big-end, and for the next practice the pistons were changed. They had to be replaced by the originals after one session, due to faults in the metal. Modifications to the lubrication system followed and, when working into the night, their primitive garage was lit by acetylene lamps of the type fitted to road bikes of the time. Thursday practice saw the AJS riders stopping several times to adjust their tappets. Initial thoughts of valve-stretch were discounted and it was decided that the 'cooperite' washers under the barrels were sinking and affecting the valve clearance. On all but one machine (that later gave trouble) they were replaced by *'cardboard washers that we cut from Hans Renold chain boxes'*.

The next series of problems came with failure of several crankpins. Inspection of their spare crankpins revealed minute cracking and there was an air of despondency in the camp. Harry tells: *'It happened about this time that brother Joe had arrived at Greeba, and after a good deal of argument and discussion, it was decided that the engines should be removed from the frames, and*

Members of the AJS team for the 1914 TT pause from their machine preparations at their Greeba base.

that Joe should visit Douglas, and see if he could either get some firm or repairer to make us half a dozen crankpins, or make them himself, if he could not find a man capable. These he must insist upon being made from ordinary common mild steel. It was arranged also that if he was successful in getting a firm to make them, he should get a supply of prussiate of potash, which we should use for flash-hardening of them'. On his way to Douglas, Joe met brother George, so all the Stevens brothers were on the Island. It took until mid-day on Saturday to get the replacement crankpins, and with all the totally dismantled bikes required to be up and running, tested and prepared for weighing-in on Monday prior to racing on Tuesday, *'super-human efforts'* were needed to get the bikes ready for Monday morning's practice.

Despite all the problems experienced in practice, the race itself turned into a triumph for the AJS concern, with Eric Williams taking victory from similarly mounted Cyril Williams in second place and Billy Jones fourth, whilst Bert Haddock and Billy Heaton (who had led at one stage) also finished the race. Celebrations were on a scale justified by a TT win, and after doing the rounds of various establishments in Douglas they returned to Greeba with half a dozen boxes of champagne that they drunk out of pint glasses.

It is worth reflecting that the AJS effort with five machines was achieved mainly with the tools, spares, etc, that they brought with them in a couple of sidecar outfits and, although the Stevens brothers and the riders helped pull the bikes to pieces after practice problems, the team had only one recognised mechanic to look after them.

AUTOGRAPH HUNTERS

One price of fame is to be the target of autograph hunters. The free and easy arrangements around the Grandstand in the 1920s and 1930s encouraged swarms of local youngsters to come to early morning practice armed with autograph books with which they pestered riders for signatures. Given the early hour and the more important pressures they were under, most riders were remarkably cooperative.

Some of the lads were selective and asked only the top men to sign, others were more concerned with quantity than quality and fell upon anyone in leathers. A few of those autograph books still exist and it is a nostalgic sensation to hold one and fan the pages to reveal the names of Freddie Dixon, Alec Bennett, Howard Davies, Stanley Woods, Jimmy Guthrie and other top men of the era.

Having returned from an early morning practice in 1933, Jock Fairweather (Cotton) tries to give the photographer his attention, whilst several young autograph hunters wait to pounce.

It can sometimes be a problem to decipher the signatures of British riders, but when Japanese riders came on the scene things got very much more difficult!

How Honda works rider Kunimitsu Takahashi signed himself.

According to Larry Devlin, one man who was choosy about giving autographs was double Lightweight TT winner of the 1950s Fergus

Anderson who would only inscribe his name in a proper book, not on programmes or scraps of paper.

Phil Read was a superstar at the TT in the 1960s and a constant target for autograph hunters. Whilst Takahashi probably spent a minute over each example of his signature, Read streamlined the process by using a rubber stamp. Autograph hunters can still be seen around the Paddock, but it is not just autograph books that get signed nowadays, for riders are asked to sign T-shirts, caps, programmes, action posters of themselves, even bare-flesh. In addition, some owners of road bikes will ask star riders to add their signatures to their petrol tanks or fairings.

Not every competitor gets the use of garage facilities. This photograph from 1973 is of one mechanic supporting three riders at the MGP. Working on the pavement or in the back of the van if wet, the only concession to comfort is a kitchen chair borrowed from their landlady.

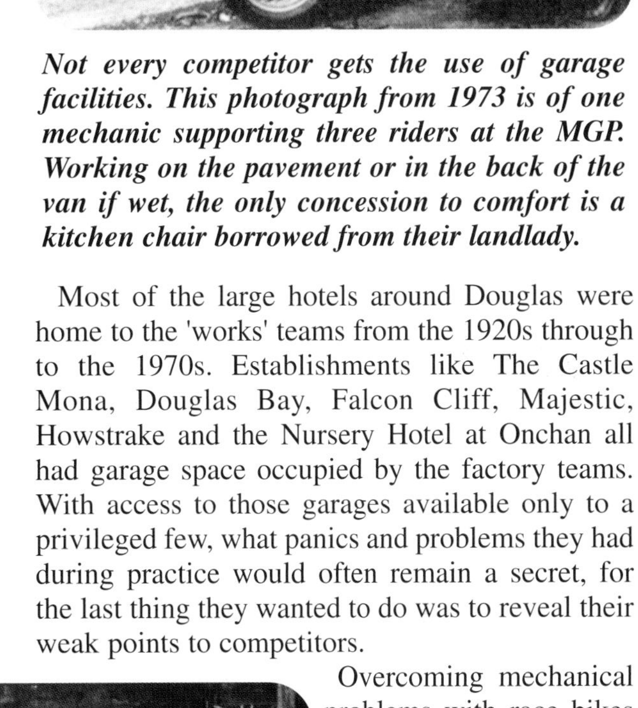

BAD PRACTICE, GOOD RACE

The above saying is part of Island racing tradition and has often proved to be true. The trials and tribulations of the AJS team during practice for the 1914 TT were recounted above in *'As Things Were'*, yet the race proved a resounding success for the marque. Many other firms and individuals have spent much of their practice periods with engines, gearboxes, brakes, suspension and other components spread around their garages in a multitude of pieces. Working in basic conditions without the accustomed back-up facilities of workshop equipment and mechanical support, some of those who embraced the challenge of racing at the TT or MGP must have wondered if they had taken on too much.

Things looks under control in the HRD garage at the 1925 TT and so they turned out to be, for Howard Davies (right) took victory in the Senior and second place in the Junior TT.

Most of the large hotels around Douglas were home to the 'works' teams from the 1920s through to the 1970s. Establishments like The Castle Mona, Douglas Bay, Falcon Cliff, Majestic, Howstrake and the Nursery Hotel at Onchan all had garage space occupied by the factory teams. With access to those garages available only to a privileged few, what panics and problems they had during practice would often remain a secret, for the last thing they wanted to do was to reveal their weak points to competitors.

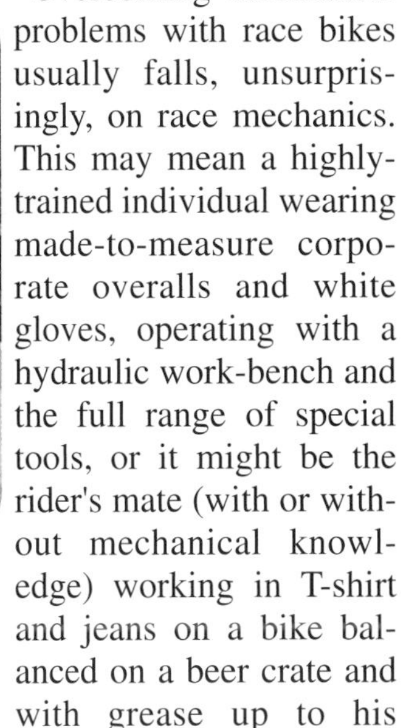

Overcoming mechanical problems with race bikes usually falls, unsurprisingly, on race mechanics. This may mean a highly-trained individual wearing made-to-measure corporate overalls and white gloves, operating with a hydraulic work-bench and the full range of special tools, or it might be the rider's mate (with or without mechanical knowledge) working in T-shirt and jeans on a bike balanced on a beer crate and with grease up to his elbows. What both usually have in common is dedication to the cause and a willingness to work very long hours. Those hours are long even when things are going well, but when things go wrong there are many tales of mechanics working until after midnight then, thinking it not worth going to bed, spending a few hours in the Casino and going from there straight to early morning practice. Slightly more worrying is the fact that some riders used to keep the same hours!

Given the extent of problems experienced during practice by many fully prepared and factory-supported riders, leaves one wondering just what troubles many privateers must have suffered. Even the very top men are not immune to troubles, for in 1979 Mike Hailwood's 14th and last TT win was achieved on a Suzuki that his mechanics had to totally strip and rebuild in a marathon overnight session that continued into the early hours of race-day.

Victory in the Junior TT of 1982 went to Con Law after an intensely troubled and 'bad practice' period that did not allow him to show his true form. So, not only did he go into the race with doubts about the bike but, starting at number 11, he knew that there were a lot of fast men in front of him. But fortune smiled on Con on Junior day, for not only did his bike go well in the race but all those who started in front of him gradually dropped out.

Whilst most people are aware that Joey Dunlop rode 'works' Hondas for most of his TT career, what was not so obvious was that Honda did not necessarily provide him with bikes for all of the races that he contested at the TT. This meant that some years Joey might be racing his own 125 or 250. This happened in 1993, the year that he achieved his fifteenth TT win and moved to the top of the list of TT winners. That record-breaking win was in the Ultra-Lightweight race on a 125cc Honda. Joey's own 125 had proved troublesome all through practice and, because of his commitment to Honda in the other classes, he was restricted as to the number of practice laps that he could put in on it and the amount of time that he could work on it. Putting out an emergency call, an engine was borrowed from James Courtney's sponsors just hours before the 125 race, and the rest is record-breaking history.

Whilst many riders have good reason to believe the adage of 'Bad Practice, Good Race', some are justified in believing that 'Good Practice, Bad Race' also applies. Life can be tough for a racer!

BEING PREPARED

Boy Scouts, or just Scouts as they are known today, have been part of the TT race organisation since its early days. The aim then was to have Scouts located within sight of each other at tricky sections of the Course like Glen Helen. They were equipped with flags and whistles with which they announced the approach of a rider and passed other basic information. In the days before telephones were in general use Scouts were also used as runners to convey information from one marshal's post to another. A note from 1927 emphasises the extent of their involvement: *'During the practising period eight Scouts under a Scoutmaster, will be on duty each morning at the starting point. On each of the Race Days as many Scouts as can be mustered will be stationed round the course. Their duty is to watch for and endeavour to prevent accidents, to capture and detain any stray dogs, to pass messages, to call for medical assistance or, if able, to render first aid, and to assist in keeping the course clear. In addition to those stationed around the course, 20 scouts will be required on Race Days at the starting point for operating the scoring boards, as messengers, etc, etc'.*

Winner of the 1925 Amateur race, H.G. Dobbs (Norton) makes a pit-stop. It was the duty of the Scout on the left to clean riders numbers.

Although Scouts are no longer used for tasks around the Course, the reference above to *'operating the scoreboards'* still holds good. It refers to the huge scoreboards facing the main Grandstand that plot the progress, lap times and the finishing positions of the leading riders in a race. With the time-keepers and auditors box close-by, information is passed from there to Scouts who pass it to those whose job it is to maintain the flow of information to the painters who constantly up-date the scoreboard during a race. Amongst the 'etc, etc,' tasks referred to was the one of cleaning riders' number plates at their pit-stops, so that they could be read by the time-keepers. Such a task was a necessary one in the early 1920s when rain could create muddy roads and dirty machines. What today's Health & Safety enforcers would think about having young lads on the track-side of the Pit Counters with bikes rushing in to refuel, is fairly easy to guess. It reflects a changing attitude to risk, something that the TT as a whole has its fair share of and that, importantly, contributes to the 'buzz' that the event gives to all concerned.

In 1935 a little pomp was added to the TT starting ceremony by getting riders to parade to the start-line behind flags of their respective countries. Carrying the flags at the head of the parade was a job for Scouts.

The rostrum where race-winners are garlanded and pop the champagne is in front of the Grandstand at Douglas, but all that the Scouts working on the Scoreboard see of this ceremony is the riders' backs. However, it is customary for the podium finishers to turn and give the Scouts a wave before walking off as a thank-you for all the work they

"Hi! The grand parade ends at the starting grid"

put in. It is a good investment, for several of today's officials started their involvement with the TT by working on the Scoreboard.

The TT organisers have relied on the support of many local organisations in the running of their events. Some others who helped them to 'be prepared' were mentioned in a 1914 race report. This told how sailors with powerful telescopes were located near the Start and Finish at the top of Bray Hill. Their job was to watch for the first rider to appear on the long straight that approached the finish and to announce his number to an official.

BENDING THE RULES

The TT rule book is a formidable document, for its development is the result of 100 years of effort by riders to outwit the organisers whilst, over the same period, the organisers have sought to counter every such move with additional regulations. Such activity has seen many petty squabbles, and quite a few serious ones.

At the first TT in 1907 some of the bikes in the race were still fitted with pedals that could be used to assist the engine on the steepest hills. Although the rule-book prescribed that *'Pedalling will only be allowed for the purpose of starting or restarting in traffic, or at sharp bends or on steep gradients. Excessive pedalling will disqualify'*, it did not prevent vigorous pedalling by those so-equipped, thus leading to protests from those who lacked such fitments.

Manliff Barrington told that at his first TT in 1934 he suffered major problems with his Lightweight Rudge 250 in practice. Being a newcomer and wanting to take advantage of every practice session, he borrowed a friend's 500 Rudge, put his own number plates on it, and went off and did several more laps while his own bike was being repaired. No one was more surprised than Manliff when his name later appeared on the practice leader-board for the Lightweight class. It did not take the organisers long to find out what he had been up to, and his practice times were scrubbed; but Manliff was not the first (or last) to change numbers and machine in an attempt to qualify.

Even 'Gentleman' Geoff Duke has been known to break the rules when looking for race advantage. In his autobiography 'Pursuit of Perfection' Geoff tells that in his first Island race, the 1949 Senior Clubman's TT, he was concerned about his ability to kick-start his Norton International at the start of the race and after his pit-stop. The race regulations allowed very little change from the standard road-going specification and the organisers had shown themselves to be very strict in the application of those regulations. Despite this, Geoff took a chance and welded an additional two inches into the kick-start shaft to provide additional leverage. He got away with it, the bike started second kick, and Geoff brought the Norton home in first place, ahead of Allan Jefferies, grandfather of TT-great David Jefferies.

A not unreasonable rule is that riders must only travel in the direction of the Course or, in other words, they must not ride against the flow. However, the rule was not introduced until the TT was moved to the Mountain Course in 1911. Prior to that, riders who were unsuccessful in climbing the likes of Creg Willeys hill either dismounted and pushed their bikes to the top or turned round, rode down to the bottom and took another run at it. At the 1938 MGP it was reported to the Clerk of the Course that Senior race winner Ken Bills had restarted his machine at Ramsey Hairpin in the reverse direction of the Course. Whatever it was that happened, a meeting of the Stewards exonerated Ken and the result stood. At the 1965 TT the experienced Mike Hailwood was accompanied in the MV Agusta team by newcomer to the Island, Giacomo Agostini. In the wet Senior race both Ago and Mike came off their machines on the tricky, climbing right-hander at Sarah's Cottage. Ago was the first to go down and he retired from the race. The next lap it was Mike's turn to drop the red Italian 'fire-engine'. With broken windscreen, flattened exhausts and an oil-leak, Mike kicked one or two other bits back into shape, bump-started the MV into life and rode away to eventual victory over Joe Dunphy (Norton). The only problem was that his bump-starting had been downhill, against the flow of race traffic. In truth, the road is wide enough at Sarahs for Mike to have restarted without getting on to the racing line, but, it was against the rules. Fortunately for Mike, the organisers did not get to hear about it and, again, the result stood.

There were no noise restrictions imposed by the race regulations in the 1930s. Had there been, then in 1937 this 250cc water-cooled, supercharged DKW two-stroke of Ernie Thomas would surely have exceeded all limits, for it is still regarded as the noisiest ever machine at the TT. However, this was one instance where noise did equate with power, for the German-built DKW marque took three 3rd and one 1st place in the years 1936-39.

The 'TT Formula I' event that opened race-week in 1980 was

Mike Hailwood exits Governors Bridge in the 1965 Senior TT, the damage sustained to his MV at Sarah's Cottage is very evident.

keenly contested both during and after the race by the Honda and Suzuki 'works' teams. Indeed, a bit of needle crept in even before the start when, in a tactical move, Suzuki-mounted Graeme Crosby managed to take over the riding number of no-show American Dave Aldana (moving from 3 to 11) and thus put himself in a position to keep an eye on the race progress of Honda's Mick Grant (No.12). The lead chopped and changed between the two of them during the race, but at the finish Grant was declared the winner by 11 seconds. The sponsor of the fourth finisher then submitted a protest claiming that the petrol tank on Grant's Honda was of greater capacity than the 24 litres permitted by the regulations. Honda admitted that the tank was capable of holding 28 litres but explained that they had put air bottles and table-tennis balls inside to reduce its petrol-holding capacity to regulation size. Mick Grant did his bit to help matters in that direction when, at the end of the race, he brought his fist down onto the aluminium tank with considerable force in what he described as a spontaneous gesture of celebration. Suzuki saw the resultant capacity-reducing dent somewhat differently, but their protest was dismissed and the win stood to Honda.

Production racing has always offered opportunities to bend the rules, for it is very difficult for the organisers to police the event. Many are the doubts and murmurs that circulate in the Paddock at each Production TT. Some are probably just 'sour-grapes' but others have foundation for, in the quest for every possible advantage, entrants are prepared to push the rules to the limit and more. Indeed the Production races of the 1970s were dropped for 1977, and in the words of former Production TT winner Ray Knight this was *'due to convoluted rules that permitted manufacturers to build any bike to specification especially written by themselves for the race'*. In further words on the subject he said *'A Production race fails completely if everybody is not quite convinced that the machines are as you can buy'*. Not everyone is quite convinced of that fact, meanwhile, as riders continue to find their way around the race regulations, the rule-book just gets thicker.

BRAKING

The Snaefell Mountain Course has always allowed riders to take advantage of their maximum speeds (something not necessarily achieved on short circuits) if the bikes they rode had handling to match. Back in the early 1950s Geoff Duke voiced the considered opinion that the twist-grip of his 'works' Norton was hard against the stop in top gear for just over 15 of the 37¾ miles of a full lap. That was an impressive statistic, but everyone was aware that all the 'go' had to be accompanied by a considerable amount of 'stop'. It was Ferodo who supplied brake-linings to most of the entry and they calculated that on one of his very fast laps, Geoff would apply his brakes 73 times, that they would be on for 2 minutes 50 seconds, and that represented a distance of 4½ miles. By comparison, today's top 600cc runners have the throttle against the stop for just under 13 miles of a lap, but the best side-cars have the throttle wide-open for almost 25 miles.

Ralph Cawthorne is pictured on his 'works' Norton at the 1922 TT where lap speeds approaching 60 mph were set on bikes still fitted with a dummy rim rear brake and a small front brake of the internal expanding drum type.

It was common up until the early 1920s for machines to be fitted with only one brake, for it was generally believed that a front brake was dangerous. Where a second brake was fitted, it was often of the stirrup variety that pulled two brake-blocks onto the front wheel rim. Today we associate such a fitting with a childs push-bike. It became a requirement for two independent brakes to be fitted in 1923 but, whatever the number and type of

Disc brakes fitted to S. Ollerhead's Douglas at the 1923 TT. Manxman Tom Sheard and Freddie Dixon rode to victory on similar mounts in that year's Senior and Sidecar events.

Freddie Frith prepares for his Island Guzzi debut, a debut that ended abruptly at Ballacraine.

brakes used, there could be vast variations in efficiency arising from factors of design and adjustment.

It was at Ballacraine in 1947 that Freddie Frith showed that, however good the design, a brake needed to be prepared, assembled and adjusted properly. Out in practice for the first post-war TT, he had the front brake lock as he slowed for the corner. Thrown through the air for a considerable distance, his eventual contact with the roadside kerb served to break his shoulder and ruin most of his racing season. Although there was no official announcement of the problem, the word went around that it was due to insufficient chamfer on the brake-linings.

Drum brakes were gradually increased in size and operating efficiency (aided by improved braking materials and metals that shed heat faster) and then developed to utilise twin and multiple leading shoes. In the last days of drum brakes, some almost filled the wheel.

The double, twin leading-shoe front brake fitted to the RA97 'works' 250 Yamaha in the mid-1960s

In a move that some saw as a reversion to motorcycling's push-bike heritage, Honda's wonderful little 50cc racers of the early 1960s were fitted with a bicycle-type caliper front brake acting on the wheel-rim.

The move to disc brakes occurred in the mid-1960s and, as with the drum brakes that came before, disc brakes were developed to provide more stopping power by increases in the number of pistons, improvements to brake pad materials and enlarging the size and number of discs used.

Such developments were not without their problems and riders recall situations where the pads would get 'knocked back' at high speed and subsequent application of the brakes would result in the brake lever coming back to the handlebars. It was an event followed by frantic 'pumping' of the brake-lever (and the rider's heart) to get the brake operational. Another modern-day problem seems to be that of 'arm-pump' that can inhibit a rider's braking or even force him to retire. Maybe it is the sheer physical effort that causes it, perhaps riding position; whatever, it can be a serious problem if it strikes.

Many riders use the practice periods to develop regular braking points at the places where they need to slow, often using a course-side marker for reference. Come race-day and newcomers sometimes find to their horror that their carefully memorised braking markers are completely obscured by hordes of course-side spectators. One tale of braking that comes in the hard-to-believe category concerns the comment made by Honda and Suzuki 'works' rider of the 1960s, Stuart Graham, who said: *'I didn't use markers as braking points at all. My braking points were the places where it felt right to brake'*. It worked for Stuart with three TT podium finishes, and it also works for multiple Sidecar TT winner and lap record-holder, Dave Molyneux. When asked how much reliance he puts on previously memorised braking points, his answer was *'none'*. Dave does all his braking by instinct, and he has lapped on three-wheels faster than anyone else, at almost 116 mph.

Dave Molyneux and Colin Hardman keep a tight line at Quarter Bridge on their Honda outfit.

CHAPTER 2

TALES OF . . .

BRIDGES

Was there ever a circuit with so many bridges as the Mountain Course? Within a mile of the Start is the tricky Quarter Bridge where riders turn sharp right and have the river and a former railway line on their left. It is a place that sees its share of incidents, particularly on the first lap of a race when riders arrive with relatively cold tyres, a full load of petrol and lots of enthusiasm. Normally a busy double roundabout for ordinary traffic (think oil and diesel droppings!), as competitors crank over they are thankful that at least the Manx Highways people use non-slip paint on the many road markings here.

Leaving Quarter Bridge, riders no longer feel the bump of what was a shallow bridge on the straight towards Braddan, although it used to be enough to get their wheels off the ground. Braking hard for Braddan Bridge they bank to the left over the former railway track and then to the right in front of the massed spectator seating.

Skilled use of the throttle will give riders good drive away from Braddan Bridge out towards Union Mills where, perhaps unknowingly, they will recross the old railway track by another bridge just after the Railway Inn. Having ridden through Union Mills, Glen Vine and Crosby, slowed for Greeba Castle and Appledene, they then tackle the sweeping left-hander of Greeba Bridge, before the flat out stretch to Ballacraine. About ½ mile before Ballacraine is the hump of a stream-crossing at Ballagarraghyn. Now much reduced, it used to get the fast riders airborne whilst flat-out in top gear.

Soon after Ballacraine is Ballig Bridge which takes the road over the River Neb. Ballig was the humpiest bridge on the Course until it was eased in the mid 1930s. Before it was flattened and straightened, Stanley Woods told how when on the right line he would ride it diagonally, left to right, saying that: *'one's right-hand handlebar would have been over the parapet of the bridge if you*

This is the scene at Braddan Bridge from some 50 years ago.

A 1920s photograph of Ballig Bridge. It was flattened and widened in the mid-1930s.

were travelling at the maximum speed and on the best line'. He omitted to mention that you had to be well and truly airborne to get the handlebar over the parapet. Stanley was a skilled rider on the best of machinery but, on the rigid bikes of the time, those who were uncertain of their skills or the strength of their frames would back-off from the unofficial long-jump competition over Ballig Bridge that was so enjoyed by spectators.

Ballig Bridge is some 8 miles from the Start and it is another 3 miles before riders come to Drinkwater's Bridge which is located amongst the sweeping 140 mph bends of the 11th Milestone. With its parapet leant on by thousands of spectators down the years, it is one of those spots that has adopted the name of a TT rider. In this case it is that of the unfortunate Ben Drinkwater who was killed there in a crash during the 1949 Junior TT. Lost amongst the bends of the 11th Milestone, Drinkwater's Bridge does not have a particularly high profile, but that is certainly not the case with the next one that riders come to - Ballaugh Bridge - for it is one of the most photographed places on the Course and has been the scene of many exciting moments as riders lacking in technique arrive too fast or make front-wheel landings. This is a spot where all-rounders like Nick Jefferies score, for they use the off-roaders method of lifting the front wheel to achieve a controlled rear wheel landing. The best that the less experienced can aim for is level flight and a two-wheeled landing.

Nick Jefferies shows the correct way to take Ballaugh Bridge

Whatever jumping

method is used, the speed and throttle control needs to be such as to minimise damage to suspension and transmission on landing, and also allow riders to avoid the projecting walls of Course-side houses that come immediately after. Interestingly, one multiple TT winner of the 1970s claimed that he deliberately made front-wheel landings at Ballaugh to avoid imposing shocks on the transmission!

Like Ballaugh, the well-known Sulby Bridge has many tales to tell about riders who have failed to get it right. Approached at extreme speed along Sulby Straight, the formerly humped Sulby Bridge forms the exit of what is now a flat, wall-bound, ninety degree right-hand bend over the Sulby River and the secret of a successful crossing is all in the braking at the end of the Straight. Those who, on account of brake-fade or brain-fade, arrive too fast to take the Bridge may be relieved by what looks like a straight-on escape route into a field. However, pre-race inspection should have shown them that there is a difference in level of three feet between road and field, making it yet another spot where off-road riding experience could come in useful.

Seems like plenty of warning, but at 180 mph the Bridge is less than 10 seconds away.

Through the flat stretch to Ramsey riders barely notice the bridge at Milntown, and with the climb of the Mountain that follows it is many miles before the next named bridge is crossed. But if they were travelling more sedately, riders would be aware that they were passing over many minor streams, particularly on the Mountain where much water flows under the Course on its way to the sea, including at the Bungalow Bridge by the Graham Memorial.

Nearing the end of a lap a rider will come to perhaps the slowest part of the Course at Governor's Bridge. Notorious for the number of riders who fall off - perhaps fall over is a truer description - it offers a close-up view of competitors trying to brake to under 10 mph and make a hairpin right-hand turn, whilst a stiff steering-damper and limited lock seek to prevent them doing so. In addition to the transition from high to low speed, the fact that the bend falls into the ensuing tricky dip and that engines want to stall, all contributes to making it a testing low-speed challenge.

One of the most photographed spots on the TT Course is Governor's Bridge and this is one of its most famous moments as Bob McIntyre (Gilera) clocks the first 100 mph lap on his way to victory in the Golden Jubilee Senior TT of 1957.

Having successfully negotiated Governor's Bridge and the ensuing dip, riders are once again able to stretch the throttle-wire to the limit for the blast along the Glencrutchery Road, where the fastest competitors hit 170 mph as they complete another lap.

BRUSHES WITH THE LAW

The TT and MGP have such a major impact on the Isle of Man that it is not surprising that their running has contributed to occasional infringements of Manx laws. At the start of one of the earliest events at St Johns, a local farmer objected to the effect the racing had on his comings and goings over the local roads and showed it by driving his horse and cart onto the Course at the Start area before the race. After fruitless cajoling from officials, boos from the crowd, the disconnection of his horse from his cart and an air of growing hostility, it took firm action from a local policeman to resolve the farmer's infringement of the official road-closing orders.

The Manx police are renowned for their tolerance during race periods. Some say, perhaps with tongue in cheek, that this is due to the substantial overtime payments they take home during TT fortnight but, whatever the reason, it does enable the events to be held in an atmosphere of high spirits that would not be tolerated in the United Kingdom. However, not every member of the constabulary enters totally into the spirit of the races. In the mid-1920s it was a requirement of Manx law for anyone in charge of a motor vehicle to sound a horn when approaching road junctions in built-up areas. It was a law that was only occasionally enforced but several TT competitors riding to and from practice were brought to Court charged with failing to 'hoot' and, to the reluctance of the Court (so it seemed), were fined 10/- (50p). Amongst those caught in 1926 were brothers Kenneth and Edwin Twemlow, both of whom were TT winners. Another year, top TT man Jimmy Guthrie was up before the High Bailiff for riding his race machine without an effective silencer. Again it was clear where official sympathy lay and there was laughter in Court when Jimmy was asked if he required time to pay the 10/- (50p) fine.

Travelling Marshals are usually considered to be amongst the more responsible of riders - but one must not forget that they are all former racers. A couple who have had minor brushes with Manx laws are Terry Shepherd and Graham Downes. Terry's occurred in 1957, the year that he was asked by Velocette to use an early race-kitted Venom on his Travelling Marshal duties. Between a couple of practice sessions he gave the unlicensed Venom a run around the roads of Douglas to resolve a small carburation problem, with the result that he was summoned to appear in Court to explain his actions. Unfortunately, Terry was catching up on a bit of sleep (after early morning practice) at the time that he was supposed to be in Court, so they sent an officer around to collect him. Anywhere else and he might have been for the 'high-jump', but everyone was quite understanding about the whole matter. Indeed, so understanding were they, that the policeman who had booked him was left feeling that he was the one who was in the wrong.

Former MGP competitor Graham Downes did his single year of Travelling Marshal duty at the 1961 MGP, where he was given a sporty and road legal AJS 650 twin to use for the fortnight. Outside his race duties he met a nice young lady on the Island (later to become his wife) and, removing the 'M' (for Marshal) plates from the bike, he took her for a fast ride around the Course. All went well until they were approaching Ballaugh Bridge at some three times the legal speed limit, when they were stopped by a policeman at the bridge and given a solemn ticking-off about the dangers of visitors travelling at excessive speeds when (supposedly) they did not know their way around the Course.

Norton used this silencer mute on their race machines when travelling to the Start area for practice in the late 1930s

The top men get the most publicity when they break the Island's laws. Lightweight 125 and 250cc TT winner Bill Ivy certainly made the headlines in the 1960s, when he appeared in Court to explain how he had managed to scrape the side of his car for a couple of hundred feet along the roadside wall at Greeba Castle. The incident gave a fright to passenger Mike Hailwood and, some say, to two young lady passengers. Bill had to pay £12 to the Court for his driving misdemeanour and somewhat more to the firm that repaired his car.

For many years Joey Dunlop was renowned for liking a tipple and one year this got him into potentially serious trouble. Stopped by the Manx police whilst driving back to his digs, he was adjudged to have partaken to excess. (Joey might not have agreed with that, as he operated to different standards than those laid down by the 'breathalyser' laws). The outcome was a hefty fine and a ban from driving on Manx roads. Happily, this did not mean a ban from racing on Manx roads.

Competitors put in many miles around the Mountain Course outside official practice periods as they strive to improve their Course knowledge or, in the case of some top riders, to impart that knowledge to others. Used to travelling briskly, they are easy prey for the radar-equipped Manx constabulary, and each TT and MGP sees a number of competitors making unsought contributions to the Manx Treasury for speeding.

Lots of foreigners visit the Island for the TT and not all are familiar with the local laws. A great many of them are German riders and to make them feel comfortable (or maybe that should be uncomfortable), German traffic police visit the Island at TT and do turns of duty over its roads.

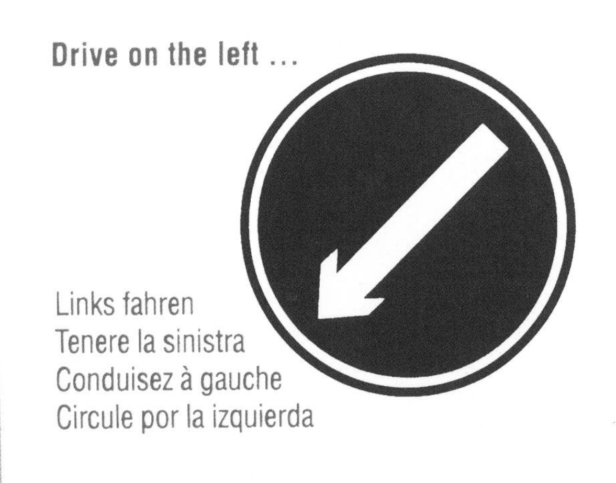

Some Manx roads signs have instructions for foreign visitors.

CAN YOU BELIEVE IT?

Rem Fowler won the multi-cylinder race at the first TT in 1907 riding a twin-cylinder Peugeot-engined Norton fitted with automatic inlet valves (opened by engine suction). He returned to contest the 1908 event using a twin-cylinder engine of Norton's own design that also featured automatic inlet valves and non-adjustable tappets. The basic steels in use at the time allowed the valves to stretch in use and, with non-adjustable tappets, all clearance could sometimes vanish after 20 miles of racing. To cope with the problem, Rem planned to carry a 6" file with the intention that he could stop during the race, file-down the valve tops, recover some clearance (and compression) and continue the race. Unfortunately, he forgot to carry his file and in his words: *'... it soon overheated, lost its compression and ran to a standstill'.* Not only did valves stretch but they sometimes broke. Riders in those early races usually carried a spare that, at the risk of burnt fingers, they could change at the side of the road in about 10 minutes.

A Norton twin-cylinder engine similar to the one used in the 1908 TT, this example being from 1910.

*

Few of today's race fans will have heard of some of the makes of machine entered in the early races. In 1910 a three-man team were mounted on the Moveo marque. Jack Loxham owned the firm and was entered on a twin, while D.B. Rea and Bert Houlding were on singles. In a later report of their endeavours, respected historian Bob Currie wrote: *'Practice periods passed off uneventfully enough but apparently Loxham was ill-at-ease with the twin and, exercising a gaffer's privilege, he swapped bikes with Houlding as they came to the starting line'*. Surely that was against the rules!

*

Whilst the Isle of Man has always been thought of as welcoming to motorcyclists, there has been the occasional aberration in official attitude. A pre-TT article in 'Motor Cycling' of May 1914 warned those who had thoughts of going to the TT with a pillion passenger: *'In the Isle of Man it will be remembered ludicrous penalties are enforced against pillion riding - £50 fines and three months imprisonment loom largely before the Isle of Man motorcyclist'.*

The manner in which many pillion passengers were carried in the days before the First World War.

Wal Handley was a man who achieved great deeds in his TT career (4 victories and 9 fastest laps), but on the first occasion he took to the Course on his Lightweight OK Supreme in 1922, no one would have suspected him to be capable of such fine performances. In his words: *'I arrived in Douglas on the Tuesday evening of the first week (of practice) and turned out to practice the following morning. I had never seen the TT Course, and when I arrived (at the Start) on Wednesday morning there was heavy mist. I pushed onto the road on my machine half pointing to Governor's Bridge and was then told that I could go. I did, at full speed - the wrong way of the Course. There was a lot of excitement over that . . . . but by the time I reached Governor's Bridge I realised what was the matter and turned round'.* Despite such a bad start to his TT career, Wal showed his class that first year by getting around in practice in a time that was less than the lap record and, come the race, he held the lead until forced to retire at Sulby on the second lap.

Later in his career Wal Handley used his TT fame to boost his motor business.

*

Maurice Davenport was an ace engine-tuner of the late 1920s and Syd Crabtree was an experienced TT runner who was desperate for a win. Eric Neliussen told how Crabtree passed the engine of his Lightweight Excelsior to Davenport to prepare for the 1929 race, promising Davenport £1,000 if he, Crabtree, won the race. That was a tremendous figure for the day (multiply it by forty for today's value) and, as Crabtree did win the race, it made Davenport a rich man.

*

The number of marshals available to the organisers in the late 1920s was far less than for today's races. This made crowd control difficult, particularly as spectators assumed that they could walk along the footpaths whilst practice and races were in progress. After a policeman 'booked' several for indulging in this potentially dangerous pastime, he in turn found himself criticised in the 'Isle of Man Weekly Times' with the words: *'When the Manx*

Legislature closed the roads for practices, it was not thought that it would affect pedestrians walking along a footpath on a straight, but only vehicular traffic on the roadway itself. The police seem to be unnecessarily officious in this paltry matter and deserve to be reprimanded for their conduct'. It was the organisers who encouraged the policeman to take out his note-book, for they were aware of the dangers and could not maintain adequate control of spectators. Indeed, if there were no marshals around, they could only hope that spectators would take heed of the polite request in the race programme, which read: *'Spectators would help the riders very considerably by refraining from crossing the road during races'.*

*

The 1930s saw increased use of light alloys in race machines in items like crankcases, carburettors and in the case of some Lightweights, in their connecting rods. There was also the beginnings of a move from steel to alloy wheel rims but, seemingly lacking confidence in the alloy-welding of the time, the rim-joint was reinforced by riveted plates.

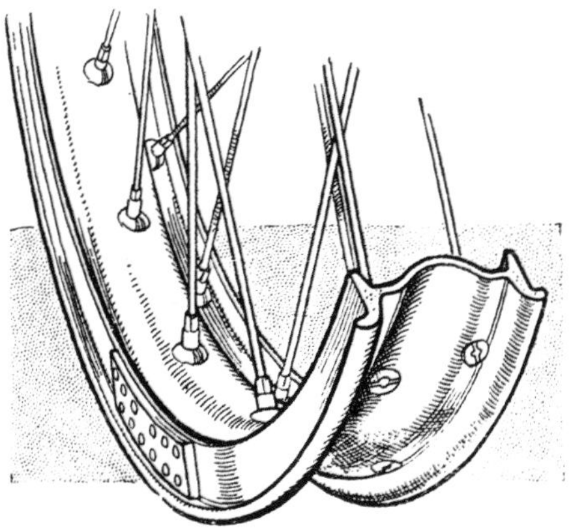

A light alloy wheel rim in 1935, showing the welded joint reinforced with riveted plates.

*

Ronnie Mead was sitting on his lovingly prepared Excelsior waiting to go out for practice at the 1947 TT when he was run into by an ambulance. The bike was badly damaged and Mead's foot was crushed, so putting him out of the race.

*

Practice at the 1959 TT was interspersed with a few light moments. Albert Moule and Terry Shepherd were both racing Nortons (as were most of the Senior entry) and Albert was embarrassed when he accidentally took Terry's machine from the Paddock at one practice session instead of his own. He realised his mistake by the time he got to Braddan Bridge and returned to the Paddock via side roads, where he found Terry standing scratching his head and muttering *'I am sure I left it just here'.* It was still the time when most competitors rode their machines up to the Paddock and, without wheelstands (which were virtually unknown), they usually leant their bikes against the Paddock fence, or against the posts which the organisers provided.

*

One man at the 1959 TT who would have had an excuse for getting confused over his machinery was sponsor Reg Dearden. Reg was a man whose name was synonymous with the Island's races in the 1950s and 60s and he probably supplied a machine to almost everybody who was anybody at the time. MGP winner George Costain rode for Reg for several years and tells how at the 1959 TT, Reg brought 22 Manx Nortons to the Island, plus a host of spare engines, gearboxes, etc. Some of those were probably unofficial 'works' Nortons, for although the company had withdrawn from racing and offered only stock versions of their Manx models for sale, they did supply 'special' engines to a few privileged riders, often doing it through Reg Dearden.

*

Mike Hailwood came to his fourth TT in 1961 with several leaderboard finishes to his name, but no victories. Arriving with 250, 350 and 500cc machines, he was on the look-out for a 125 and approached Honda. They claimed all their bikes were allocated so Mike accepted that he would just have three rides. But Mike's father, Stan, then brought his financial muscle to bear, telling Honda that if they supplied Mike with a bike he would stock Hondas in his Kings of Oxford dealerships across Britain. All that Honda could offer was a tired practice bike but Stan took it, the incredible Mike rode it to victory, and doing so left the Honda 'works' bikes ridden by Luigi Taveri, Tom Phillis, Jim Redman and Sadao Shimazaki to follow him home. He then took wins on his 250 and 500 (becoming the first person to achieve a hat-trick of TT wins in a week) and was leading the 350 race until his engine failed half a lap from the chequered flag.

'Catch me if you can' says Mike Hailwood as he streaks away from the opposition on his six-cylinder Honda 250 on which he took TT and World Championship wins.

*

Someone who had an exciting time just getting to the Island to ride in the 1963 TT was Swiss sidecar driver Florian Camathias. Driving up through England his van broke-down near Hinckley. With his prime concern being to get to the Island, he unloaded his BMW racing outfit and he and his passenger climbed into their leathers and set off for Douglas on open pipes. There was a slight hitch at the Mersey Tunnel when they could not produce money for the toll, but they were let through, made it to the boat, crossed to the Island and, for good measure, won the Sidecar TT!

*

By the end of practice week at the 1981 TT, riders in all classes had completed 1824 laps and 68,820 miles. One man who rode his share of those practice miles only to be left bitterly disappointed at the end of the week was Eddie Roberts. His Honda blew its engine in the final practice session and it looked as though he was out of the opening Formula I race. Then a German visitor offered him a ride on his road-going Z1000 Kawasaki, complete with high-rise handlebars. Eddie did not even get to learn the generous visitor's name before he raced the bike to 28th place at an average speed of 91.96 mph.

Eddie Roberts exits Governors Bridge on the borrowed racer.

*

It has been the trend for some years for the TT races to be contested by production-based bikes. These may not provide spectators with the raw excitement of specialised race machinery but, initially, they had the advantage of being relatively cheap for the manufacturers to produce and for riders to run. Senior MGP winner of 1992, Alan Benallick, moved up to the TT in 1993 and his Honda RC30 ran all practice sessions, the Formula 1 race (finishing 11th) and the Senior (7th) with one oil and filter change, plus replacement of worn tyres and brake pads. No other mechanical attention was required in the 32 laps (over 1,200 racing miles) that Alan completed. The Honda even finished the TT fortnight on the same chain, and came back for more punishment in later years.

Alan Benallick was still riding an RC30 at the 1997 TT, taking it to 7th place in the opening Formula 1 event.

As is always the way with motorcycle racing, the use of production-based bikes has become ever-more expensive as those with the deepest pockets engage in no-expense-spared missions to win. Now the fastest bikes will not last two races, requiring expensive rebuilds that are almost impossible to achieve in the short interval between races.

*

At the 2003 MGP, local rider Terry Crane made use of a toe-clip of the type that cyclists use to keep their feet firmly on the pedals. His was fixed near the right footrest and served not only to keep his foot in place but also his false leg. Perhaps a star rider of the early 1980s, John Williams, could have benefited from one of those clips. Riding with an ill-fitting boot during practice, he lost the boot from his foot somewhere on the Course and finished the lap without it.

CLOSE FINISHES

The time difference between finishers in some of the early TT races could often be measured in a generous number of minutes, for few riders completed a race without some form of mechanical problem and punctures were frequent. Stopping to replace an inner-tube (spare tubes and tools were usually carried) could take 15 or 20 minutes, but it would not necessarily put a rider out of contention, for his opponents might well have had to stop to take a link out of a drive-belt, or even to change an exhaust valve. The earliest close finish occurred in the 1913 Senior where the relatively unknown Ray Abbott raced off into the lead on his Rudge. Still at the head of the field on the last lap, he was within 100 yards of the Finish when he overshot the right-angled bend at St Ninian's crossroads (at the top of Bray Hill). He turned, rejoined the Course and finished the race, but his little excursion cost him victory which went to Tim Wood by just 5 seconds.

Through the 1920s and 30s races became much closer-fought affairs, riders no longer carried tools (except for a plug spanner) and stopping with a mechanical problem was usually enough to put a competitor out of contention. But it really is amazing that after racing for up to 265 miles, two riders, who probably never saw each other during the race, could finish within seconds of each other. This was doubly difficult to believe when they were riding completely different machines. The 1935 Senior TT was one of the greatest races of all time and the two main protagonists, Jimmy Guthrie and Stanley Woods were on very different machines. Jimmy's single-cylinder Norton with girder front forks and rigid rear end was up against Stanley's Moto Guzzi V-twin with an early form of rear suspension. Although, due to their widely differing starting numbers, they were almost a quarter of an hour apart on the road, they were only 4 seconds apart on corrected time after the 3 hours and 7 minutes that it took them to complete the 265 mile race.

Close finishes are perhaps a little more understandable when riders are mounted on identical machines, and that was the case when Luigi Taveri won the 1964 Ultra-Lightweight race by 3 seconds from Jim Redman, with both riding 'works' Hondas. But even then things were not really equal, for ultra-slim Luigi weighed about 4 stone

Luigi Taveri tucks himself away on his 50cc Honda. Luigi was 125 World Champion in 1962 and later rode four and five-cylinder 125s for Honda as well as 50 and 250cc machines.

(56 lbs/25 kg) less than the conventionally built Jim. Luigi may well have had to add weight to his machine, for it was in the era when minimum weight limits were set for riders, nevertheless, there remained a big difference in the load carried and it must have had an impact on machine performance, for as well as the obvious effect of the engine having to haul more weight, the bigger rider would not have been able to tuck away behind the fairing as efficiently as the smaller one - something that was critical to get top performance out of a 125.

The weight difference between Luigi Taveri and Jim Redman was probably the same as between Luigi and Mike Hailwood, yet three years earlier Mike had managed to push Luigi into second place by 8 seconds when they both contested the 125 TT on Hondas. Manufacturers have probably experimented over the years to determine the effects of rider weight on machine performance and it would be interesting to see some data.

A Production machine race was introduced at the 1967 TT with classes for 750, 500 and 250cc machines. In the smallest class Bill Smith and Tommy Robb were on Bultaco Metrallas and from the drop of the flag at the Le Mans type start, they rode them wheel to wheel for the 113 miles of the three lap race, with Bill snatching victory from Tommy by just 0.4 of a second.

That Le Mans type start was an exception to the customary interval starting system employed for most Island races. With interval starts riders challenging for the lead often do not see the person who they are contesting it with for the entire race. But there have been occasions when riders (when sent off in pairs) have left the line together, ridden the whole race together and finished together. One such event was the Production Class C event of 1986 when Gary Padgett beat Malcolm Wheeler by just one second and another, with even closer finish, was the Classic Senior MGP of 1992. Previous Classic winners Bob Heath and Bill Swallow were separated by just 0.2 of a second after a titanic tussle in which they were never more than a couple of bike lengths apart for the whole race. With total confidence in each other and able to race at maximum speed, Bob was first across the line at a record race average speed of 102.84 mph.

The closest finish - 1992 Classic Senior Manx Grand Prix

This is how they started the 1992 Classic Senior MGP, with Bob Heath (no.1) and Bill Swallow (no.2) given the instruction to move up to their starting positions by Alex Downie.

This is how they raced - Bill Swallow just ahead at Governors Bridge

This is how they finished - Bob Heath takes the narrowest of victories.

It is difficult to see how one could expect a closer result than that between Bob Heath and Bill Swallow. Indeed, most of those who saw them battling for 4 laps thought that a dead-heat would have been a very satisfactory result. The rare occurrence of a dead-heat did occur in the Lightweight 400 race in 1999. Nick Jefferies and Geoff McMullan tussled for 4 laps and 151 miles in their attempts to claim third place, but at the finish they could not be separated on time.

Close finishes are not limited to the solo classes, for sidecars have also had the time-keepers double-checking their watches. Surprisingly, the mass-start sidecar races held on the Clypse Course between 1954 and 1959 did not, as mass-starts are supposed to do, generate close racing for the lead, and each of those races was won by a margin of over a minute. The first close finish to a sidecar race occurred in 1966 when Fritz Scheidegger (BMW) won by 0.8 of a second from Max Deubel (BMW), and in 1989 Dave Molyneux (Yamaha) won by a similar narrow margin when he took his first victory by 1.2 seconds.

The fact that riders can be racing within a split second of each other whilst separated by a mile or more on the Course is just one of the aspects that makes Island racing so different from short circuit racing.

COMMUNICATIONS

The present day system of round-the-Course radio and telephone communications from marshals posts to Race Control, from marshal to marshal, from rider-counting points to Race Control, rescue-helicopter to Control, Travelling Marshals to rescue-helicopter, etc, ensures that little in the way of a race incident is missed by the race organisers. It is all a far cry from the system employed at the first TT held on the Mountain Course in 1911, when, in truth, the organisers were almost completely in the dark as to what was happening once riders left the Start area. Using the technology of the day, a marshal might be able to get a Course-side Post Office to use their telephone to send a message to Race Control, but even this could only be done during races, for the Post Office would not be open during early-morning practice, so there really was no communication in 1911. A dedicated telephone was installed at Ballacraine in 1912, plus one at Ramsey and one at Creg ny Baa, but as few people were familiar with the use of the instrument, each was attended by a trained telephonist to operate it.

By the mid-1930s there were 12 dedicated telephones around the Course, but they came with the strange warning from the organisers that *'intercommunication by telephone between marshals is most undesirable'*. A dozen telephones was still insufficient to spread messages to all parts of the Course (there was no Manx Radio and the only public-address system was at the Grandstand), so Scouts continued to be used as runners to convey information between marshals posts. Even the messages that did pass were not always totally accurate. George Paterson was a man who raced at the TT for nearly 20 years but one year the organisers lost track of his whereabouts, with his last sighting supposed to have been at Creg ny Baa. A search was instigated on the stretch after the Creg without success. With concerns growing as to his safety, it was eventually discovered that he had spilled at the Gooseneck which is some 10 miles before the Creg.

Communicating with Race Control from a Course-side telephone.

It was in the mid-1930s that Travelling Marshals were introduced and they were provided with a list of private houses on the Course which had telephones that they might make use of. It was not until 1956 that their bikes were first fitted with radios, and they were bulky steel clad items that added 37 lbs (17kgs) to the weight of each machine. The glass valves of the time (no transistors) did not take kindly to the rough treatment they received over the Manx roads and they particularly disliked the after-effects of jumping Ballaugh Bridge. Whilst the 1956 experiment proved the worth of radio communication (subject to some black-spots), there was no regular provision of radios for Travelling Marshals until the early 1980s.

Travelling Marshal Bob Foster's radio-equipped Triumph at the 1956 TT. As well as the bulky box on the carrier, there was a tank-mounted control panel/handset and a handlebar-mounted speaker.

The number of dedicated telephones available for use by marshals increased to about 75 by the mid-1980s, and they were housed in green wooden boxes at the side of the Course that involved much commissioning work for the telephone authorities before each event.

The number of telephones continued to increase and hand-held radios were introduced on some parts of the Course to allow 'intercommunication' between marshals in the same sector, rather than as a link to Race Control. As mobile phones came into widespread use during the late 1990s, many marshals made use of these until, in 2004, elements of the race organisation first made use of TETRA the Island's latest radio communication system, this use spreading in 2005 to the whole race organisation.

CONSISTENCY

It is easy to understand how a rider can circulate for lap after lap on a short circuit and record times within fractions of a second of each other, for he is doing what a top rider ought to be able to do, and that is to hone his skills with a particular machine and ride to the limit over relatively few corners for a short distance. A short circuit rider's progress may occasionally be hindered by a back-marker, but there are usually sufficient marshals waving blue flags at the slow rider for him to get out of the way. But things are so very different on the 37¾ mile Mountain Course, for no two laps of riding will offer exactly the same conditions (and the blue flag is not used). To expect even the best TT riders to lap in consistent times might seem too much - but they often do so. A top rider who starts at the front should enjoy fairly clear roads for much of the race, but he is likely to catch tail-enders before the finish and they will affect his lap times, for it can sometimes take half a mile or more on some parts of the Course to pass. Even subtle changes in the wind direction, or an isolated shower, can cost a few seconds - and will an engine deliver exactly the same output for an entire race? Ignoring the effects of fuel stops, a rider can be thought to be riding remarkably consistently if he delivers lap times over the Mountain Course that are within 10 seconds of each other.

In the great Senior TT of 1935 Stanley Woods beat Jimmy Guthrie by just 4 seconds over 7 laps and the story of their respective race strategies can be seen in their lap times. Both were under no illusions as to whom they had to beat and Jimmy, full of confidence in his tried and tested Norton, rode virtually flat out for the whole race, delivering lap times of: 26 minutes 53 seconds (standing start), 26:31, 26:28, 27:32 (refuelling stop), 26:39, 26:31, 26:40. But Stanley did not have such confidence in his mount and chose not to ride flat-out in the early stages. He was aware from his signals that Jimmy was pulling away from him, but the knowledge that he had to make his Moto Guzzi last for seven laps made him ride with restraint. Increasing his revs and speed from the middle of the race in controlled fashion, he threw caution to the winds on the last lap and gave the Guzzi its head. Seriously over-revving it as he came down the Mountain,

Superstars of the 1930s racing scene. Stanley Woods (below) - Jimmy Guthrie (above)

Stanley prayed that it would hold together until he crossed the finishing line. It did, and victory was his by 4 seconds. Once again his lap times revealed his race strategy: 27:21, 26:50, 26:33, 27:22, 26:26, 26:28, 26:10.

At the 1961 Senior TT, Mike Hailwood rode his Norton to victory over Bob McIntyre and lapped with remarkable consistency over the six laps of the race: 22:30, 22:16, 22:16, 23:09 (fuel), 22:18, 22:33. Mike won by nearly two minutes and it is possible that, knowing his lead, he eased the pace a little on the last lap, or may be he encountered backmarkers. Bob Mac was equally consistent, running in: 22:50, 22:35, 22:34, 23:35 (fuel), 22:44, 22:39. Mike's consistency is all the more remarkable when you consider that he was riding four different capacity classes in 1961: in the 125, 250, 350 and 500cc TTs, on bikes that had different handling, braking, number of gears, gearchange positions, and performance characteristics.

Consistency by Mike Hailwood (no.5) at the head of the Leaderboard at the 1963 Senior TT. It was an unusual race for the way the first six places remained unchanged until the last lap when no.8 Alan Shepherd dropped out.

Ten years before Mike's 1961 performance came an even more remarkable one from Rhodesian Ray Amm. With a reputation as a bit of a wild man, his was not the first name to spring to mind when thinking of absolute consistency of riding, but in the Junior TT of 1951 he recorded the remarkably similar times (excluding his standing start and refuelling laps) of 26:23, 26:21, 26:23, 26:24 and 26:21 during the 7 lap race. What made his performance the more surprising was the fact that he was a Newcomer riding in his first TT.

Geoff Bell and passenger Keith Cornbill took a double win in the two Sidecar races at the 1992 TT. Each race was over 3 laps and in Race A their winning average speed was 101.50 mph, whilst in Race B it was 101.49 mph. That represented a time difference of 0.6 of a second between the two races, each of which was over 113 miles. Like the solos, sidecars are seeded with the top runners starting at the front and, with their additional width, this can be a big help, for it often needs a good stretch of road and the cooperation of the outfit being passed, for overtaking to take place. The additional difficulty of overtaking with a 'chair' can certainly be regarded as a barrier to achieving consistent lap times.

A diffrent example of consistency is the way some riders fit the TT and MGP into their race programmes year after year. 'Paddy' Johnston rode every year from 1922 (above) to 1936, then came back for three more races in the post-war period, finishing in 1951.

Bill Beevers raced from 1934 to 1960 and usually rode in two solo classes. But that was not enough for him, and from 1955 he raced a sidecar as well. Of the same era was Albert Moule. His Island career started in the MGP of 1936 and he moved to the TT in 1948. Thereafter, in his familiar blue and black-ringed helmet, Albert rode until 1967 when he was prevented from continuing by the upper age limit for riders in International events enforced by the FIM. It was believed that Albert managed to achieve a few more years racing after he reached the limit by 'losing' several years from the age shown on his entry form (if not from his birth-certificate). The organisers recognised the huge experience of Bill Beevers and Albert Moule and they were both enlisted as Travelling Marshals after retiring from racing. Others with long TT careers were Tommy Robb, Bill Smith, Arthur Wheeler, Joey Dunlop and Nick Jefferies, whilst at the MGP Dennis Parkinson rode from 1932 to 1953. Dennis was a five-times winner of the MGP but nowadays the organisers operate to an un-written rule that prevents a winner from competing again. Many riders who start their Island racing careers at the MGP extend them by moving on to the TT. It has even become the fashion that when they have finished at the TT they now return to compete in the Classic races at the MGP - something that the rules do allow. Consistency of appearance at the TT and MGP extends beyond the racers, for many of the organisers and marshals have contributed long years of service. And then, of course, there are the long-term spectators . . .

COUNTDOWN TO THE START

The TT and MGP meetings run under sets of procedures that have been refined over a period of 100 years. Prior to the start of every race there is a 180 minute countdown period that incorporates the following tasks:

180 minutes	Scrutineering commences.
120 Minutes	Clerk of the Course on duty with prepared schedules. Early weather report from Met Office.
110 minutes	Both Deputy Clerks of the Course on duty.
95 minutes	Inspection car proceeds with Clerk of Works who is in direct contact with control.
90 minutes	First course report from 2 Travelling Marshals in Ramsey, having covered the

course in opposite directions.

60 minutes All Travelling Marshals have given their first reports.

55 minutes Clerk of the Course obtains latest weather report from Met Office.

50 minutes Clerk of the Course communicates all relevant information to the Jury/Stewards and indicates whether the race will start on time or a delay is expected.

45 minutes First signal (klaxon). Competitors take possession of their machines and may start engines.

35 minutes Senior police officer on duty. Radio checks to Travelling Marshals at their pre-race locations. Score-board, clocks control operators and scouts on duty.

30 minutes Road closed. Second signal. Riders and machines proceed to their pit. Duty doctor in control Helicopter doctors on duty. Civil Defence and Raynet radio controllers on duty.

25 minutes Clerk of the Works reports to Clerk of the Course after inspection lap. Travelling Marshals move to their race locations. Control officers on duty at pits telephones.

20 minutes Race log and press release typist on duty. His Excellency, the Lieutenant Governor, arrives. 12 Sector marshals phone in reports. Time keepers and audi tors on duty.

17 minutes Weather report and 'course condition' information relayed to competitors.

15 minutes Third signal. Competitors lined up on starting grid in start order.

10 minutes Travelling Marshals report in from their race locations. Barrier reports received.

5 minutes Control tower telephonist on duty. Fourth signal. Competitors stand to machines. Official check of clothing and helmet straps. Timekeepers and start-line control officers told to start on time.

0 minutes START RACE.

The 180 minute countdown allows for most problems to be identified and rectified without interruption to the pre-race procedures. However, events sometimes occur that cannot be rectified and they can cause the start of the race to be delayed. The most common of these is the effect of adverse weather. Exactly when the countdown is put on hold on account of the weather is a decision for the Clerk of the Course after he has assessed its effect on the racing. It may be one hour before the scheduled start time, or it can be as close as five minutes to the start.

The Tower at the Grandstand that houses the Race Control office.

Given the length and nature of the Mountain Course, it is not surprising that things sometimes prevent the smooth flow of pre-race countdown procedures. Despite all the pre-race publicity, cars are occasionally left parked on the Course after road-closing times and they have to be moved before a race will be allowed to start. Locals know that they must keep animals under control, but they sometimes stray. Normal incidents in Manx life like house-fires, road accidents, or serious illness do not stop just for the races, and when they happen around practice or race times, it means that rescue-service vehicles must sometimes be allowed access to the Course, with resultant delay to the racers. This is yet another example of where the TT differs from a conventional circuit that operates under conditions of controlled access behind high security fencing on private land. Such delays to racing activity can be very frustrating to all concerned, not least to the organisers and to 'non-racing' Manx residents, but they are part and parcel of TT racing.

COURSE IMPROVEMENTS

The present day TT meeting may be run over almost the same 37¾ miles that the early competitors used, but today's roads would barely be recognised by those TT pioneers. Even when the races returned after their enforced absence during the First World War, Graham Walker described conditions as *'soul-shattering'*. He went on to say: *'Beyond a few tarred stretches between the Start and Union Mills, the remainder consisted of narrow and incredibly dusty lanes of dazzling whiteness, whilst up the Mountain the track consisted of two loose ruts with moss in the middle'.* He claimed the Mountain climb could only be excelled by: *'the excruciating purgatory of the Sulby Straight, which made me literally sick three times during the race. Whereas nowadays a rider prays for a long straight so that he can rest muscles tensed in cornering, the opposite was the case in 1920 - we prayed for corners to give us an excuse to ease down after the battering we received on the faster straights'.*

The rough road conditions of the early TT meant that many riders wore body-belts of the type that are now only used in off-road competition. They were still in common use up until the end of the 1930s as Les Dear (Velocette) shows in 1939.

An interesting array of machinery awaits the start of the 1922 Senior TT - no.4 is Walter Brandish (Triumph), no.5 Clarrie Wood (Scott), no.6 Alfie Alexander (Douglas) and no.7 George Tucker (Norton).

Much of the day-to-day traffic that used the roads of the early 1920s was still horse-drawn and punctures from horse-shoe nails were frequent for the racers. One report of the time said: *'On the Sunday before racing, a party of motorcyclists collected a "hatful" of nails and other "puncturing instruments" between Ramsey Hairpin and the Gooseneck'*, whilst Stanley Woods recalled how a bunch of Scottish lads used to bring brooms and sweep the Course on race-days on the approach to Creg ny Baa.

Road conditions gradually improved (as did suspension systems) to give competitors a slightly easier ride, but, paradoxically, there came a time when riders began to

Frank Applebee (Scott) passes Kate's Cottage on the perilous descent of the Mountain in 1912.

complain about the sort of improvements that eased bends and smoothed bumps - and they are still complaining. Quite when this critical moment of the Course being 'just right' might have occurred is not known. It probably depended on whose opinion was asked. Riders arrived at the TT in 1935 to find road improvements that they estimated were worth 10 seconds a lap and the effect of such improvements on lap speeds has proved an endless topic for debate down the years. Geoff Duke's high speeds had everyone talking at the 1951 TT and, as Editor of 'Motor Cycling' and himself a past TT winner, Graham Walker added the opinion (and a great deal of imagination) that if Duke had ridden his 'works' Norton over the same roads that 1911 winner Oliver Godfrey (Indian) rode at an average speed of 47.63 mph, he would have been pressed to average 62 mph - his actual race-winning speed was 93.83 mph in 1951.

It used to be the custom for the motorcycling

This is the view from Signpost Corner looking towards Bedstead in 1927. Today it is much changed with a mini-roundabout at Signpost, a much widened road down to Bedstead and the fields full of houses.

magazines to produce a useful page-filling report in February or March about the latest Course improvements. As an example, in early 1954 they wrote (with pictures) of widening at Governor's Bridge, slight easing of the right-hand bend at Appledene after the demolition of a roadside cottage, setting back of the high stone wall on the right-hand side of Handley's, easing of the exit from Ballaugh Bridge by repositioning the boundary wall to The Raven, widening the left and right-handers at Kerromoar, substitution of railings for the stone wall on the inside of Signpost Corner and widening of the road down to Bedstead. Although TT fans may have regretted those alterations to their hallowed Course, many of them were actually made for the benefit of the ordinary traffic that traverses the Manx roads week in and week out when they are not being used for racing.

A review of the Course at the time of the TT's Golden Jubilee in 1957 described it as having been transformed over the previous 50 years into *'one of the finest highways in the world'*. Despite the claim, a steady flow of 'improvements' have been carried out during its second 50 years of use. Writing in 1974, one critic of improvements to the Course pointed out that the easing of bends and flattening of bumps resulted in greater strain on engines, as they were flat-out for more of the time. Ten years later Geoff Duke voiced the opinion that circuit changes alone had been responsible for increases in lap speeds of 8 mph over those recorded in the mid 1950s. But despite all the work that has been carried out since 1911, the TT Course is still comprised of very ordinary roads and with the increased speeds involved it remains a major physical challenge to riders, for the machines of today offer little respite from the struggle to keep them under control. There are many places that remain relatively rough and bumpy, and whilst the average rider may allow such conditions to govern his speed, the top men know that they have to overcome them without abating speed.

DIFFICULT STARTING

Machines used in the first TT were single-speed without a clutch and so required to be push-started. To get a bike going, the rider made use of a decompressor lever which lifted the exhaust valve off its seat, so allowing him to push 'in gear' but with much reduced resistance from the engine. When sufficient speed had been gained, he released the decompression lever and hoped the bike would fire.

When clutches came into use, push-starting (comprising run and bump) was retained for race starts. Pushing and bump-starting of a dead engine was a far more tricky and unpredictable process than the engine running, clutch start of today's racers. Riders used to rehearse their starts, for every bike demanded its own particular technique and no one wanted the humiliation of failing to get going in front of the crowded Grandstand. For a bump-start the procedure was - with petrol turned on and bottom gear selected - in the last few seconds before the drop of the flag the rider would pull the bike backwards to get it against compression. He would then pull in the clutch-lever, watch for the flag to drop and, praying that his boot soles would not slip, heave the bike into forward motion. After running a few steps he dropped the clutch, the engine fired, he would jump on side-saddle, increase revs, feed in the clutch, swing into his riding position, change into second, pull down his goggles, flatten himself on the tank and blast off down Bray Hill. If the engine failed to fire he had to repeat the whole time-consuming process. That was the technique for most of the large capacity bikes, but some of the small two-strokes would allow the rider to sit astride the bike, paddle off with his feet when he received the starting signal, drop the clutch and be away in an undulating scream of revs and slipping clutch, often accompanied by clouds of smoke as the engine cleared itself of two-stroke mixture.

Gary Hocking has push-started his Norton into life and prepares to swing into the saddle at the start of a practice lap.

Whilst bump-starting was still the required method to be used at the TT in the 1940s and 1950s, riders in the Clubman's classes that were run from 1947 - 1956 were excluded from this provision. On virtually showroom sports models, Clubman's competitors were required to kick their machines into life at the start of a race and (for several of those years) repeat the process after pit-stops. Many would probably have preferred to push-start, for not all bikes were keen to fire and dodges like squirting lighter fuel into the carburettor before kicking were tried by some.

Many riders have told of difficult starting that involved pushing a reluctant bike from the Start to the top of Bray Hill, but Harold Daniell claimed that he had to push to the bottom of Bray before he could get his four-cylinder AJS to start in the 1936 Senior. There have even been riders that have pushed as far as the Quarter Bridge. There they would usually find some joker who would ask if they intended to push for the remaining 37 miles of the lap. Most were too shattered to provide the deserved response, and it was usually the moment that they decided to retire.

Engines have to be cut during a pit-stop and it is always a worrying moment for a rider when he comes to restart. With hot engines rarely at their most co-operative after a pit-stop, if carefully rehearsed starting techniques get forgotten in the heat of the moment, then precious seconds gained by skilful riding out on the Course can easily be lost. The ultimate blow in such situations - and it has happened - is that the engine refuses all attempts to restart it, forcing the rider to retire.

When John McGuiness won the Singles race of 2002, he lost time in getting the bike to fire after his pit-stop. The problem was solved when he remembered that he had used the kill-switch to stop the motor - but had forgotten to switch it back to the 'run' position. John also had several TT rides on the big Ducati twins of the early 2000s. Not only were they notoriously difficult to start from cold, but there was a good chance that their riders would not be able to get the bikes going again with just a push-start after a Pit-stop, so Ducati obtained dispensation to use the garden-roller type powered-starter in the Pits. Amateur timing suggested that it added 5 seconds to the time their rider was stationary.

DISQUALIFICATION

Disqualification is not only a blow to a rider's race hopes, for it brings with it the stigma of cheating. In the 1911 Senior race the experienced Charlie Collier (Matchless) was disqualified from second place, an event that he described as *'to my mortification and embarrassment'*, after taking on petrol outside the two official refuelling stations (Braddan and Ramsey), and Jake de Rosier (Indian) lost his leader-board finish for borrowing tools out on the Course to adjust his valve-gear.

Jake de Rosier (Indian) in 1911. Although disqualified from the Senior race, he did take victory in a Flying Kilometre race along Douglas Promenade, averaging 75.57 mph.

Howard Davies fantastic ride to victory in the 1921 Senior (500cc) race on a Junior (350cc) AJS saw him escape disqualification on a matter that might have seemed a technicality, but it was one that was an infringement of the rules. Seemingly, the tyres on his Junior machine were a fraction of an inch under the size specified for machines in the Senior race. No one protested and the organisers took no action, so Howard kept his win. He is still the only man to have achieved such a giant-killing victory.

Henry Tyrell Smith comes to grief at a narrow Glen Helen in the 1929 Senior TT.

For many years riders were required to weigh-in their machines on the day before they raced. At the weigh-in the names of the ancillary components fitted would be logged by the organisers; things such as tyres, carburettor, sparking-plug, etc. In a particularly strict interpretation of the race regulations, Italian rider Pietro Ghersi was stripped of a podium place in the 1926 Lightweight race when it was seen at the post-race inspection that his Moto Guzzi was fitted with an Italian Fert sparking-plug instead of the Lodge make that had been specified at the weigh-in. Ghersi was 'excluded from the results' of the race rather than disqualified, it was an action that allowed him to be officially credited with the lap record that he had set in the race.

Henry Tyrell Smith came to the Island in 1929 with two years previous TT experience and, in many peoples eyes, a fair chance of a race win. Seemingly living up to expectations, he led the Senior race on his Rudge until, in his words (from 'Story of the TT' by Geoff Davison): *'I had a lead of about three minutes, I think, when I came to Glen Helen on the fourth lap. It was a pretty tricky bend in those days and I took it a shade too fast. The exhaust-pipe touched the road and spun me round. I crashed into the bank, was winded and tore my leathers badly. They carried me into the hotel and pinned my clothes together. After a bit I got my breath back, but had a nasty pain in my chest. However, I came out of the hotel to see what was doing and found that someone was holding my machine with the engine running, strictly contrary to regulations. They sat me on it and, still very muzzy, I let in the clutch and carried on. I believe that the officials had more than half a mind to stop me and they would certainly have been quite justified in doing so, for it was discovered later on that I had cracked three ribs. I was very glad that they didn't however, for I was just able to carry on and I was very glad to finish third'.* The action of the marshals at Glen Helen would, in the eyes of officialdom, have been regarded as *'outside assistance'* and thus could have brought about disqualification In this instance it did not and third place no doubt offered some consolation for Tyrell Smith's three cracked ribs.

Mass exclusions took place after the Amateur races of 1929 (predecessors of the MGP) when 21 riders lost their awards following an ACU enquiry which revealed that the rules prohibiting riders acceptance of retainers or bonuses had been broken. It was an occurrence that also threatened to break the event, but out of a rewording of the rules (the originals had been unrealistically strict) the Amateur race was reborn as the Manx Grand Prix, that still runs under the auspices of the Manx Motor Cycle Club.

In the first ever TT race to be run on a Sunday (1966), Fritz Scheidegger was excluded from first place in the Sidecar class for using Esso fuel instead of the Shell/BP provided by the organisers. After a protracted appeal he was reinstated as the winner. Scheidegger made no secret of the fact that he was using Esso. Bob Light recalls that he was helping Fred Hanks with 'The TT Special' (it was Fred's first year as Editor after taking over from Geoff Davison) and was on hand at the weigh-in, making a note of all the makes of components, etc, used by the riders. Bob asked Fritz what petrol he was using and he replied *'Esso Golden'* and that was what Bob entered on his record card - a fact that he was asked to verify by the organisers, shortly after the race. It had been an extremely close-fought race, with second place man Max Deubel less than a second behind Scheidegger, and it was one in which BMW showed their dominance of the three-wheeler class at the time by taking the first eight places.

The receipt by a rider of 'outside assistance' is enshrined in TT and MGP history as a reason for disqualification from a race. Later to go on to TT victory and become Sidecar World Champion, George O'Dell rode his first TT in 1970 with Peter Stockdale in the chair. Electrical problems put them out of the opening leg and an oil-pipe burnt through by the exhaust looked like putting them out of the second at The Bungalow. Borrowing a pen-knife, George cut and remade the oil-pipe but was then faced with the fact that he was desperately short of oil. Undaunted, he found a plastic bag and, with the help of a willing spectator, drained oil from the tank of the fellow's road-bike, transferred it to his own machine and rode home to collect a Finisher's Award. As he was a Newcomer, perhaps George had conveniently forgotten the ruling about not accepting outside assistance. However, whatever the rules say, there is another force at work in such situations, for the determination of riders to fix their stricken machines is a reflection more of their overriding will to get to the finish than a deliberate attempt to break the rules on outside assistance. Having said that, spectators are always prepared to offer tools and emergency petrol supplies when a rider stops near them in a

Fritz Scheidegger (BMW) and John Robinson on their way to victory at the 1966 TT.

race and, for their part, despite the rules, riders find it difficult not to accept such well-meaning offers. When the TT races lost their World Championship status in the conventional racing classes, they were allowed to run events counting towards the Formula 1, Formula 2 and Formula 3 World Championships, and the first Formula 3 race on the Island in 1977 attracted controversy. The 'Formula' events were for machines similar to the ones that any competitor could buy (highly expensive 'works' racers were thus excluded) but, right from the outset, there was debate as to what was permitted. Second man home behind John Kidson in that F3 race of 1977 was Derek Loan, but he was later disqualified after it was discovered that the carburettors he used were not covered by the rules of homologation. Other well known riders to suffer disqualification for perceived infringements in Formula races were Phil Mellor (1981), Barry Woodland (1984) and Steve Parrish (1985). It is told elsewhere in the book how Mike Hailwood escaped disqualification from the 1965 Senior race after he had bump-started his MV Agusta in the reverse direction of the Course, but at his come-back in the 1978 races he actually volunteered for disqualification from that year's Senior. Mike knew that he had taken on extra petrol on the Mountain on the last lap to get to the Finish and that this was against the rules that banned the receiving of 'outside assistance'. Plenty of other people must have known what he had done, but nobody told the organisers - except Mike.

Mike Hailwood accelerates his Martini Yamaha out of Governors Bridge, 1978 Senior TT.

CHAPTER 3

TALES OF . . .

DID YOU KNOW?

Although riders wore plain black leathers for many years, the general move to coloured leathers (starting with a daring contrasting stripe down the arm) occurred in the late-1960s. However, it was not the first time colour had been seen, for back in 1910 Frank Phillipp turned out in leathers dyed purple to match his Scott machine, a few years later Rudge entries rode in green, and American Putt Mossman turned up in 1936 in leathers that were described as *'once white'*.

During the 1930s many riders stayed at 'The Cunningham Young Men's Holiday Camp' above Douglas. Qualifications were needed to get in, with the rules stating: *'Only youths and men of good moral character are eligible for admission to the Holiday Camp'*. The £2.10 per week charge for full board made it popular with the younger cash-strapped racers.

*

The Swedish Husqvarna firm were late arriving for practice at the 1934 TT with their 350 and 500cc v-twin racers, due to an accident that befell the lorry carrying the bikes whilst loading ship at Gothenberg. A cable snapped, the lorry fell to the quayside, finished upside down, and the bikes had to go back to the factory for emergency repairs. Husqvarna's best finish at the TT was Ernie Nott's third place in the 1934 Junior, although Stanley Woods held second place in the same year's Senior race until he ran out of petrol.

*

For many years competitors worried about the reliability of sparking plugs, and it was common practice for a rider to carry a spare plug in the pocket of his leathers and a plug-spanner tucked into the top of his boot. The TT Course was very bumpy and it was not unknown for the plug-spanner to be missing from the rider's boot at the end of the race. Some preferred to carry the spanner taped to a frame rail but this was outlawed in 1951 and spanners had to be carried in a container.

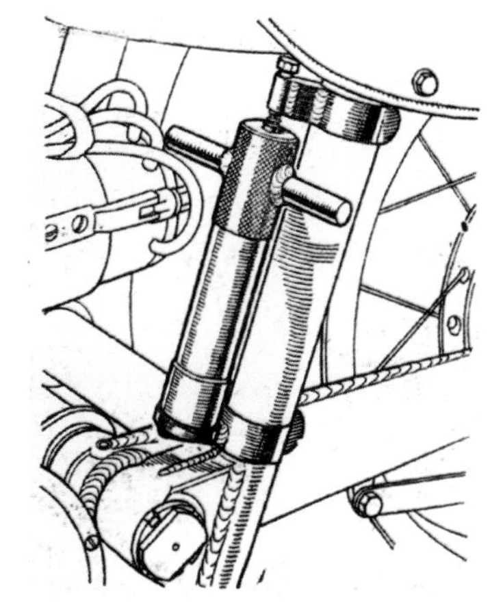

Les Graham's 500cc MV Agusta of the early 1950s carried a plug spanner clamped to a frame rail. Les had four plugs to worry about on the MV.

Geoff Duke's first application to ride in the TT (the Senior Clubman's race of 1948) was turned down due to his lack of racing experience, even though he was a 'works' rider in Trials and Scrambles for Norton at the time.

*

A newcomer to the BBC's race commentary team at the 1949 TT was Murray Walker, who joined his TT-winning father, Graham, to broadcast the races to the world. A motorcyclist in his own right, Murray is a great supporter of the TT and MGP.

*

Norton designed a four-cylinder racing 500 in conjunction with the BRM car-racing concern in the early 1950s. Although some bench-testing was carried out, it never made the track to counter the increasing threat to Britain's single-cylinder racing engines from the four-cylinder machines of the Italian MV Agusta and Gilera concerns.

An artist's impression of the proposed Norton four-cylinder racer.

*

Castor oils such as Castrol 'R' were used for engine lubrication by almost the whole entry in the Junior and Senior classes during the 1950s. Although Castrol 'R' has always been the best known variety, all the other oil companies were able to supply a castor-based oil. Nowadays it is just the occasional traditionalist at the Classic MGP or a runner in the TT Historic Parade who chooses to use castor oil, causing older spectators to sniff the air with nostalgia at the unique aroma.

*

A race for machines of 50cc ran at the TT from 1962 to 1968. The 'tiddlers' were required to cover 3 laps and the fastest lap speed around the Island on a 50 was put up by Ralph Bryans on a 'works' Honda at 85.66 mph. Unfortunately, there was a huge performance gap between the 'works' bikes from Honda, Suzuki, Kreidler, and those of the private runners on Itoms and such-like. In the first running of the race, ten of the private runners were timed at less than 60 mph on the Sulby Straight.

*

The rescue-helicopter came into use at the 1963 TT and the first man to benefit from its services was Tony Godfrey. Tony fell from his Yamaha at Milntown and sustained serious injuries, but his swift transfer to Hospital by 'chopper' probably saved his life.

*

Stunt rider (and much more) Dave Taylor entertained the crowds in the interval between races at the 1977 TT with his attempts to ride a lap of the Course on the back-wheel of his Honda moto-crosser. He almost succeeded, being forced to drop the front-wheel on just a couple of occasions.

Safety-orientated moves at the 1990 TT saw riders being started singly at 10 second intervals, rather than in pairs, and, to reduce speeds in Pit-lane a

'Stop Box' was created at its entrance. Riders are now required to come to a standstill and put one foot down in the 'Stop Box' before accelerating away to their Pit.

Determined not to overshoot the Stop Box at the Pits, Phillip McCallen nearly overdoes the 'stoppie'.

*

Joey and Robert Dunlop came from a family of 7 children, all of whom were known by their middle names. Joey was William Joseph Dunlop and Robert is Steven Robert Dunlop.

*

It is difficult for the ordinary road rider to imagine what it must be like to lap the TT Course at an average speed of over 125 mph, as the very best riders do. But that figure conceals the fact that the average varies over different stretches of the Course. From the Start to Ballacraine top riders are estimated to average 133 mph, from Ballacraine to Kirk Michael 126 mph, Kirk Michael to Sulby Crossroads 136 mph, Sulby Crossroads to Ramsey 123 mph, Ramsey to Bungalow 120 mph and Bungalow to Finish 115 mph.

DOUBLES

First man to win two TT races in a week was Wal Handley. It was in 1925 when he took the short-lived 175 Ultra-Lightweight race and the Junior. It was a year that saw a spectacular jump in average race speeds, due partly to improved road conditions arising from the surfacing of much of the Mountain section of the Course.

*

One of the strangest doubles was that of Eric Lea, the winner of the Junior and Senior Amateur races of 1929 - strange because he came home in second place in each race but finished up being declared the winner of both. Velocette-mounted in the Junior, he finished 12 seconds down on Harry Meageen (Rex Acme), only to see Meageen disqualified for receiving outside assistance with a push-start at Hillberry (after trying to ride the latter part of the race with a broken throttle cable). In the Senior, Lea was on a Norton and finished some 7 minutes in arrears of J.D. Potts (Grindlay-Peerless), but Potts was later disqualified for infringing regulations about receiving Trade support.

Eric Lea, ultimate winner of both the Junior and Senior Amateur races of 1929.

*

Stanley Woods shocked British manufacturers at the 1935 TT when he took Italian Moto Guzzi machines to a double victory in the Lightweight and Senior races. No foreign machine had won a TT (and reaped the subsequent world-wide publicity) since Indian took the first three places in 1911. Moto Guzzi had previously knocked on the door of Lightweight victory on several occasions, but in 1935 Stanley barged it open with his double winning ride.

*

The talented Bill Lomas managed a unique double TT win in 1955 when he won the Junior TT on a Moto Guzzi racing on the Mountain Course, and two days later he piloted a single-cylinder MV Agusta to victory in the Lightweight TT over the Clypse Course.

*

Bob McIntyre won both Junior and Senior races at the Golden Jubilee TT of 1957 and set the first 100 mph lap in the process. Come the prize-giving ceremony after the Senior and Bob explained: *'I was a happy man that night. Not so much because of the 100 mph laps that were to be so publicised but because I was the only other Scot apart from Jimmy Guthrie to bring off the Junior and Senior double'.*

*

To win a MGP in September of one year and then go on to win a TT in June of the next has always been seen as a sign of star-rider quality. Few have achieved such a double, but amongst those who did were Geoff Duke and Phil Read, and both went on to prove their outstanding abilities with more TT wins and World Championships.

*

Prolific 'double' men in the 1960s were Jim Redman (Honda) with three consecutive Lightweight 250 and Junior wins from 1963-65 and Giacomo Agostini (MV Agusta) with three consecutive Senior and Junior doubles from 1968-70.

Doubles were not so frequent in the 1970s although Phil Read managed a couple before and after his 5 year break from the TT.

Giacomo Agostini an the three-cylinder MV Agusta.

*

Riding in some International TT races serves to bar a rider from subsequently taking part in the 'proper' MGP, although he can still enter the Classic races at the meeting. Manxman Richard 'Milky' Quayle had already gone down the promising young rider route with a double MGP win before moving on to the TT, but he then added a new form of double to the record books in 2002 when he first won the Lightweight 400 TT and then went on to win the Senior Classic MGP in August/September of the same year.

Following his unique 'double', Richard 'Milky' Quayle is interviewed at the end of his winning ride in the 2002 Senior Classic MGP by Manx Radio's roving-mike, with wife Lydia and sponsor Andy Molnar sharing the occasion.

*

TT doubles are still regarded as a bit special but a select few have won three races in a week - Mike Hailwood, Steve Hislop, Joey Dunlop, David Jefferies and John McGuinness - whilst Phillip McCallen is the only rider to have won an incredible four races in one week.

EARLY MORNING PRACTICE

Loved by some, disliked by many and even loathed by a few, early morning practice was a legendary part of the TT meeting and for many years it extended over two weeks. Even that was not enough for the first riders and they could be seen thundering around the 15½ mile St Johns Course, that included the narrow streets of Peel, at all hours. Threats of prosecution brought this under control, and when the races were moved to the Mountain Course in 1911, things were a bit more disciplined.

Not all the early race teams stayed in Douglas, because Triumph and Levis took accommodation in Peel, whilst Scott chose Ramsey. For the convenience of those teams not based in Douglas, their riders were permitted to join the Mountain Course for practice at Ballacraine and Ramsey, although they would only be timed from the Start and Finish point at Douglas. But it was not only riders who could join in at Ballacraine, Ramsey, etc, because before 1928 the roads of the TT Course were not closed to ordinary traffic during the official early-morning practice sessions. It is difficult to imagine, but horse-drawn fish carts, lumbering lorries, cyclists, etc, could, and did go about their normal business. It was a recipe for disaster and in 1927 Archie Birkin was killed in a collision with a fish-van at the bend just outside Kirk Michael that now bears his name. Thereafter, the Road Closing Orders that reserved the use of the roads for competitors during racing were extended to cover practice periods.

It must have been a wearying business getting up so early for practice over a period of two weeks, not only for those connected with the racing but also the inhabitants of Douglas whose sleep would be rudely awakened by the sound of racing bikes being ridden to the Start. Indeed, the noise in some of the enclosed back-alleys of Douglas where riders kept their bikes must have been awful to residents when they were bump-started on open-pipes. And for the many people living on the edge of the Course, a Manx Norton going past at full-bore offered a guaranteed wake-up call. However most of those who lived within earshot of the racing soon learnt to turn over and go back to sleep.

The timetable for early morning practice varied slightly down the years. In the mid 1930s an official car would complete a lap to close the roads and the first rider would be despatched at about 4.30 am. To cater for such early risers the Falcon Cliff Hotel advertised *'guaranteed practice calls at 3.45 am with refreshments'*. An even earlier start was required by some of the officials and marshals, for they had to be up by 3.00 am. Not

The Scott team on Ramsey Promenade 1923.

everyone was the best of early morning risers and Travelling Marshal of the early 1950s, Len Parry, took unusual precautions to ensure that he woke on time. Upon retiring to bed at Mrs Cringle's 'Studley House' establishment on Douglas Promenade, Len would tie a piece of string around his foot and lower the other end out of his front bedroom window. Fellow Travelling Marshal and guaranteed early riser, Fred Hawken, would give the string a tug as he passed on the way to where he garaged his bike.

In the final years of early-morning practice, the roads were closed at 5.00 am by virtue of the official Road Closing Orders, and the first rider was despatched at 5.15 am at the TT - slightly later at the MGP. Being up so early presented an unfamiliar world to many, but even experienced riders were shocked when they read the information board displayed to them before one morning practice at the 1964 MGP. It told them that conditions were generally good *'except for frost here and there'*. A newspaper wrote of riders gathering for the same session *'in brilliant moonlight'*.

The first evening practice was introduced in 1937 and, thereafter, the number of evening sessions increased and the number of morning ones reduced. Strangely, some riders vied for the 'honour' of being first away in early morning practice and amongst the most successful of those in immediate pre and post-war years was privateer Les Higgins. It was Les who was first on the line with his Velocette on the morning of Monday 29th May 1947, for what was the first post-war TT. It was a nostalgic moment for him and for some of those watching, because he had been first man away in practice for the last TT meeting before war broke-out in 1939, eight years earlier.

Whatever peoples views on early morning practice, it did offer an experience that was unique in motorcycle racing. Nowadays, the first practice session is held on a Saturday evening, but it used to be the case that the first session would be early on Monday morning. Newcomers and old hands would be up at an early hour, climb into cold and stiff leathers and set off to the Start area in the dark. Today that is usually in a van, but in years past they used to ride their racing bikes up through the streets of Douglas. Then, after the bustle of scrutineering they would have to try and get their minds around the fact that they were expected to go out and deliver high-speed laps in the just breaking dawn. The attitude of Newcomers to their first practice lap varies. Many admit to being petrified at the prospect of tackling Bray Hill at speed, let alone the remaining 37 miles. Nearly 50 years ago Arthur Burton had an entry on a 500 BSA Gold Star and wrote of lying in bed shivering *'from fear not cold'*, before his first practice. After completion of his first lap he took stock: *'I was wet, cold, and yes, rather pale, but I was still in one piece, and the BSA had been marvellous. I'd done it! My first lap of the Island. Felt ten feet tall'*. But recent Newcomer to the TT, James McBride, showed no lack of confidence when asked how he felt prior to setting off on his first lap. He replied: *'I own the race-track'*. Certainly, with no speed limits to observe, nobody pulling out from side-turnings and everyone travelling in the same direction, it must be a fantastic feeling to have 37¾ miles of road available to race over.

Riders prepare for a damp and cold early morning practice session at the 1947 MGP.

Hardy spectators shared the unique experience of early morning practice, for they could easily find themselves an empty viewing spot, sit listening in the silence of the Manx countryside and then, faintly, pick up the distant sound of a racing motorcycle. It was something that could only happen on the Island. The sound would come ever closer, until machine and rider leapt into view. That first rider would quickly be followed by many others with just a few seconds between them, for the roads are usually much busier during practice than they are in a race.

A chilly early-morning practice session of the mid-1960s, as a few hardy spectators watch Chief Travelling Marshal Allan Killip take his BSA around the Gooseneck above Ramsey.

Early morning sessions were abandoned for one year as an experiment in the 1970s but they soon returned, although the organisers gradually reduced the number of sessions to three (Monday, Wednesday and Friday) with the option to include Saturday if felt necessary. Recognising that conditions are sometimes less than ideal so early in the day, riders were no longer timed during morning sessions at the MGP. However, most felt that they still offered valuable track time, for a major part of the TT challenge is in getting the bike set up for the TT Course so that the rider can make use of its maximum performance - and that can take much time. Just one example is that of fastest Newcomer in the 1995 Junior (at 111 mph), Jared Gillard from New Zealand. He was faced with 9 wet practice sessions (out of 12) over the daunting Course that he had come so far to learn and race over. Nevertheless, the early sessions did allow him essential Course-learning time which he obviously used to good effect in the race. It was with relief that he saw his race-day dawn fine and sunny and it moved him to say: *'beats the hell out of 3.45 am rises to make 4.30 am scrutineering for 5.15 practice'.*

Come 2004 and early morning practice was abandoned at the TT and MGP, although the organisers had a couple of emergency sessions reserved in case they lost any evening ones. There were mixed views on the matter and also mixed reasons put forward by the organisers for dropping them. Whilst evening sessions were extended slightly (into the gathering dusk) and sessions added after race-days, it was difficult to believe that there was not an overall loss of practice facility over the testing Mountain Course.

ENGINE COOLING

Once they reached their designed operating temperatures, there used to be a risk that motorcycle engines would lose power as they gained heat. This was particularly noticeable with the early all-iron engines that incorporated fairly basic metallurgy in vital components such as pistons and valves. For most of those primitive machines the only thing that kept their engines at reasonable operating temperatures was the cooling effect of air as the bikes were in motion. The first TT Course was chosen to be testing, but not over-testing, to the clutchless,

The Assembly area at the Start is busy as riders and machines await an evening practice session.

single-speed, air-cooled engines of the day, nevertheless, the ascent out of Glen Helen was very difficult and needed every ounce of their limited power. Rex machines were just one of the makes that were troubled by this hill. In an attempt to ease the problem, the Company came to an arrangement with a lady who lived in a cottage near Laurel Bank (on the flat before the climb) to keep a bucket of cold water available for use by riders of Rex machines. They would stop, ladle water over their engines to cool them, and then set off for the ascent. Whether this would have been classed as 'outside assistance' (forbidden by the race regulations) if it had come to the notice of the organisers, is open to debate.

Two-strokes are even more sensitive to the effects of power loss from overheating than four - strokes, and the only two-strokes in the early races were Scotts. Advanced for their time, Scotts were well aware of the problem. Not only were they partly water-cooled from the outset, they were also good enough to take victory at the 1912 & 1913 TTs.

Water-cooling had an obvious weight penalty and most manufacturers tried to avoid it. The fast and successful ohv AJS machines of the early 1920s had their barrel fins copper-plated before being blacked - all in pursuit of cooling. Through the late 1920s and 1930s, engines made greater use of metals with better heat shedding ability that were also beneficial when used in components like brake drums. Whilst occasional machines were water-cooled in this era, manufacturers, seemingly, still tried to avoid it.

What is just as important as avoiding overheating is ensuring that engines are brought up to a reasonable temperature before the start of a race, although it was not until 1935 that riders were allowed to warm their engines before the start. Even with that concession, many an engine has suffered from too enthusiastic a use of the riders right-hand in a race that sees the start followed by the fast descent of Bray Hill, then after a brisk stretch through Braddan and on to Union Mills, the engine is fully loaded by the climb of the Ballahutchin out of Union Mills and the flat-out section that follows through Glen Vine and Crosby.

Riders were first allowed to warm-up their machines in 1935. They did it by riding them up and down the Glencrutchery Road round strategically placed dustbins. Warming-up under those controlled conditions should have been a safe procedure, but prior to the 1938 Junior, C.B. Sutherland managed to tangle with Les Higgins and fell from his machine. While the rider escaped unscathed, his bike suffered brake damage that prevented him from taking part in the race. What a

Two water-cooled racers. Left: Frank Phillip made fastest lap of the race in the Senior TT of 1911 on his Scott. Right: Walter Rusk sits astride his water-cooled and supercharged AJS V-4 before going out to practice for the 1939 Senior TT. This machine was said to be the heaviest in the race at 405 lbs/184 kg whilst the race-winning BMW claimed to be only 305 lbs/138 kg.

disappointment that must have been.

Some riders tried to ease the problem of starting with cool engines in the 1950s and 1960s by filling them with pre-warmed oil on the Startline, whilst the NSU team of the early 1950s even used generators to duct hot air on to their motors to warm them before a race. Riders of air-cooled machines were never really confident that they were not going to suffer early engine seizure until they were past The Highlander and on the way to Ballacraine on the first lap. In the same era came the increased use of streamlining, and that could help or hinder the cooling process, depending on the efficiency of its design.

Geoff Duke going through the warming-up procedure in 1955 on his Gilera. The four-cylinder engine needed a thorough warm-up as it held one gallon of oil.

As with road-bikes, the engines of most new race machines moved over to water-cooling in the 1960s and 1970s and that is, generally, the way things remain. But that did not solve all the problems, particularly on the highly-tuned two-strokes that, to cope with differing ambient temperatures, often came to the line with pieces of duct-tape stuck across their radiators. Unbelievably, not just the size but also the position of that duct-tape was absolutely critical and could mean the difference between race success or failure.

Chris Palmer's 125cc Honda makes use of vertical strips of yellow duct-tape on the radiator to achieve optimum temperature during practice at the 2004 TT.

EXHAUSTS

Perhaps the single most important factor to cause friction between motorcyclists and the general public over the last 100 years has been exhaust noise. With riders taking the simplistic view that noise equals power, generations of them have either tampered with their standard exhausts and silencers or fitted the loudest 'after-market' device they could lay hands on. Unfortunately, the main reason behind such noisy and anti-social behaviour has been the ordinary riders' perceived need to copy the racers.

The Tourist Trophy races were created to encourage the development of the touring motorcycle and in the first few years of the event competing machines were required to be fitted with effective silencers. Many motorcycles of the day had a foot-operated restrictor baffle in their

Left: The straight-through exhaust of Stanley Woods Norton was fairly standard for the early 1930s. Right: The substantial megaphone fitted to a Velocette single at the 1949 TT.

silencers to reduce noise in town, but once in the open-country this 'exhaust cut-out' could be de-activated and the machine could run on an open pipe. Such devices were not permitted at the early TT races, because silencing had to be effective throughout the event. But the requirement for silencers only lasted for a couple of years and by the time the TT moved to the Mountain Course in 1911, riders were free to race on open pipes (although, theoretically, silencers had to be fitted whilst practising until 1927).

The straight-through exhaust pipe, that for many years extended as far as the rear mudguard, began to be superseded in the 1930s by a shorter pipe finishing in a megaphone, with multi-cylinder machines seeming to need a slightly less extreme form than single-cylinder models. Like so many

The AJS Porcupine twin experimented with various small megaphones.

'new' technical developments, someone had tried megaphones many years before (one being ABC in 1920) but had failed to develop the principle.

Four-cylinder MV Agustas went for long tapering megaphones, but four-cylinder Gileras of the same era chose straight-through exhaust pipes of constant diameter.

It was not uncommon through the 1920s and 1930s for TT competitors to carry out unofficial testing of their bikes on the Manx roads. The Ballamodha straight between Castletown and Foxdale was a popular location, although with the growth in use of megaphones, most riders chose to use the Mountain. Such activities were less common in the post-war period, although they still occurred. Care was needed, as was shown by Phil Read in race-week of 1977. Testing prior to the Senior race, Phil took a tumble at Brandish, damaged his shoulder, put himself out of the race, and received admonishment from the organisers. Nowadays, such testing is done with a semblance of control at Jurby Airfield.

There is little doubt that, on a race-track, the sound of a motorcycle engine working to its limits on open pipes adds greatly to the enjoyment of those present, although some thought that the pre-war, two-stroke DKWs were so loud as to be too much of a good thing. The TT Course has echoed to the noise of every great racing motorcycle down the years but in 1965 the new sound that bounced from the Course-side walls and spilt far and wide over the Manx countryside was that of Honda's new six-cylinder 250. In the hands of Jim Redman,

Four-cylinder MV Agustas went for long tapering megaphones, but four-cylinder Gileras of the same era chose straight-through pipes of constant diameter.

the rasp from its six tapered megaphones sent a shiver down the spine of those listening, and momentarily deafened the riders he passed.

Jim Redman rounds Quarter Bridge preparing to open the throttle and thrill spectators with the sound from his 250cc six-cylinder Honda.

Production racing was introduced in the 1960s, for which silencers were required. Manufacturers did their best to derestrict the performance muffling effects of their silencers whilst keeping within the rules and noise limits. Production racing has been in an out of the TT Programme, but for several years after their reintroduction in the 1990s, Production machines could be fitted with after-market exhausts and silencers, but then it was ruled that they had to retain their standard devices.

So, although in the Production classes the TT can be said to have gone full circle on the issue of 'proper' silencing in the past 100 years, when listening to some of the 'old' bikes that take part in the Classic Parades at each TT, it is understandable why many people get nostalgic for the sounds of the open-piped singles, twins, threes, fours, fives, sixes and eights of yesteryear. However, what those who heard those open-piped multis in their prime know (and younger listeners may not), is that the noise that emanates from those valuable engines under the controlled and limited revs conditions of Classic Parades, does not match the spine-tingling intensity of sound that came forth when they were raced without restraint in the heat of competition.

Stanley Schofield issued these long-playing records of TT sounds of the 60s and they provide a true reminder of the wonderful noises that emanated from the race machines of the day.

FACTS AND FIGURES

The TT is a paradise for statisticians, for not only can they juggle with lap and race times but the interval starting system creates an additional complication to occupy those who enjoy a little mental arithmetic with their racing. In the first two years of the races even petrol consumption figures were calculated and published, and factors such as the respective weights of machine and rider were also made known.

*

The record books of TT racing are littered with the names of riders who, in theory, were good enough to achieve a win over the Mountain Course but failed to do so. A well-known rider of the 1920s was George Dance (he even has a style of tank knee-grip named after him). Always expected to challenge for a win, he invariably did so, but in 8 TT races (two of which he led), he only finished in one. His greatest disappointment must have come in the 1923 Junior race when he was leading until 4 miles from the finish, only to strike mechanical problems.

*

After the 1959 TT it was announced that the Clypse Course would be dropped and all classes would race on the Mountain Course, so in 1960 the Sidecar TT was held over the traditional 37¾ miles for the first time since 1925. It was hardly surprising that 1960 winner Helmut Fath broke 1925 winner Freddie Dixon's lap record of 57.18 mph by almost 30 mph with a fastest lap of 85.82 mph on his BMW outfit.

First appearing at the TT in 1961, it took Yamaha several years before they achieved the reliability necessary to win a TT. Phil Read gave them their first solo victory in the Lightweight 125 race of 1965, and Mac Hobson and passenger Mick Burns provided the first sidecar win for a Yamaha powered outfit in 1976. Yamaha have since been consistent winners and have well over 100 TT victories to their name.

*

Some riders labour for years and fail to even record a finish over the Mountain Course, others have somewhat better records. Geoff Duke recorded a win in the Clubman's TT and a win in the MGP before moving on in 1950 to tackle the TT proper. Thereafter, in 11 TT races his lowest finishing position was 4th (with 3 retirements). When MV Agusta were in their prime (and relatively unopposed for several years), Giacomo Agostini rode Junior and Senior mounts in 16 races and his lowest finishing position was 3rd (again with 3 retirements). It is difficult to imagine riders coming into today's TT and being so quickly on the pace as Duke (2nd in his first TT race) and Ago (3rd on his debut).

One of Giacomo Agostini's rare TT retirements came in the 1971 Junior, when the MV three ground to a halt in Parliament Square.

*

The total mileage covered by riders during practice and racing is huge. It is a figure that can vary with the number of entries, number of practice periods available (they have varied down the years) and race distance, but a few examples from the TT are: 1990 - total of 4,615 laps, a distance of almost 175,000 miles, the figures for 1996 were somewhat reduced, being 3823 laps and approximately 145,000 miles. The lap split in 1996 was: laps in practice 2112, in races 1711. In 2004 it was 3065 in practice and 1780 racing laps, a distance of nearly 183,000 miles.

When Soichiro Honda sent the first of his company's bikes to contest the Isle of Man in 1959, it was with the aim of (one day) achieving a TT win. But even someone as foresighted as Mr Honda could hardly have dreamt that when Jim

Moodie won the 1998 Production TT it would give the Japanese company their 100th TT victory. Nick Jefferies tells that one of Mr Honda's favourite sayings was: *'If you are winning TT races you are selling motorbikes'*. That is why the event has always been so important to the Japanese company.

*

For the average TT fan the thought of lapping the Mountain Course at 100 mph can only remain a distant dream. But whilst that figure has had a magical attraction for the past 50 years, even Newcomers are now clocking 110+ mph laps in their first year. (Incredibly, Guy Martin lapped at 114 mph in his first practice session in 2004 and finished his TT fortnight with a lap of 122 mph and 7th place in the Senior race.) Many men have now beaten the 120 mph figure and such speeds were common-place to the great Joey Dunlop. Whilst someone probably has records of exactly how many TT laps he rode, it is known that on the way to establishing his record of 26 TT victories, he put in over 250 laps in excess of 110 mph and over 30 at 120 mph.

Joey Dunlop (Honda) on his way to another 120 mph lap during the 1999 Formula 1 race when he finished in second place.

FEATHERBED NORTON

Through the 1930s and 40s Norton were known to produce respectable handling race-bikes, within the restraints imposed by plunger rear suspension (introduced on the 'works' racers in 1936) and their progressively developed telescopic front forks.

Models of the time were fitted with what was known as their 'garden-gate' frame, but it was subject to frequent breakages when stressed over the bumpy road circuits of the day. It was also expensive to produce, was heavy, and by the late 1940s had reached the limits of development. The result was that the company found itself in danger of losing ground to other manufacturers in matters of handling and, therefore, in race results.

Rex McCandless was a freelance engineer who offered Norton a solution to their problem and gave them something that became a legend in motorcycle racing - the Featherbed frame. Although the 'production' Manx Norton offered to customers for £347 in 1950 was still fitted with the 'garden-gate' frame (it did inherit the double overhead camshaft valve gear of earlier 'works' bikes), Rex came up with a double-loop welded frame fitted with swinging-arm rear suspension for the 'works' racers that he claimed would improve Norton handling. The one place that could be guaranteed to reveal if his claim was correct was the TT Mountain Course. Over the winter of 1949/50 a test was arranged with Geoff Duke and Artie Bell riding examples of the old and new-framed racers over part of the Mountain section of the Course - all done on open roads under the benevolent eye of the local constabulary. The test showed Norton that the new McCandless frame was a considerable improvement on the old and, in the words of Gordon Small: *'he gave them a motorcycle rolling-chassis which allowed their outdated single-cylinder engine to be competitive*

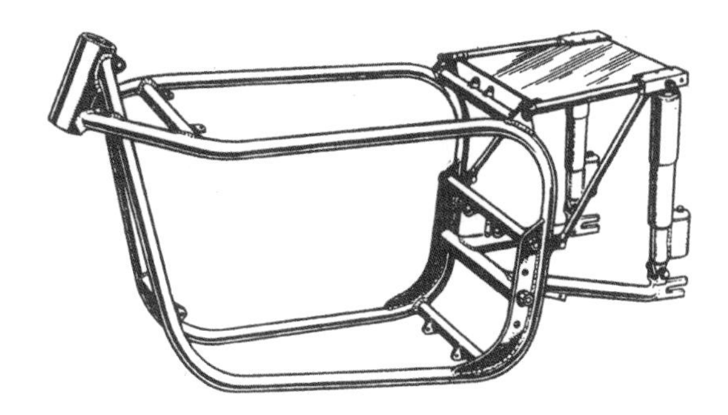

The Featherbed frame designed by Rex McCandless. Norton modified his design in several ways before using it on their race machines.

years after it deserved to be'. After further testing at the bumpy Montlhery circuit in France, the first McCandless framed Norton made its debut at Blandford at the end of April 1950, where Geoff Duke took it to victory in the 500cc race at record breaking speeds. It was a feat that he went on to repeat in the Senior TT, following Artie Bell's win in the Junior.

One of the other 'works' Norton riders at the 1950 TT was Harold Daniell and it was he who, in saying that the new frame and suspension was so comfortable that you could fall asleep on it, went on to coin the expression 'Featherbed'. It is the name by which the McCandless frame, in race and roadster form, has gone down in motorcycle history.

FINANCIAL REWARDS

Some riders have made their fortunes from racing at the TT whilst others have invested every penny they owned in contesting the event (sometimes more than they owned) and finished up poor. It is only in the last 20 years that the prize money available has allowed riders to make money directly from racing at the TT, and those racers who grew rich in earlier years did it either from the retainers paid by factories for their services as 'works' riders, or from the bonus payments paid by the Trade as reward for racing success.

This gives an indication of the lifestyle that top-racer Phil Read had to support in 1976, although there was not quite room to include his Cessna 172 aeroplane on the lawn for the photograph.

Most riders at the first TT of 1907 were mounted on 'works' models supplied by manufacturers and they competed for a prize of £25 to the winner of the single-cylinder and multi-cylinder races, with £15 going to the second placemen and £10 for third. A smaller prize of £5 went to the first private owner in each class. They were quite appreciable amounts for the time and whilst the organisers had raised money from private subscriptions to pay the running costs of the first event, in 1908 they appealed for help to road-riders of the day with an announcement reading: *'Motorcyclists who feel disposed to assist the ACU in awarding some cash prizes to the successful competitors in the Tourist Trophy Race, should forward a postal order for one-shilling or twelve stamps to the secretary of the Auto-Cycle Union'*. The response is unknown, but by 1909 the first prize was up to £40 and it had climbed to £120 by the mid-1920s. However, somewhere along the way the system was changed so that the prize money was paid to the successful rider's entrant, rather than to the rider himself.

Compensation for the fact that a rider who was entered by someone else (as all the top riders were) no longer received prize-money, came from the growth in payment of bonus money based upon race results. Such money came from the 'Trade' which comprised motorcycle manufacturers, component suppliers (sparking plugs, chains, carburettors, etc), plus the petrol, oil and tyre companies. With average race speeds exceeding 60 mph by the early 1920s, such companies desperately wanted to be associated with the high-speed glamour of TT success that made headlines around the world, and they were prepared to pay to gain that association. It was probably the peak era for bonus payments, for they were closely linked to companies' sales and most of those went into decline in the depressed trading conditions of the late 1920s. Payments were rather more modest when things improved in the mid-1930s.

Good riders could expect to be paid a retainer by the factory that they rode for. Charlie Dodson was the first Sunbeam home in the 1925 Junior race. On the strength of that performance he was signed by Sunbeam as a 'works' rider at £600 pa, with Sunbeam taking any prize-money that he won. Charlie's first TT win was the wet 1928 Senior when, after falling at Keppel Gate on the sixth lap and splitting his crash helmet from front to back, he was surprised to arrive at the finish and be greeted as the winner.

Charlie Dodson pictured at the 1934 TT where he retired in all three of his races.

Taking a small digression here - the widespread payment of bonus money in racing almost brought about the downfall of another event over the Mountain Course, the one that is today known as the Manx Grand Prix. Started in 1923 and always intended to be a race meeting for amateurs without payment of prize money or Trade support, it was initially known as the Manx International Amateur Motor Cycle Road Race Championship (usually abbreviated to the Amateur race). Trouble came to a head in the late 1920s with many riders breaking the ultra-strict rules that banned any form of trade sponsorship and, as a consequence, the ACU threatened to withhold the issue of permits for the Amateur races. Organisers, the Manx MCC, rewrote the rules for 1930 to allow riders a little more freedom to receive support, and renamed their meeting the Manx Grand Prix.

When the TT returned after war-time absence in 1947, prize money was announced as £250 for the Senior and Junior races, although the next year it was £200. Inevitably, the races were run in an atmosphere of post-war austerity and that seriously reduced the Trade bonuses available to successful riders. But not all rewards to riders were of a financial nature. When Moto Guzzi-mounted Fergus Anderson won the 1952 Lightweight TT he received a telegram from the President of Moto Guzzi, Giorgio Parodi, saying *'Bravo, Bravissimo. I kiss you!'* - it is strongly suspected that Fergus would have preferred a cash reward. Whilst there were less earnings for the stars in the early post-war years, enthusiastic privateers continued to pay their own ways, as they had always done.

The TT has always been an expensive meeting to contest, both for manufacturers and for riders. Competitors had to pay sizeable entry fees (a large element of which was to cover insurance), travel costs to the Island, accommodation for a lengthy two weeks, plus the above average costs associated with running their race machines over a far greater mileage than at an ordinary Grand Prix meeting. But everyone recognised that the TT was not an ordinary meeting, for it was acknowledged as staging the greatest races in the world. The prestige to be gained from TT victory brought many British and foreign manufacturers to compete on the Island and, as each class at the TT counted for its respective World Championship (that grew in stature from the late 1940s), the organisers were assured through most of the 50s and 60s of receiving top class entries. Perhaps that made them complacent, for by the late 1960s the prize money for winning the world's greatest road race, the Senior TT, was still only £200. It was a time when regular World Championship riders had formed themselves into a Grand Prix Riders Association with the aim, amongst other things, of increasing prize money and improving track safety. Many were dissatisfied with both of those aspects of the Isle of Man races and looked for improvements to the long-running races, saying *'tradition is not enough'.*

Criticism of the TT's finances during that period of unrest persuaded the ACU to make public the cost of running the races. On paper it looked as though the organisers could not afford to pay more prize money but they under-estimated the threat to their event that was to arise from the growing strength of 'rider power'. Continuing to pay in 1970 the same level of prize money as in the late 1940s (they had grudgingly introduced a payment of £15 towards each rider's expenses in the early 1960s), they eventually bowed to rider pressure and offered increased prize-money at the 1971 meeting (the Senior TT winner taking £750 instead of £200). But the ground-swell of discontent with the TT amongst a few of the top riders continued to gather force and would not go away.

In 1973 many of the top men were absent from the TT and at the end of 1976 the meeting lost its World Championship status. Although the GP riders' increased concerns over safety had a bearing on this loss of status, an earlier pre-emptive move by the organisers to provide much increased financial rewards from the event might well have retained more of the stars. A few good GP runners continued to contest the TT but road and circuit racing became increasingly polarised through the 1970s.

1952 Lightweight TT winner on a Moto Guzzi was Fergus Anderson. He was 43 years of age, it was his first TT win and he was followed home by team-mate Enrico Lorenzetti (Moto Guzzi) who is seen here congratulating him.

But thirty years on from the loss of its World Championship status the organisers consider that the TT is a successful race meeting. Much of that success has been achieved through the payment of greatly increased start money to entice the stars of road racing, and a better basic contribution towards expenses for every rider, plus huge increases in prize money. However, whatever their aspirations, not every competitor is going to get a bite of the big prize money and much of the present-day meeting's success is down to the fact that there still exists a breed of racing motorcyclists that simply want to race on the roads, and the height of their ambition is to take part in the event that, after 100 years, continues to be known as the Tourist Trophy.

A man who has earned his living from road racing for many years is Ian Lougher. Riding everything from 125 to 1000cc machines, he has had six TT victories in his career.

Total prize money payable today is close to £400,000. A rider who leads from start to finish of the premier Formula 1 or Senior races can win £20,000, and a total of approximately £75,000 is paid out to riders in each of those races. What a winner can achieve in trade bonuses tends to remain a secret nowadays, but the huge amount of sponsor advertising on riders' machines, leathers, helmets, etc, suggests that rewards are there to be had, although things are not always as they seem in that area. Race fans might reasonably assume that the rash of product stickers carried by the top men indicate that they are making use of the products named on those stickers - but is it always so? After the 1992 TT Ferodo felt a little aggrieved, for they claimed that the first three riders in each race used Ferodo discs and brake pads, even though the fairings of some of the top runners suggested the use of products belonging to other manufacturers. Presumably those other manufacturers had simply bought advertising space on the fairings and left spectators to think what they might.

David Jefferies shows off his sponsor's colours to good effect in 2000.

Whilst the trend is for even today's ordinary runners to have fairings and leathers bedecked with advertising, whatever that may appear to suggest the certainty is that it is the top riders who leave the TT each year with the most money and, nowadays, some of them are well rewarded by the event.

FIRE

Petrol vapours, hot engines and ignition sparks make a highly combustible mixture, particularly when provoked by racing incidents like split petrol tanks or clumsy refuelling at the Pits. At the very first TT of 1907, Oliver Godfrey's bike burst into flames at his Pit-stop. Despite the stout efforts of a Manx policeman who tried to smother the flames with his overcoat, Godfrey's bike was too badly damaged to allow him to continue. Three years later in 1910, a race report read: *'Creyton was on fire for a full mile at Kirk Michael before the flames extinguished themselves'*, yet he still brought his Triumph home in third place. Another early rider, Hugh Mason, had his Matchless burst into flames whilst refuelling in 1912. It was extinguished by everyone around throwing sand on it from a nearby heap. The sand put out the fire but was hardly the best of lubricants for the bike's exposed valve-gear.

Noel Pope's Velocette is on fire as he rounds Governor's Bridge with a leaking petrol tank in the 1935 Junior TT.

When Stanley Woods made his TT debut on a Cotton in the Junior race of 1922, his race was jeopardised by a petrol fire in the Pits that spread to his leathers. Fortunately, no great damage was done and Stanley was able to continue and finished 5th. Perhaps the problem in his Pit was aggravated by the fact that the present rule requiring riders to cut their engines at pit-stops, was not in force in 1922. It is believed that Stanley's experience hastened its introduction.

Although the organisers have always been concerned about the danger of fire in the Pits, they do have trained firemen on duty there, something that is not possible at many other spots on the Course. A quick calculation shows that if a fire-extinguisher were positioned every 100 yards around the 37¾ miles it would require 666 extinguishers.

Tony Wright chose a spot where a fireman was located when he fell off his BSA Gold Star in the Senior MGP of 1960.

Geoff Davison rode a borrowed Scott in practice at the 1925 TT and as he approached the Bungalow on his first lap he sensed the bike was slowing and, in his words: *'I glanced down and was horrified to see that the motor was on fire beneath me. Thinking very quickly, I shut off the petrol, turned right at the Bungalow, down the Sulby Glen Road, knocked the gear into neutral shoved my feet on the handlebars, and coasted down the hill, relying on the wind to keep the flames from the tank and the petrol pipe. This worked perfectly, for everything that could burn - HT wires, and so on - had burnt itself out by the time I reached the Sulby Glen Hotel. I was a little proud of myself, for had I stopped at the first sign of fire, the model would have been a complete write-off'.*

John Hartle's walks away from his MV Agusta after it caught fire during the 1958 Senior TT at Governors Bridge.

The all-conquering MV Augusta fours of the late 1950s were nick-named 'fire-engines' on account of their bright red finish, but that counted for nothing when John Hartle's MV burst into flames as he left the Governor's Bridge dip during the 1958 Senior. Forced to abandon the bike, John and marshals had to stand-by as the intense fire consumed the expensive 'works' MV at the roadside.

A similar incident befell Steve Cull on a Honda RS500 two-stroke in the Senior TT of 1988. Setting a new lap record of 119.08 mph, he looked set for victory until slowed by a holed expansion chamber. But worse was to follow when the bike burst into flames near Creg ny Baa and was almost burnt out. Overcoming their disappointment, at dinner that evening Steve's pit-crew presented him with a fireman's helmet and an extinguisher.

Fires are not just confined to the bikes and racing. Alan Chadwick was riding a 125 Honda in the 1963 TT and was camping in the riders area behind the Grandstand that is often called 'The Paddock Hotel'. While preparing breakfast in his tent the pipe on his gas-bottle split and the whole of the interior of the tent went on fire. He was lightly singed, most of the contents of the tent were saved, but breakfast was ruined. Fortunately, the bike was outside the tent and was not damaged.

A Travelling Marshal will very quickly be on the scene of any racing incident on the Course and he carries a small fire-extinguisher in his emergency pack. But that was of little use to the one who attended one post-crash conflagration that resulted in the sending of the legendary radio message to Race Control: *'The road is on fire but the racing line isn't'*. Back came the reply: *'That's OK then, carry on racing'*.

FIRSTS AND LASTS

Charlie Collier (Matchless) became the first of many illustrious names to be inscribed on the Senior Tourist Trophy when he won the 1907 event in a time of 4 hours, 8 minutes and 8½ seconds at a race average speed of 38.2 mph and a fuel consumption figure of 94½ mpg. He received a winner's prize of £25.

*

Scott-mounted Eric Myers surprised onlookers when he became the first to kick-start his machine at the start of the 1909 TT. For most machines of the time it was necessary to run and bump them into life. Even when kick-starters came into general use on road bikes, racing machines were generally bump-started. The exceptions to this were the Clubman's and Production races, where riders were required to kick-start them at the beginning of the race and (for the first few years) at their Pit-stops. At the start of the 1961 Lightweight event Fred Stevens became the first rider to get his TT race under way by use of an electric starter. When he received the signal to go, Fred just thumbed the starter-button of his converted Honda roadster and pulled away, leaving his starting partner pushing down the road to get up sufficient speed for bump-starting.

*

The first TT victory by a foreign machine was in 1911 when Oliver Godfrey brought his Indian into first place. The same year brought the first TT fatality when Victor Surridge was killed in a crash near Creg Willeys during practice. Unfortunately the Surridge incident was a double-first, because he became the first person to be killed in the Isle of Man in an accident on the road involving a mechanically-propelled vehicle.

*

Crash helmets were first made compulsory at the TT in 1914, by which time the Start and Finish had been moved from the bottom to the top of Bray Hill, where the slight downhill gradient was ideal for competitors to bump-start their machines.

Oliver Godfrey push-starts his Indian from near the top of Bray Hill at the 1914 Senior TT.

There were nine Royal Enfields entered for the 1914 Junior race, one of which was ridden by Fred Walker and he led the race for the first two laps. He was then delayed with tyre trouble and, in trying to make up lost time, came off a couple of times. However, he was allowed to proceed and finished in 3rd place. But, seemingly dazed from earlier crashes, he carried straight on at the finish, ploughed into a barrier, and was killed.

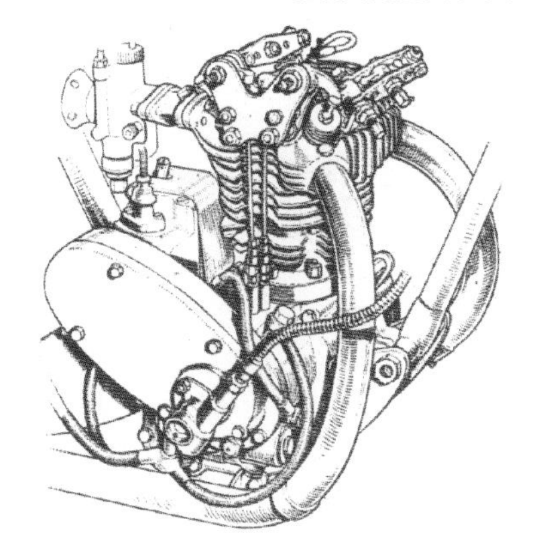

The 250cc Rudge engine that won the 1934 Lightweight TT - note the exposed push-rods and valve-gear.

*

The first tie occurred in the 1914 Senior event when Oliver Godfrey (Indian) and Howard Davies (Sunbeam) finished in joint second place. It was also the first time that Davies and Sunbeam had contested the TT.

*

The first overhead-valve Norton to be ridden in a TT was that of Ralph Cawthorne in 1922, but the other Nortons in the race were all side-valves. None of the Nortons were a match for the mount of Alec Bennett, even though his Sunbeam proved to be the last side-valver to win a TT.

*

Tom Sheard was the first Manxman to win a TT when he took his AJS to victory in the 1922 Junior. The following year he was first home in the Senior on a Douglas. As an aside, the three winners of the 1922 TT, Geoff Davison (Lightweight), Tom Sheard (Junior) and Alec Bennett (Senior), were chosen to represent Great Britain in the off-road International Six Days Trial in Switzerland, although Tom chose not to take his place in the team.

*

The 1928 Senior race gave the experienced Harry Brockbank the chance to record both a first and a last. It was the custom to offer the previous year's winner the opportunity to start at number 1 the following year. As 1927 winner Alec Bennett did not want to be first away, Brockbank was given the honour on what was his 16th and last TT race.

*

Rudge had a spectacularly successful year in 1930, taking the first three places in the Junior race and first two in the Senior, but they were the last victories by push-rod engined bikes in the Junior and Senior classes. Thereafter the wins went to engines of ohc design, although a 250cc push-rod Rudge won the Lightweight TT in 1934.

First man to lap the Mountain Course at 60, 70 and 80 mph was Jimmy Simpson and in addition to those impressive achievements he also set eight record laps. However, he was often too fast for the race machines of his day, for they could not stand the pace that he set and he was only victorious in one TT, the 1934 Lightweight, when he headed home a Rudge 1,2,3, in front of Ernie Nott and Graham Walker. Jimmy's first TT was in 1922 and in 1925 he rode in the Junior, Senior and Sidecar races for AJS. In total he raced in 26 TTs and in his victory year of 1934 he also came second in the Junior and Senior classes on Nortons.

Jimmy Simpson on his 350 Norton at the 1932 TT. He was forced to retire in the Junior race but brought his 500cc Norton into a fine third place in the Senior.

Stanley Woods victory in the 1935 Senior on a Moto Guzzi was the first by a sprung-frame machine. Stanley vanquished British makes like Norton, Velocette and Vincent HRD, the latter being the only other make in the race with a sprung-frame.

*

In 1937 Omobono Tenni (Moto Guzzi) became the first Italian rider on an Italian machine to win a TT. Austin Munks victory in the 1947 Lightweight MGP on his Moto Guzzi was the first MGP win by a foreign machine.

*

The Lightweight 250 machines first appeared in 1920 in a separate class run with the Junior race, but in 1922 they were given their own race. Thereafter, a Lightweight 250 TT event took place every year up to 2002. During the 1960s the class probably had more research and development poured into it than the hitherto all-important 350/500 classes and through the 70s and 80s the top two-stroke 500s were derived from earlier 250s. However, with the growth of production-based racing at the TT, the pure 250 racing class went into decline. The last time that the 250s competed for their own Tourist Trophy was in 2002. After that they ran with the 600s in the Junior TT for a couple of years, with a separate prize being awarded to the first 250, but now they are no longer catered for.

*

After a delayed start due to bad weather, the 1954 Senior race eventually got under way, although it was not long before it started to rain. Race favourite was Geoff Duke on a Gilera but he stopped for petrol at the end of the third lap and lost the lead to Ray Amm (Norton) who went straight through. With the weather worsening the organisers, for the first time at the TT, decided to stop the race at the end of the fourth lap and Amm was declared the winner.

*

First man to set a 100 mph lap was Bob McIntyre when he rode his four-cylinder Gilera to victory in the Golden Jubilee TT of 1957. Derek Minter became the first to do it on a single-cylinder machine when he achieved 101.05 mph on his Steve Lancefield tuned Norton in the 1960 Senior.

*

In 1958 MV Agusta achieved a first by winning all four solo classes. John Surtees claimed the Junior and Senior double over the Mountain Course, while Tarquinio Provini won the Lightweight 250 and Carlo Ubbiali the Lightweight 125 over the Clypse Course.

*

From the start of the Travelling Marshal service in

1935 until 1975, members had always ridden British-built machines. But a shortage at the 1975 MGP saw former Senior MGP winner Roger Sutcliffe become the first Travelling Marshal to do duty on a foreign bike. In this case it was a Rickman Kawasaki, but in 1977 Honda stepped in to support the service and its machines have been used ever since.

*

It was in 1977 that the 100 mph lap was first achieved by a sidecar outfit. George O'Dell and Kenny Arthur did it 'unofficially' in practice, then Dick Greasley and Mick Skeels were the first to do it in a race, although O'Dell subsequently set a faster time in winning the race.

*

The event that rounded-off TT week in 1977 was the Schweppes sponsored, four-lap Jubilee Race. Joey Dunlop was in only his second year of TT racing and was allocated riding numbers in the 30s by the organisers in the races that he entered - obviously they did not rate him too highly! Entry to the Jubilee Race was by invitation only and Joey would seem not to have received an invite, for his name did not appear in the original programme for that event. However, a few strings must have been pulled, and when Jubilee race-day arrived a revised entry list was issued and Joey was on the starting line. Come the finish of the race and he was on the top step of the podium, having taken his privately entered Yamaha TZ750 to his first TT victory. It was a winning feat that Joey was to repeat another 25 times in his TT racing career.

On the last lap of his victorious ride in the 1977 Jubilee race, Joey Dunlop found time to stop in Parliament Square and check his rear tyre.

*

A separate Newcomers class was introduced at the 1978 MGP, something similar having been tried in the late 1950s but then dropped. The three classes for Newcomers of 500, 350 and 250cc, were run concurrently on the Wednesday morning of race-week (having been postponed from Tuesday) over four laps. Just as the MGP proper has seen many of its winners go on to TT success, so, many of those who first raced to victory in the Newcomers races have gone on to racing glory. Names such as Phil Mellor (1978), Norman Brown (1981), Carl Fogarty (1985), Colin Gable (1987), Phillip McCallen (1988), Mick Lofthouse (1990), Jason Griffiths (1991) and Richard Britton (1997). Perhaps the most talented show of raw racing talent destined for TT glory was on display at the 1983 Lightweight Newcomers race, when Robert Dunlop, Steve Hislop and Ian Lougher took the first three places.

*

Anyone looking for results of the Production Class A and Class C races (usually run together) for the 1987 TT will not find any, the reason being that adverse weather caused them to be abandoned. With no time for them to be rearranged, they simply were not run. It was another 'first' at the TT.

*

Few would dispute that TT week of 1996 belonged to 32 year old Phillip McCallen. TT greats like Mike Hailwood, Steve Hislop and Joey Dunlop had already made the record books by taking three wins in a week, but McCallen became the first man to take four TT victories in one year, all on Hondas. Setting the pace in practice, come race-week he started with a win in the opening Formula I race, and used the same RC45 to take the last race of the week, the 'Blue Riband' Senior event. Wins on his 900 Fireblade in the Production race and CBR600 in the Junior made up his quartet of victories and earned him £35,000 in prize-money.

Phillip's only defeat of the week came in the Lightweight where he lost out to Joey Dunlop. Mind you, he was leading that race until he holed his exhaust and dropped to fourth place. With Joey also taking the Ultra-Lightweight race, Honda all but swept the board in the solo classes with record-breaking performances from the two Ulster stars. The only other make to get a look-in was Yamaha, when Jim Moodie took one of their big bangers to victory in the Singles race.

*

A few TT races have been stopped on account of the weather but until 1999, so it was widely reported, none had been stopped because of a racing incident. Paul Orrit 'starred' at the 1999 Formula 1 race with a frightening fall from his machine near the bottom of Bray Hill that was captured on video for the whole world to see. The incident occurred on the first lap so the organisers halted the despatch of any more competitors from the Start and those who were already racing were red-flagged at Sulby Bridge. From there they travelled back to the Grandstand behind Travelling Marshals for a restart of a shortened to 4 laps race.

But 85 years before Paul's fall, H Vaughan Knight (Chase) also fell at the foot of Bray Hill in the Senior TT of 1914 and the organisers halted the start of further riders for 5 minutes whilst they made the track safe. He was relatively unhurt. 1914 was an unusual year because riders were given race numbers which were different from the ones they used in practice.

*

There have been many combinations of members of the same family who have competed in Island races, but in winning the Lightweight 250 race at the 80th anniversary running of the MGP in 2003, Norman Kneen joined his twin brother, Mike, as an MGP winner and they thus became the first 'twin' winners. Mike's win was way back in 1980 when he rode a Yamaha to victory in the Junior, but Norman had to try for 25 years before he achieved the success that had eluded him for so long. The two belong to a family of five brothers all of whom have contested the Manx Grand Prix.

Philip McCallen's four 1996 TT victories

1996 Formula One

1996 Junior TT

1996 Production TT

1996 Senior TT

CHAPTER 4

TALES OF . . .

FLAG SIGNALS

The only flag used by the organisers in the first races was a red one. A report of the time said *'when this was displayed competitors either stopped or proceeded slowly, according to the vehemence of the waving'*. The purpose of flag signals is, essentially, to warn competitors of dangers on the Course. The organisers quickly got to know where the dangerous points were and appointed flag marshals to them for each race. In the early 1920s, Dunlop equipped the flag marshals with a white coat and a Dunlop sash, thus earning them the nickname of 'Dunlops'.

Harry Harris (HRD) rounds Ramsey Hairpin in 1925 with a 'Dunlop' Flagman in the background.

Today, every flag-marshal has six different coloured flags, (Yellow, Yellow and Red stripes, White, White with Red Cross, Red, Green) with which to warn or advise riders, whilst on some parts of the Course they also have Sun and Fog flags to inform of impending problems with visibility, and a black flag with orange circle that is used to stop a rider during a race. In addition, races are formally started with the Manx flag and the end of the race is signalled by use of the chequered flag.

Six of the flags used during today's races on the TT Course.

In the early 1920s marshals had just two flags and competitors were told that the red flag meant stop and the white one required caution. By the mid-1930s they were still using two flags but they were:

Blue - When waved, 'danger'.
When motionless, 'keep close to your left side of the course'.

Yellow - 'Complete and immediate stop'.

Riders vary in the amount of attention they pay to warning flags. Back in 1935 it was reported after a couple of incidents at Laurel Bank: *'the blue flag was flown slowing down riders, and today they understood what it meant - which is more than they seemed to know yesterday!'*, and the degree to which today's competitors take heed of warning flags still varies, whatever *'the vehemence of the waving'*. The organisers now recommend that riders slow to 30 mph under a waved yellow flag but such a blanket-rule cannot be expected to work when there is no realistic provision for enforcement. Nevertheless, flag-marshals who stand in the road waving flags for the benefit of riders are far from impressed with the many individuals who continue to thunder past at 100mph+. (Far too close, too fast and too frequent for him to record their numbers.) It is understandable for a competitor not to want to lose time and revs by slowing unnecessarily, but it is not only his safety that he puts at risk when he ignores such flags, for it can also be that of the marshals and medics who have to venture on to the Course to attend to a fallen rider. However, whilst with the current system a competitor, rightly, gets blamed if he ignores a flag signal, it should also be recognised that a flag marshal cannot convey to riders the exact degree of severity of the hazard that awaits around a blind bend using the same flag-on-a-stick technology as 100 years ago, even if he now has a choice of six flags rather than the one of earlier days.

A point that does have to be watched by a flagman if *'vehement waving'* is indulged in, is to ensure that the flag is firmly fixed to the pole that he is holding. In an incident reported in 'The TT Special' in 1979, Malcolm Lucas came off his Yamaha when it seized, the flagman waved the yellow with vigour, the flag flew off the pole, blew over the face of a following rider, and nearly caused another incident.

FROM THE STARTLINE

Before racing commences at the TT and MGP there is a week of practising to allow riders to prepare themselves and their machines for the challenge ahead. For the old hands this is an enjoyable business that allows them to get back into the swing of Island racing, but what about newcomers? Though difficult to believe, in past-times the opening lap of practice could be the first time some newcomers had ever been around the Course, whilst, in contrast, others made a careful pre-event study of the whole 37¾ miles before turning a wheel in official practice.

Come first practice and the reality of what newcomers have let themselves in for strikes home. Waiting in a huge crowd of riders for the Starter to give the nod that first time, what goes through a rider's mind? Are they all as pessimistic as 1985 MGP runner Ian Alexander who recalled thinking: *'why am I queuing up here to kill myself?'*. Hopefully not, but there is little doubting the trepidation that many riders must feel at the thought of launching themselves down Bray Hill. But after a lap to settle themselves, most come in with a big grin and bubbling the same words as the previously pessimistic Ian Alexander: *'fabulous - wouldn't have missed it for the world!'*.

With practice over it is not long before race-time arrives, and before the start of each race riders have to be marshalled into their correct positions, in what can be very tense times. Although most are ready with their machines well before their starting time, there have been a few who made a habit of late arrival and one of those was Joey Dunlop. Spectators almost got used to hearing commentator Geoff Cannell say:*' There's one minute to the start but there's no sign of Joey. His bike's here but . . . . . . ah, here he comes now!'*.

Waiting for the signal to go - a tense moment.

The Manx MCC always have a Guest of Honour at their MGP meeting who is usually asked to flag the first riders away at the start of a race. One year it was Geoff Duke, a vastly experienced man, greatly respected for his MGP and TT exploits. In the moments leading up to the off, the official Starter checked that Geoff knew that the correct starting signal was a quick upward jerk of the flag, and Geoff responded by saying: *'Like this?'* twitching the flag. That was all the two highly-strung riders on the line needed, with a scream of revs and biting clutches, they had the startline dignitaries stepping smartly backwards as, flattening themselves on their tanks, they were away down the Glencrutchery Road. The startled time-keeper belatedly pressed the button on his watch, but there was an element of approximation in the first lap times of those two riders.

Nowadays TT riders are sent off singly at 10 second intervals, but at the MGP riders are still started in pairs. Here Colin Breeze (1) and Jason Griffiths (2) wait for the signal to start the Senior Classic MGP of 2002.

The days of run-and-bump starts are long gone and today they are clutch starts with engines running. Such is the pent-up tension waiting to get out at the start that, particularly with the first few away, full-power wheelies and wheelspin are common. One thing you can be sure of - nobody stalls their engine on the line!

GETTING TO THE TT

The TT races quickly established their popularity with motorcyclists, although in the event's early years the only real contact that the ordinary enthusiast had with it was by reading the motorcycle press. In an attempt to keep race fans in the picture the magazine 'The Motor Cycle' arranged for cablegrams to be sent to prominent UK motorcycle dealers whilst races were in progress. They contained up-to-the-minute race positions and results which the dealers then posted in their showroom windows. 'Motor Cycling' was equally determined to involve its readers in the TT scene and organised day-trips to the 1914 Senior TT by rail and boat from several parts of Britain. Such trips went on to run for over 50 years and became a traditional method of seeing the Senior race for the many enthusiasts who could not manage a week's holiday at TT time.

The majority of the competitors coming to the early Tourist Trophy races would also have brought their machines by train to Liverpool's Lime Street, then wheeled them the short distance to the loading stage for the Isle of Man boat. Travel by train was an accepted way of life over long distances in those days, indeed, the idea of the TT races is said to have been conceived by a group of enthusiasts on the return train journey from a motorcycle race meeting in Austria. Not every train journey undertaken by those intrepid continental racers went smoothly. Henry Tyrell Smith (later to win the 1930 Junior TT) recalled a trip from Rotterdam to Leipzig in the 1920s, when *'On the frontier of Luxembourg, at a tiny station called Trois Vierges, just as the train moved off, I was rewarded with the pleasing sight of my motorcycle and precious box of tools being wheeled along the opposite platform back in the direction of Holland'.*

Although the Isle of Man's location in the middle of the Irish Sea has been seen as a problem by some visitors, for others it was part of the overall TT adventure.

George Brown was a man who set the British racing scene alight in the late 1940s with his short circuit performances on the legendary 1000cc Vincent called 'Gunga Din'. But George also entered a rather more standard Vincent in the Senior class of the 1948 Clubman's TT. Reading his account of tackling that Island race shows how things were; he said: *'Transport to the IOM for my machine and luggage, etc, provided a difficulty (not owning a Utility Waggon), but this was overcome by sending my luggage and etceteras on in advance and riding my machine (220 miles) to*

Liverpool and the boat. On arrival at Douglas I dealt with the taxation of the machine - at the same time getting a temporary driving licence'. It is difficult to imagine a modern-day competitor contemplating a visit to the TT without the back-up of a van, awning, generator, tools, tyre-warmers, spares, support team, etc. And what is this business that George Brown had to go through of taxing his machine and getting a temporary driving licence? From the 1920s to the late 1950s, owners of visiting vehicles were required to pay Manx road-tax for the duration of their stay. The vigour with which this was enforced varied down the years, as did the amount - from 2/6 (12½p) to 5/- (25p). Owners were then issued with something called an Exemption Registration Certificate. A temporary Manx Driving Licence was also required, costing 1/- (5p). What George was not aware of was that race competitors could, with a bit more form-filling, obtain exemption from those temporary licensing regulations.

Three 125cc Mondial racers are swung ashore from the Steam Packet Co's vessel at Douglas in 1951.

An exception to the rule that modern-day competitors require a major support and logistical effort to ride the TT was given by Peter Small when riding his Suzuki GSX-R750 into 41st place in the 1998 Production Race. Showing that it was genuinely fit for the road as well as the track, Peter rode the Suzuki from his home in Idaho to Vancouver where it was air-freighted to Gatwick, from there he rode it to the Island. After a busy fortnight's TT racing, Peter set off on the Suzuki to tour Germany, Italy and Slovenia.

Some spectators book their TT visits in very good time, others, due to work/family commitments, cannot do so and sometimes it can be a last minute decision to go. That can cause problems in getting a boat crossing, finding accommodation, etc. One such enthusiast of the mid-1980s also wanted to keep the cost down and decided to go by 'moped'. But this was no ordinary moped for it was powered by a clip-on type engine of the 1950s attached to a folding paratrooper's bicycle of the 1940s. Taking advantage of a cheap rail and boat excursion fare, the intrepid fan took the folded machine in a bag as hand luggage, re-assembled it in Douglas and had cheap transport for a few days stay.

Before the advent of the modern 'Roll-on and Roll-off' ferries it was a requirement for all bikes to have their petrol tanks pumped dry before they were allowed on the boats to the Island, much to the discontent of their owners. Riders who were members of the RAC would find a patrol man stationed on Douglas quay who would give them sufficient petrol to get to a filling station. Others had to hope that there was enough left in their tanks to do so.

Many fans cannot afford a long stay on the Island to see the races and the Steam Packet Company's day-excursions by boat have always been popular. In their heyday the Company would bring 11,000 people over for Friday's Senior TT. Making their way on Thursday evening to Liverpool, Fleetwood, etc, they would board one of the boats for the Island which, by the time it sailed, was full of recumbent bodies.

The early landing of thousands of visitors in Douglas on Senior race day saw the Island's cafes awake and ready to receive them. Some would then opt for a pre-race coach tour around the Course, while others would take advantage of the free motorcycle show presented by thousands of machines parked along Douglas Promenade. Then it was off to secure a vantage point for the day's racing, perhaps taking a coach out to a favoured spot, walking to the Grandstand or, for those with really strong nerves, going to one of the accessible but truly frightening spectator places like the bottom of Bray Hill. After the racing had finished and the Roads Open car had been through, it was time for the day-trippers to start the journey in reverse.

Breakdowns on the way to the Island have beset plenty of motorcyclists, ancient and modern, and the 'must get there' tales are legion. Indeed, many a TT fan has been towed onto the boat with a dead bike, with the aim of fixing it after arrival in Douglas.

In 1985 many spectators were faced with a major change to established travelling arrangements, when most of the Isle of Man Steam Packet Company's sailings to the Island were switched from Liverpool to Heysham, some fifty miles further north. Such a change of port did not affect the many TT enthusiasts who travelled from Ireland, amongst them being Joey Dunlop. But Joey did not travel to the Island by Steam Packet boat anyway, instead he made arrangements with a friend who owned a fishing boat to bring him, brother Robert, some of their racing bikes and a group of friends, from Belfast to Douglas. In 1985 this resulted in what Joey describes as the most frightening experience of his life when the boat, 'Tornamona', sank just outside Belfast, taking the bikes to the bottom. Passengers and crew used a life-raft to get to nearby rocks, from where they were rescued and, eventually, so were the bikes. It was hardly the most promising start to a TT fortnight, but a mere thirty-six hours after the sinking, Joey was out in practice on 'works' Hondas, setting the pace, re-acquainting himself with the Course and experiencing the usual changes that included major road improvements at Quarry Bends.

With a high concentration of speed-hungry motorcyclists on such a small Island, it is inevitable that there are accidents at TT time, some serious, some not so. Falling off a bike (fast or slow) can be expensive in repairs. Occasionally one sees an unlucky faller who has left his battered machine outside his digs on Douglas Promenade, complete with a notice explaining how it got to this state and a bucket inviting contributions toward repairs. No doubt reflecting that *'there but for the grace of God go I'*, many enthusiasts throw in a few coins to ease the unlucky rider's financial pain, whilst he tries to find someone with space in a van who will take his broken bike home for him.

Surprising as it may seem, the majority of TT visitors do not come by bike. With total visitor numbers over the TT period being in excess of 40,000, figures from the Steam Packet Company show that they ship about 12,000 motorcycles, plus 3,500 cars and vans, many of the latter carrying several bikes. Some of the bikes brought to the Island consist of exotica that only come out to rub handlebars with everyday machinery at special occasions like the TT or MGP.

These BSA Rocket Gold Stars are the sort of Classic exotica that can be seen at the TT.

GONE MISSING

One of the most important tasks of the race organisers is to keep track and account for every rider that they let onto the Mountain Course for a practice session or a race. It is a considerable responsibility, because a busy evening practice can see 375 riders going out during the session, and this can involve them doing multiple laps, calling in to the Paddock for adjustments or change of machinery, and also breaking down and occasionally falling off at various points around the 37¾ mile lap. It is a recipe for confusion but, like many aspects of Island racing, it operates under systems that have been refined and developed over a period of 100 years.

The main checks on riders are implemented by the Timekeepers and Race Control staff at the Grandstand and they are augmented by 'counting-points' at defined locations round the Course, where the passage of every rider is logged. Such points are in radio or telephone contact with Race Control. In addition, if a rider stops, falls or pulls out anywhere on the Course, the nearest marshals post will convey the fact to Race Control. If a rider somehow avoids all those checks and Race Control become concerned as to his or her whereabouts, they will instigate a search from the point at which the rider was last recorded. This will be by way of marshals operating on foot in the area, or by motorcycle-mounted Travelling Marshals.

Travelling Marshal Des Evans speeds away from Parliament Square on his Honda Fireblade.

The facilities available to Race Control to search for a lost rider are far better today than they used to be, due to improved communication systems and the far greater coverage of the Course by marshals. Indeed, the Travelling Marshal service was introduced in 1935 to improve the search facilities for missing riders, after the unfortunate Syd Crabtree fell from his machine in 1934 and was not found for 40 minutes.

There had been less serious cases of riders going missing before the Syd Crabtree incident, one of which involved George Rowley, a TT competitor from 1925 to 1939. George told a tale from the 1929 Senior TT relating to his retirement at a remote spot on the Mountain with clutch trouble. The nearest point of 'civilisation' was The Bungalow Hotel and he set out to walk there. After trudging for what seemed like half an hour, he had not reached it, but he did come across several ambulance-men carrying a stretcher and looking for a lost rider. Somewhat against his wishes, George allowed himself to be persuaded to walk back the way he had come, as the rescue party thought that his expert knowledge of where a rider might have fallen off would be useful to them. After another half an hour of trudging in heavy boots and leathers, they arrived at George's abandoned machine. One of the ambulance-men noted that the number on the stricken machine was the same as the number of the rider that they had been sent to search for. With a silent curse, George realised that he had earlier removed the numbered waistcoat that every rider wore while racing, and was carrying it in his helmet.

Riders who experience a problem in one practice session - such as a mystery mis-fire - often do not know if they have solved it until they go out in the next one. If the problem still exists they may abort the lap and pull off the Course at somewhere like Ballacraine, intending to use the backroads to get back to the Paddock to try and fix the problem. But not all riders know the backroads sufficiently well to achieve this. Occasional riders have been spotted, literally way off course, including one trying to ride his mis-firing machine along the Promenade at Port Erin, which is approximately 12 miles from the nearest point of the TT Course.

Syd Crabtree made his TT debut in 1922 and this 1934 photograph shows him the Excelsior Mechanical Marvel.

Is this AJS rider heading back to his garage after practice, or has he dropped out of a race? He is certainly well off the TT Course, for he is riding along Douglas Promenade.

Experienced riders would often keep going with a malfunctioning bike until they could stop at a Course-side pub. There they could be sure of refreshment and, sometimes of greater importance, warmth and shelter. Their whereabouts would usually filter back to the organisation - but not always. During the long Thursday afternoon practice session at the 1966 TT the logging of retirements was not 100% effective and George Cullen's mechanic was forced to set off and look for him without having been able to discover exactly where he had retired. This meant slow progress looking in every gateway and pub until he found George at Ramsey. Loading the bike and starting for Douglas, they struck trouble with the van and eventually got back to the Grandstand in an unofficial lap time of 5 hours and 13 minutes.

The people who staff the Race Control office all have vast experience of managing the racing, but there are many problems that can only be dealt with by marshals on the spot - if there are any marshals on the spot! The Mountain stretch of the Course is long, inhospitable and relatively thinly populated with marshals; it can also be damp and misty. All those conditions applied during Thursday afternoon practice at the 1995 MGP. It was a year in which promising local lad Richard 'Milky' Quayle was riding and he had already created some excitement by unofficially breaking Phillip McCallen's long-standing Lightweight MGP lap record earlier in the week. On the Thursday afternoon 'Milky' had excitement of all the wrong sort when he went wide after Brandywell, ploughed through a wire fence, and he and the bike finished down the bank and out of sight of the road. With a broken leg and wire tangled about him, he lay there helpless as rider after rider streamed past. Shouting was a waste of time but, in desperation, he did manage to throw his helmet up the hill and onto the road where it was seen by a passing rider and help was summoned. No doubt the organisers logging of riders would eventually have shown that 'Milky' was missing, but he admits to feelings of desperation as he lay there in the mist.

HAILWOOD's RETURN

The few people who noticed were somewhat surprised when great rider of the 1960s, Mike Hailwood, appeared at an evening practice for the 1977 MGP mounted on a Padgett's Yamaha fitted with a Travelling Marshal's 'M' plates and a camera. Apart from a couple of demonstration laps on road bikes, this was the first time he had ridden a real racing bike on the Course since 1967.

Behind the borrowed leathers, helmets and camera is Mike Hailwood, leaving Governors Bridge on the 'M'-plated Yamaha during evening practice at the 1977 MGP.

Mike duly completed a lap, with a few stops for interviewing, filming, etc. and, on completion, expressed himself a little shocked at the speed of the Yamaha. Anyway, he then disappeared and everyone thought that was it - a one-off ride by the twelve-times TT winner, with a bit of filming done on the way.

The 1977 TT had been a very good year for race-fans and, as they often do, many of them booked their hotels and guest-houses for the following year before they left. They were the wise ones, for by the time of the 1978 TT, every establishment was showing a 'No Vacancies' sign. The reason was that 'Mike the Bike' Hailwood had announced that he was returning to race at the TT. It was eleven years since he had ridden an Island race and, despite Phil Read's successful return in 1977, many doubted that Mike could do the same, for, unlike Read, he had been away from bikes for many years. But, whatever their thoughts, legions of older fans flocked to Mona's Isle to see his return, while those who were too young to have known him in his hey-day were just as keen to see what they had been missing. Television crews and journalists flew in from all over the world.

Phil Read (Honda) knows that Mike Hailwood (Ducati) is coming past on the approach to Brandywell, a section of the Course that is now known as Hailwood's Height.

Although Mike (and the other riders) had only six practice sessions, no one could have been disappointed at the outcome of his return, for in a stunning display of riding skill he took an unfancied Ducati to victory in the Formula 1 race, leaving experienced opponents like Phil Read, John Williams, Alex George, and Chas Mortimer trailing in his wake; plus what journalist Ted Macauley described as *'a pack of youngsters on thoroughbred race machinery, howling after his reputation'*. It was truly a quality win, because the Ducati twin had no real TT history and delivered probably 20 bhp less than the main opposition. But Mike was a master of getting into a fast and smooth race rhythm, and his reward was to stand on the top step of the winners podium once again.

Mike Hailwood's victory in 1978 saw him set race and lap records for the TT Formula 1 class, and in doing so he lapped faster than he had done in his prime, even though, in his words: *'Truthfully, I was well within my safety limits, seven-tenths, well below 100 per cent effort, and with plenty left in hand had I needed it'*. It was a highly emotional time for all involved, and Mike's performance served to both confirm and add to his already legendary TT status.

Although Ducati were pleased to take that famous victory in 1978, they had been half-hearted with their support and most of the effort on Mike's machine was put in by Steve Wynne and Pat Slinn of Sports Motorcycles, who carried out the whole operation on the strength of a handshake with their famous rider - no contract. Yamaha did seem to realise the publicity value associated with his return and provided three 'works' bikes for him to ride in races other than the Formula I class. However, despite the fact that this was the first time they had given unqualified factory support to the TT for ten years, the Yamaha effort failed to impress and their bikes were sidelined with niggling problems.

Enticed back to participate in the 1979 TT, Mike found that Ducati were a little more interested in his efforts, but that they had produced a bike that was probably worse than the one used in 1978, by doing unhelpful things like reversing the direction of the gearchange. Mike was determined to enjoy what he announced as his last TT, and although he narrowly lost out to Alex George in the big-money Classic race (by 3.4 seconds), he took a comfortable win on his Castrol Heron Suzuki in the Senior, setting new race and lap records, and again recording his own personal fastest laps of the TT Course. Second place man was the experienced Tony Rutter who told Mike after the race *'When you came by, I tried to keep up with you, but no-way . . .'*. With the Senior win giving him his 14th TT victory, Mike's legion of fans must have wondered just what he would have done to the record books if he had not been absent from the Island races for eleven years. Those same fans greeted with mixed feelings the news at the 1979 event that he was finally retiring from racing at the TT. Of course, they would have liked to have seen him race again and add to his total, but they were aware of the dangers of the Mountain Course, and so many were secretly happy at his decision and wished him a safe retirement. Two years into that retirement, Mike was killed in a car accident when on a family errand. It was a cruel twist of fate that a lifelong racer on two and four wheels should meet his death in a road traffic accident.

In this 2002 photograph H stands for Hailwood but this is Mike's son David doing a TT lap of honour on a BSA Rocket 3.

IRISH RIDERS

Back in 1908, Dubliner Charles Franklin became the first Irish TT rider and he was joined by Tom Greer in 1909. Since then there has been a continuous flow of competitors across the Irish Sea to contest the TT and MGP races. Competing on public roads is second-nature to today's Irish racers as most of their meetings are held over highways and byways, with closed circuit racing being less common. However, road-racing was slow to get underway in Ireland and although there were early races, it was not until the early 1920s that it really became established. Their events were loosely organised affairs, for not only were the roads not closed to other traffic during practice but they frequently were not closed to other traffic during races! The local constabulary usually co-operated in manning major junctions and keeping the roads as clear as possible, but really it was a bit of a free-for-all.

There is little doubt that Irish riders took to this 'between the hedges' form of racing, and it was understandable that they looked across the sea to the races being held over the Isle of Man's TT Mountain Course. As an indication of the talent available in Ireland, the 1922 Senior TT was won by Alec Bennett and it saw the debut of riders like Stanley Woods and Jimmy Simpson, both of whom would go on to fine racing careers, plus Charlie 'Paddy' Johnston who, as well as winning the 1926 Lightweight on a Cotton, continued to compete in the TT until the early 1950s.

How 'Sallon' saw perhaps the greatest TT rider of his time, Stanley Woods, who rode to 10 TT victories.

Three of the finest Irish road racers. Left to right: Phillip McCallen, Ralph Bryans and Tom Herron

They were followed by other Irish riders who went on to TT wins such as Henry Tyrell Smith, Manliff Barrington, Artie Bell, Cromie McCandless, Reg Armstrong, Ralph Bryans (who became Ireland's first World Champion), Tommy Robb, Tom Herron, Norman Brown, Con Law, Steve Cull, Joey and Robert Dunlop, Brian Reid, Eddie Laycock, Johnny Rea, Phillip McCallen, Adrian Archibald and Ryan Farquhar. There were, and still are, many other fine Irish riders in both the TT and MGP, and although they may not all achieve victory, they contribute much to the Island races.

In all there have been just over 20 individual Irish winners of solo TT races (many of them multiple winners) and one sidecar winning team of Lowry Burton and Pat Cushnahan. Probably the greatest of all Irish TT winners was Joey Dunlop. Indeed, in many peoples' eyes he was the greatest of all TT riders with his 26 victories.

These Manx stamps were issued in 1996 to commemorate some of the Irish winners of the TT.

ISLAND VISITS

There are some riders whose first experiences of the TT have been as spectators, whilst others have arrived to race without ever having seen the Course. Coming into the first category was Irishman Stanley Woods. Just 17 years old when he came over to watch the TT with his friend Paddy Johnston in 1921, Stanley was right when he turned to Paddy during a race and said *'I could do that'*. There was the small matter of obtaining suitable race machinery, but Stanley turned his agile mind to the problem and wrote to several manufacturers saying that he had a 350 for the 1922 TT and could they supply him with a 500. At the same time he wrote to others saying he had a 500 and could they supply him with a 350. The ploy worked and Cotton offered him a 350 and a contribution towards his expenses, subject to receiving satisfactory references. Stanley gave the writing of those references his personal attention and thus secured his ride. Taking a highly creditable 5th place on the Cotton in the Junior of 1922, he returned to race another Cotton in 1923 and showed his class by winning the Junior race. Thereafter he took 5 wins for Norton, 2 for Velocette and 2 for Moto Guzzi. With those 10 wins he held the title of the rider with the most TT victories for nearly 30 years, until displaced by Mike Hailwood in 1967.

Coming in the category of those riders who had never seen the Course before their first TT ride was Alex 'Jock' Phillip. Indeed, he only received 8 days notice of a ride being available in the 1,000cc class of the 1949 Clubman's TT, following another rider's late withdrawal. With little time to do more than give his bike a quick fettle, he then rode it 330 wet miles to Liverpool and crossed to the Island. A crash at the Waterworks on his second practice lap resulted in a broken finger and, of far greater importance to him, damaged front forks. Fortunately, he was loaned a pair and completed the rest of practice with 'the bike running like a train'. Come the race and Vincent-mounted Alex was badly affected by a new ruling that prohibited Clubman's bikes from refuelling. This caused wholesale retirements on the last lap, including that of the young Scotsman. With the rules changed for 1950, Alex returned with the Vincent determined to make an impression. This he certainly did, for a report in 'Motor Cycling' (whose reporter was watching at The Highlander public-house) said: *'A. Phillip brought the house to its feet with a simply staggering performance. He took the whole section - down the hill, across the bump and out to Hall Caine's Castle Bends - with the throttle hard against the stop'*. Alex went on to win the 1,000cc Clubman's class of the TT in 1950 and with the riding style shown in the photograph below, it is hardly surprising.

An all-action shot of Alex Phillip (Vincent) at Barregarrow during his winning ride in the 1,000cc Clubman's TT of 1950.

Giacomo Agostini was a young Italian hot-shot at the time of his TT debut in 1965. Although he completed 17 early pre-practice reconnaissance laps, when he went out for his first official practice lap of the Mountain Course, 'Ago' probably wished that he had stayed home in sunny Italy. On a very wet and misty Manx morning he set off on his MV Agusta 'four' knowing that the eyes of the motorcycle racing world were upon him, for he was the man whom Count Agusta had employed to bring the World Championship back to Italy. Ago started sensibly and completed his first lap at a modest average speed of 75.48 mph, yet a mere two years later he was to hurl the MV round at a record-breaking 108.38 mph in his unsuccessful struggle with Honda-mounted Mike Hailwood in the 1967 Senior TT.

Due to make his Island racing debut in the 1969 Senior MGP, Mick Grant had both heard and read much about the 37¾ mile Mountain Course but had never seen it. Thinking of doing a little Course learning, he borrowed a road-bike before the event and with wife-to-be Carol on the pillion, set off for the Island. The bike was not in the best of health, having a suspect big-end and being generally out of sorts, but Mick had to make it hang together because he was *'skint'*. In his words: *'all we had was this rattly old bike, two sleeping bags and about 3/6 (17½p) in change'*. Sleeping rough for their short stay on the Island they covered fewer laps than they wanted to, owing to the suspect big-end and the fact that the bike had to get them back home again. Nevertheless, they managed to get it around the Course a few times and Mick went away with a reasonable idea of how the corners were strung together.

Mick's entry in that 1969 MGP was on a race-prepared Velocette road bike, but with a top speed of about 110 mph he was not destined to make a big impression in his first Island race. Hindered by a lengthy pit-stop with ignition trouble, he finished 48th out of 48. As he said: *'after that things could only get better'.* History tells us just how much better, for he went on to take many TT wins through the 1970s and 80s.

Mick and Carol Grant after another of his Kawasaki TT victories.

Many racers from abroad dream of contesting a TT race, even though they have never seen the Course, and one rider at the 1989 TT having his first ever view of the Island was American Chris Crew. He had brought his GSXR Suzuki from San Francisco to race and later described his experiences in 'The Northern California Motorcycle Guide'. Of early practice he wrote: *'You have to be willing to bet your life that you know where the next corner is going over the crest of the next hill'.* It was a stern baptism for the American newcomer who experienced major problems in practice, was faced with the cost of an engine rebuild, coped with last-minute panics before the race, but was then rewarded with a race finish and an award for the fastest Newcomer.

Whilst Chris Crew wrote his own words for 'The Northern California Motorcycle Guide', around 200 journalists, 200 photographers and 70 television personnel were accredited by the TT Press Office to spread the story of the 1989 TT across the world. Amongst them was long-time reporter for 'Motorcycle News', Norrie Whyte, who had been visiting the TT since 1960. Like most people, Norrie's visits started as a spectator. He recalled how he set out from a village that was *'a blob on the A75 in south-west Scotland'* to follow several more experienced villagers in their annual pilgrimage to the TT. His train trip from Dumfries included long waits at intermediate stations, before arriving at Fleetwood and getting his first experience of the Isle of Man ferry. First sight of the racing was from the balcony of the shop at the bottom of Bray Hill and it was an experience that left him slightly stunned. Most spectators take time to graduate to such a scary spot to watch from, but no one had told Norrie what to expect and in his words: *'I'll never forget my first TT sighting - I've never experienced the same feeling'.* Turning into a regular at the TT, Southern 100 and MGP meetings, Norrie's reports saw race news and results spread far and wide. Later he calculated that he had spent well over two years of his life watching Island racing. Unfortunately, he is no longer with us to relive the thrill of his first TT but, although new generations of spectators have taken his place, the bottom of Bray Hill is still a place that is best recommended only to those of strong nerve.

Pressman Norrie Whyte gets the race details from Percy Tait after the 1975 Classic TT.

A racer who was not one of the well-known stars but who came all the way from New Zealand to contest the 1995 Junior TT was Jared Gillard. Impressed with what he saw, in fact *'awesome'* was how he described his first reaction to the Course, he went on to say *'I couldn't take the smile off my face for about an hour after my first practice'*.

Spectators know that they can get close to the race action at the TT. Here they watch Robert Price (Yamaha) at Quarter Bridge.

For every racer at the TT there are hundreds of spectators and they all have their own stories to tell. It used to be the custom for large numbers from individual motorcycle clubs to take over complete hotels and groups of mates still come over together, as well as many individuals. It is not uncommon for regular visitors to see the same people on the boat crossings or at spectating points that they have seen in previous years. Conversation then usually takes up from where it left off on the previous occasion, for whatever they ride and whatever their degree of interest in the racing, they are all present for what, today, is called the 'TT Festival'. The same situation pertains at the MGP where many visitors come as much for the supporting motorcycling activity as come for the actual races.

JAPANESE RIDERS

Japanese motorcycles have dominated the TT races for the last 45 years, but Japanese riders have made less of an impression. The first Japanese rider to contest a TT was Kenzo Tada, who rode the 1930 Junior race on a Velocette and finished in thirteenth place. His was very much a solo effort, but his connections with the TT did not end with his one Island racing appearance, for back in Japan he contributed much to the formation of a national motorcycling body that eventually affiliated to the FIM and so offered a route into the western world of racing to one of the most significant entries in TT history, that of Honda motorcycles.

Honda made their TT debut in 1959, travelling from half a world away with bikes, riders, spares, mechanics, managers and - wary of western unknowns - a doctor and cook. Based at the Nursery Hotel in Onchan they were an oriental curiosity to onlookers, but with their thorough organisation and mechanical reliability, they were also viewed as a team with potential by several of the more perceptive British riders like Bill Smith and Tommy Robb, both of whom introduced themselves to Honda at the Nursery Hotel.

Bringing only 125 cc machines for their debut on the Clypse Course, Honda entered four Japanese riders: Giichi Suzuki, Junzo Suzuki, Naomi Taniguchi and Teisuke Tanaka. They were joined in the race by American Bill Hunt who worked for Honda in America. The Hondas were not as quick as the race-winning MV Agustas but they showed commendable reliability, taking 6th, 7th, 8th and 11th places and winning the manufacturer's team award. Their only non-finisher was Bill Hunt who fell without injury.

Naomi Taniguchi (seated on bike) with other members of the Honda team at their TT debut in 1959.

In 1960 all races were held on the Mountain Course and Honda brought twin-cylinder 125s and four-cylinder 250cc machines, augmenting their teams with established Commonwealth riders Bob Brown and Tom Phillis. Spurred by the efforts of Honda, Suzuki also came to the 1960 TT with three 125cc machines for Japanese riders, but they finished well down the field.

Toshio Matsumoto on his 125cc Suzuki Colleda at the 1960 TT.

Faster than in 1959, Honda again made a good showing with a best place of 5th in the 250 race by Moto Kitano. It was Yamaha's turn to join the Japanese TT invasion in 1961 with entries of five riders in both Lightweight races. However, 1961 was the year when Honda came good at the TT, taking wins in both 125 and 250 races with Mike Hailwood and filling the remaining podium places. The only downside for Honda was that all of those podium places went to 'westerners'. Best Japanese finishers were Sadao Shimazaki (Honda) who took 5th place in the 125 and Kunimitsu Takahashi (Honda), 4th in the 250.

The remaining years of the 1960s saw the Japanese firms taking regular TT wins in the 50cc class (introduced in 1962), 125 and 250. From 1963 they extended their dominance to the 350s, and in the last two years before Honda withdrew from racing at the end of 1967 they also won the Blue Riband Senior 500cc race.

The Japanese had established themselves as the major players in what was a golden era of motorcycle racing. Phil Read was Yamaha's top man for several years and wrote: *'We swept through a showpiece of classic racing competition that was boosted by an open cheque-book, the like of which we may never see again'.*

The dominance of Japanese machinery at the TT saw Honda, Suzuki and Yamaha using their cheque-books to repeatedly leap-frog each other in performance and so share the victories, but their successes were never quite matched by those of the Japanese riders and the only Japanese rider to win a TT was Mitsuo Itoh who rode his Suzuki to victory in the 50cc race of 1963.

Mitsuo Itoh at Governor's Bridge on his way to victory in the 50cc race of 1963.

Several attempts were made to boost the number of Japanese winners and one of those was during the 50cc race at the 1967 Diamond Jubilee TT. Suzuki were favourites for the event, and they wanted Yoshimi Katayama to win. That was fine in theory, but in the race Katayama had to make an early stop to change plugs. In his book 'Japanese Riders in the Isle of Man', Ralph Crellin tells how *'Team-mates Hans-Georg Anscheidt and Stuart Graham rode as slowly as they could to let him catch up. Catching the dawdling pair at Ramsey he took the lead up the mountain, but, looking back at his teamsters, he drifted into the ditch alongside the*

Mountain Mile and crashed, retiring unhurt, leaving Graham to win from a slowing Anscheidt'.

When the Japanese manufacturers withdrew from fully-supported racing towards the end of the 1960s, Japanese riders disappeared from the TT. There have been occasional Japanese entries since and they included world championship contender Takazumi Katayama who rode for a couple of years in the mid-1970s. In 1976 the only Japanese pairing to have contested the Sidecar TT, Matsato Kumano and Isao Arifuku, found themselves out-paced on a Yamaha four-stroke twin. Thereafter there have been occasional private entries, including that of Katsugi Ono in the MGP Senior Classic race of 1988 and, of late, Jun Maeda has contested the TT with promising results. But it seems strange that although the Japanese manufacturers began their return to the TT in 1977 and the entry lists have been largely filled with their machinery ever since, Japanese riders have failed to add to the single TT victory of Mitsuo Itoh, way back in 1963.

Jun Meada leaves Parliament Square during the 2005 Superbike race.

JOEY DUNLOP

Though small in stature, Joey Dunlop stands head and shoulders above other TT competitors with 26 victories to his name. No 'focused' one-class specialist, he achieved his record-breaking wins on machines from 125 to 1000cc, comprising two-strokes, four-strokes, singles, twins and multis, all ridden over a period of over 25 years during which he suffered his share of racing injuries (but not on the Island) and associated personal tragedies.

A Paddock shot of Joey Dunlop (above) as he looks forward to his TT return in 1990 after missing the previous year due to injuries sustained at Brands Hatch, and (below) Joey prepares to tackle his first TT lap for two years.

Joey had a close circle of friends, but outside those he sought little contact with other racers or with the publicity that came with race success. It was Carl Fogarty who explained: *'He doesn't do anything to impress anyone else, he just does what he is comfortable and happy with'.* If that meant that he remained an enigma to other publicity conscious racers, Joey did not care. When asked how well he knew his fellow Honda team-mate, Steve Hislop replied: *'We spoke about ten words a season'*. Asked a similar question, David Jefferies response was: *'Well, I think I know you better than I know him, and we've only spoken a couple of times'*. But while Joey remained relatively unknown as a person to fellow competitors, they were very much aware of his capability as a racer. TT winner Roger Burnett rated him: *'Without doubt, the best road racer that the world has ever seen, or ever will see'*. Geoff Duke said: *'He's one of the all-time greats'* and Barry Sheene explained another facet of Joey's character that was unusual for a 'works' racer, with: *'He's not frightened of a bit of hard graft or getting his hands dirty'*. Indeed, if there was a last minute decision on the grid to change to a different type of tyres, it was usually Joey who wielded the spanners.

Joey getting his knee down to carry out an adjustment before going out for practice on his Honda at the 1996 TT.

In the latter part of his career Joey's public image softened. There would sometimes be a smile, a reasonably detailed explanation of events to an interviewer, and he could be seen in Honda's corporate race-wear.

A winning smile - Joey seems at ease in this picture taken after the 1995 Senior TT.

That was not always the way, but then racing had been extremely hard graft in his early days. Living in and out of the back of a van, there was always dirt under the finger-nails, a cigarette hanging from his lips and, usually, just a yes or no response to questions. Yet throughout his career he was a winner, for, as well as his TT successes, he notched almost 50 victories at the Ulster GP and numerous others at every recognised road circuit at home and abroad.

His total of TT victories might have been greater if he had not run out of petrol on a couple of occasions while in the lead, but he also showed that he could ride through problems that would have stopped a less determined rider. During the 1980 Classic TT the tank strap of his thirsty TZ750 Yamaha broke on the first lap and for the rest of the race Joey held the huge eight-gallon tank on with his arms and knees, whilst also pulling up to first place. Losing time at spots like Ballaugh Bridge where he could not jump because of the loose tank, he lost much more time and the lead to Mick Grant at his pit-stop (Mick used a quick-filler for a 12 second stop, Joey's was a gravity type and he was stationary for 53 seconds). Undaunted, he gradually pulled back the time he had lost, took the lead on the last lap, set a new outright lap record of 115.22 mph, and won the race. It was a win that persuaded Honda that it would be better to have Joey riding for them, rather than against them, and he duly did so, although in another unconventional twist, it is said that for much of his 20 year association with Honda he rode on the basis of just a verbal agreement - no contract.

A factor that could affect Joey's performance on a particular day was whether he was in the mood for racing. Quite open about the position, he would know by the time he arrived at Quarter Bridge on the first lap of a race whether he was going to go well. Former 'Voice of the TT', commentator Peter Kneale, was a good judge of Joey's mood and performance and if he sensed that it was the Ulsterman's day he would say that *'Joey's got his race face on'* and that usually meant that his fellow competitors were left fighting for the lesser positions. One such race, that Joey rated as one of his best, was the 1995 Lightweight TT where he was riding a Honda 250. He told reporter Norrie Whyte at the finish: *'The bike went 100 per cent, the conditions were 100 per cent - dull and cool - and once I got going I was 100 per cent'*, and that was an almost unbeatable combination over the Mountain Course.

By the time of the 2000 TT Joey (who described himself as full-time publican and part-time racer) was 48 years old and was a veteran of 25 years of TT racing. But instead of slowing with age, he actually set his fastest ever TT lap that year when he took three race wins to bring his total number of TT victories up to 26. The motorcycling world was stunned to hear of his death three weeks later in a rain-soaked 125cc race in far-off Estonia. At his funeral, 50,000 people attended to pay their respects to the family man who was awarded the MBE and OBE for the care that he showed for others, but who was known to all simply as 'Joey'.

LADY RACERS

Motorcycling in general has had lady participants from its early days and before 1914 manufacturers produced ladies models of their machines, with dropped frames designed to make riding easier for those dressed in the voluminous garments of the time. Some ladies competed on their machines in road trials, long-distance trials and even Speedway, but lady racers were few and far between in Britain and unknown on the Isle of Man. But it seems that there must have been some who wished to challenge the Mountain Course, for as far back as 1936 'The Motor Cycle' poured scorn on the exclusion from TT entries of *'female persons'*, and they asked the ladies *'how long are you going to stand for this?'*. It turned out to be quite a long while with, along the way, discouragements like the report in the 1948 MGP issue of the 'The TT Special' saying: *'Women who have been agitating for female riders in the TT will be interested to learn that no women Pit Attendants will be allowed'* (at the MGP). So not only could they not race on the Island, they could not even help in the Pits, something that was quite allowable elsewhere.

In 1954 Inge Stoll-Laforge hit the headlines by becoming the first female to compete in a TT race, when she passengered Jacques Drion to fifth place in the Sidecar event. Some wondered what all the fuss was about, for Inge was a regular passenger at Continental events.

Inge Stoll-Laforge was the first lady to compete at the TT when she rode as passenger in the 1954 Sidecar race.

At the time of Inge's entry the TT regulations specified that a rider (or driver as they were described) had to be a 'male person' over 18 years of age, but the wording for sidecar passengers was that they had to be 'persons' over 18 years of age. Whether it was intended that females should be allowed to passenger or whether it was a slip in the drafting of the regulations is not known. Many females have occupied racing sidecars at the TT since Inge, with Rose Hanks and Julia Bingham both gaining second places and sharing the glory of standing on the podium. But the cruel side of such racing has been shown by two female passenger fatalities at the TT (and Inge was later killed whilst racing on the Continent).

Eventually the TT regulations were relaxed and in 1962 Beryl Swain became the first female solo TT competitor in the 55 year history of the races.

Beryl Swain on her Itom in 1962. She was the first lady solo competitor in the TT races.

Mounted on her Itom in the newly introduced 50cc class, Beryl finished 22nd in 1962 and was said to have received more publicity that year than Mike Hailwood.

Beryl Swain's appearance in 1962 did not result in a flood of similar entries, for soon after her ride the FIM again banned women from International events. Although the rule was later rescinded, there has been no more than a trickle of ladies in the TT and MGP during the intervening years. Among them have been Hilary and Gail Musson, Margret Lingen, Kate Parkinson, Pam Cannell, Sandra Barnett, and fastest lady of all at the TT and MGP, Maria Costello, who has lapped at almost 115 mph and took third place in the Senior MGP of 2005. Wendy Davis made a little piece of history in 1997 when she became the first female driver to contest a Sidecar TT. With Martyn Roberts in the chair, they finished both races, whilst in 2004 Ruth Laidlow and Helen Sutherland crewed their 600 Baker outfit to a finish.

Fastest lady around the TT Course is Maria Costello, here shown on a Honda in the 2003 MGP.

CHAPTER 5

TALES OF . . .

LEARNING THE COURSE

Is the TT Mountain Course the longest race circuit in the world? There can be few other claims to the title, and the task of learning its 37¾ miles of twists, turns and gradients in sufficient detail to risk life and limb on two-wheels has always been the biggest challenge in motorcycle racing. It took incredible vision by the race organisers of 100 years ago to plot a Course of such length, and it is worth acknowledging that the primitive and less reliable motorcycles of the pre-World War One period were actually required to cover a race distance equivalent to (and sometimes greater than) today's sophisticated machines.

Despite the quite lengthy period allowed for practice, riders have always supplemented the official practice sessions with many laps of the Course outside the official hours. Initially extending over two weeks, by 1935 practice was down to 10 early morning sessions but it was said of newcomer Otto Steinbach: *'he does six laps in the morning and six laps in the afternoon on a road bike to learn the Course, plus official early morning practice on his race machine'.*

Otto Steinbach shown to be cutting things a bit fine at Braddan Bridge on his NSU.

When Honda first entered the TT in 1959 they brought road bikes with them and the Japanese teamsters in their futuristic (for the time) jet helmets, became a familiar sight as they circulated the Clypse Course on many daytime learning laps.

Naomi Taniguchi brings his 125cc Honda around the corner at the Manx Arms on the Clypse Course in 1959.

It is said that riders must serve an apprenticeship of several years riding the Mountain Course before they should expect to challenge for a win, and the freely available advice to newcomers has always been to 'make haste slowly'. Not every newcomer takes such advice, for by nature they are confident individuals who believe that they are as good, or better, than the next rider, and this has often led to their undoing. TT and MGP winners like Manliff Barrington, Harold Daniell, Ken Bills, Don Crossley, Bob McIntyre, 'Milky' Quayle and others, have all explained how they created holes in the course-side hedges in their early Island races. Each of them lived to race (and win) another day, but some dashing young racers with more enthusiasm than course knowledge have been less fortunate.

The underlying principles of learning the Course are still to seek the best tuition, complete as many laps as possible, and try not to go too fast too soon. The need for tuition was brought home to Travelling Marshal Albert Moule when the fallen rider he attended at Creg ny Baa during the 1964 MGP told him: *'I forgot the corner'.* He forgot a right-angled bend approached downhill at near maximum speed! Today it is compulsory for all newcomers at the TT to take part in an official instructional lap on a coach, where they receive advice from experienced former racers on how to ride the Course. (Sidecar newcomers go on a different coach to solo competitors.) Gone are the days when a rider's first sight of the Course might be on his first lap of official practice. These coach trips are still nicknamed 'Crossley's Tours' after the man who started them, former MGP winner and Travelling Marshal Don Crossley. But that single compulsory instructional lap must be supplemented by many voluntary laps, for former racer Ray Knight (a man who has ridden countless thousands of racing miles at the TT) considers that there are still 264 bends in a lap, despite the many road improvements that have been carried out down the years. It was Steve Hislop who summed up the difficulty of getting all those bends right when he said: *'There has never been and there never will be a perfect lap of the TT Course'.*

Peter Darvill with Francis Beart who prepared the AJS on which he won the 1963 Junior MGP.

Many riders seek to learn the Course in stages, and one of those was Geoff Duke. Arriving a week before official practice was due to start in his debut year, Geoff concentrated on learning the stretch from the Start to Kirk Michael, followed by Kirk Michael to Ramsey and then Ramsey to the Finish. Some consider that doing their learning laps on a bike is the only way, while others are happier to learn with steady laps on four-wheels, (they know that they will get throttle-happy if they go on a bike). What every newcomer accepts is that far more laps have to be covered than are available during official practice sessions. Learning laps outside official practice usually involve many stops, retracing of steps and consideration of alternative lines. Bill Hindes accompanied Peter Darvill on his first trip to race at the MGP in 1957 and recalled a learning trip with several riders in a car when, at Ballaugh Bridge, *'one of the lads actually insisted in laying down in the middle of the road to study the "Line" completely oblivious of passing traffic - the locals stood by and kept their thoughts to themselves as this was obviously not the first time they had witnessed this form of lunacy'.*

A top racer of the 1950s and 1960s was Derek Minter and, even after he had been racing the TT for several years, he would go round in his van as often as possible, frequently stopping and walking the corners. Derek was convinced that the reason so many riders came to grief on the Island was that they did not learn the Course thoroughly before trying to race over it. Derek was the first man to lap at 100 mph on a British single, and he also won the Lightweight TT of 1962 on a Honda, so he was a quick rider. His belief in the need for thorough Course knowledge was reinforced by his view that: *'Really and truly your mind was one step ahead of your body. You're in this corner but your mind is actually in the next corner so you know what part of the road you need to be on when you get there'*. With the massive increase in speeds that have taken place since the 1960s, that approach must be even more relevant today.

Another top-man who felt that there was always something to be learnt from a lap of the Course was Joey Dunlop. By 1986 he had been competing and winning at the TT for 10 years. Nevertheless, a report of the time told of one day during practice week when he had been out on the Formula 1 bike during early morning practice, and out on two of his other bikes during evening practice. Not content, he and brother Robert then went out and completed two laps in a car. In the words of his Manager of the time, Davey Wood: *'Joey likes to do this very late at night, as he still feels that he can learn something every time'*.

Top riders are often asked for advice on how to ride the Course and that of eleven-times TT winner Steve Hislop was: *'work at the bends to get the best out of the straights so that you can carry the speed with rhythm and flow, that's the key to TT success'*. His advice was almost the same as that given by six-times winner John Surtees some 35 years earlier and in respect of learning the way Steve added: *'there's no real secret, it's just about putting in the time and having an aptitude for it'*. There are riders who favour a certain part of the Course, and Joey Dunlop liked the twisty *'between the hedges'* stretch from Ballacraine to Ramsey better than the featureless miles over the Mountain, while David Jefferies really enjoyed the Mountain, saying: *'As I come out of Ramsey, it's tail up and head down. I just go for it and blast over the Mountain as one section'*. Phillip McCallen was a rider who did not believe in favouring a particular part of the Course, saying: *'start to like or dislike sections and you start slowing down here, going faster there and you're soon in trouble at a place like the TT'*. But the response of Michael Rutter to the question of what he liked best about the Course was a not quite so serious, with: *'I enjoy the bit where I come in for a pit-stop'*.

Many riders watch videos of the races to pick up tips on how to ride the Course, but sidecar- racers need to be careful with their viewing because three-wheelers take a different line to solos in some places, and they also have to learn the racing line as a team. Rob Fisher is a ten-times winner of the Sidecar TT and reveals that, prior to his Island debut in 1993, he watched a video of the 100 mph lap achieved by rally driver Tony Pond (Rover Vitesse) on four-wheels, every day as the time for the TT approached. A couple of sighting laps in a van before first practice produced sound advice to Rob from Geoff Bell, with Geoff telling him which spots to treat with caution, rather than which spots to tackle at speed. Delighted with a fifth place in his first race, Rob describes how *'we hit the beer tent to celebrate'*.

Inexperienced riders often hope that they will learn how to ride the Course by hanging on to the tail of a faster rider who passes them, but that can turn into a frightening experience and should only be done with caution. MGP and TT winner Nick Jefferies is hugely experienced over the Mountain Course and acted as Rider Liaison Officer for many years. He is often asked about the benefits of

Rob Fisher was quite confident that he knew his way around by the time he rode to victory with Rick Long in the 2002 Sidecar TT.

tagging onto a faster rider or a Travelling Marshal by newcomers, but his advice to them is not to try and stick on anyone's tail. What he does tell them is to try and learn something from everyone who passes. Things such as how, and from which point they set themselves up for a series of bends, their general body language, where they open the throttle, etc, can all be beneficial.

New for the 2004 MGP was that the opening lap of practice was reserved for Newcomers. They rode it under the control of Travelling Marshals who headed batches of them in a swift but steady ride around the Course, and the same procedure was extended to TT Newcomers in 2005.

The length of the TT lap is part of its attraction, but when it comes to its learning, it must be a sobering thought for a would-be competitor that one lap of the Mountain Course is equivalent to the combined lap distance of all the varied circuits used in a year of World Championship Grand Prix meetings.

LESSER LIGHTS

The formidable challenge of winning a Tourist Trophy race has been tackled by many of the biggest motorcycle manufacturers down the years, but not all have been successful. However, failure on the part of some of the big boys has not discouraged smaller manufacturers from seeking to get their names engraved on one of the famous figures of Mercury that constitutes a Tourist Trophy. The heading 'lesser lights' is not used disparagingly here, but to reflect the fact that even when the races were run on the Short Course prior to 1911, there were competing manufacturers like Triumph who were producing 3,000 motorcycles a year being challenged by names like Roc who produced a relative handful.

Some of the lesser lights were aware that they had no real hope of achieving a win, but they did know that the TT was the best possible showcase in which to display their products to the motorcycle world. While victory was only a dream, participation in a TT race was enough to give their motorcycles a measurable edge over the opposition in the eyes of prospective buyers. Association with the TT was even sought by those who did not take part and many manufacturers catalogued a 'TT Model' that, just prior to the First World War, became a recognised title for a machine with sporting pretensions that lacked pedals, had a flat or slightly downturned handlebar and, maybe, a slightly tuned engine.

With over two-hundred firms turning out motorcycles in Britain in the 1920s, it was a difficult task for a manufacturer to get serious thoughts of his machine into the heads of potential buyers, but participating in the TT was one way of doing so. A typical race year of the 1920s could see entries from 20 different makers in the Senior TT, 25 different in the Junior and 12 in the Lightweight. In later years those firms who did compete would often produce sporting roadsters that they labelled 'TT Replica'. Usually having some justification for comparison with a firm's competition models, they were an attempt to make commercial capital by creating a link with prestigious TT race activities.

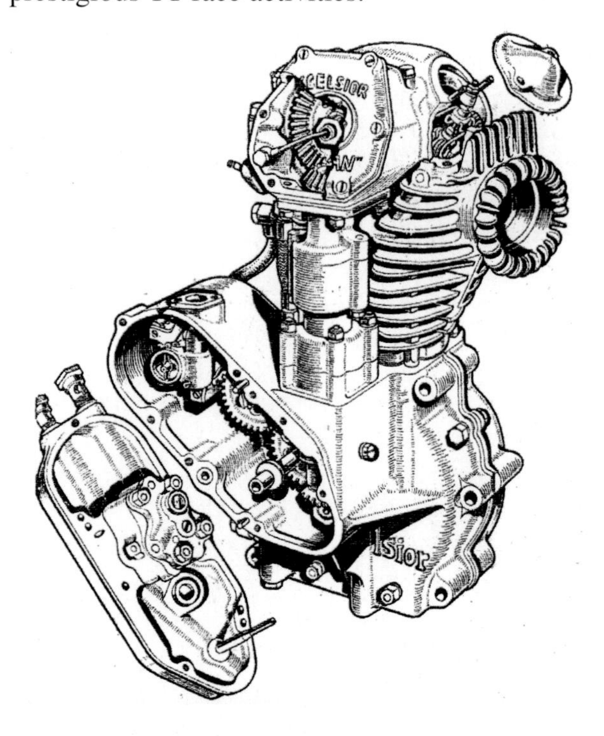

Excelsior went as far as to name their sports model of the 1930s the 'Manxman'. This illustration is of the engine fitted to their 1938 machines that took second and third places in that year's Lightweight TT.

Although the majority of manufacturers sought TT glory as an aid to promote wider sales of their road-going models, even a TT win was not sufficient to guarantee long-term commercial success. Howard Davies was an established name on the TT scene as a rider in the 1920s and, after deciding to turn manufacturer and produce his own machines, he had made less than 100 bikes at the time of his stunning win in the 1925 Senior TT (and second place in the Junior) on his HRDs. Boosted by those TT performances, Howard Davies company, HRD Motors Ltd, successfully expanded its output in its next few years of operation but, despite taking another TT win with Freddie Dixon on a 350 in the 1927 Junior, it could not balance its books in the difficult trading conditions of the late 1920s and went out of production at the end of 1927.

There have been other individuals who were dissatisfied with the standard race models available and so built their own. For this they either used proprietary engines which they sought to improve and modify, or built complete machines to their own designs. An example of the former was Chris Tattersal who campaigned his CTS at the TT from 1930-1953, whilst home designed and built machines included the REG, LCH and LEF of the early 1950s. Most of those were 250s and the results of their TT efforts were plenty of retirements and an occasional top six placing at some considerable distance behind the winners. That is not to belittle their efforts, for some were quite successful on short circuits, but it is an indication of the difficulties facing the 'lone wolf', particularly in a long race like the TT.

One TT winner who might be classed as a 'lone wolf' was Maurice Cann who took a single win in the 1948 Lightweight race, although some argued that a time-keeping error robbed him of an earlier win in 1947. Riding much modified Moto Guzzis, the difference between Maurice and many others who chose to modify standard products was that his bikes were actually faster than the bikes produced by Moto Guzzi, even faster than their 'works' machines.

Lino Tonti was an Italian who made use of existing products to produce his Linto in the late 1960s, by utilising two 250 Aermacchi engines on a common crankcase as a parallel twin. They were raced at the TT by riders like Alberto Pagani and Jack Findlay without great success. However, they did take second place behind MV Agusta in the 1969 constructor's World Championship.

The Aermacchi based engine of the 500cc Linto.

Innovations and improvements to standard products were not limited to solo riders, for sidecar drivers have always been a creative bunch. Helmut Fath was not satisfied with the BMW flat-twin engine that was the top sidecar power unit for so long, even though he had driven one to victory in the 1960 TT. Taking several years to produce his own URS four-cylinder engine, he was unable to do better than take 4th and 3rd positions in three TT outings with the URS in the late 1960s, although he proved its worth by taking it to a sidecar world championship title.

Even when Yamaha dominated the solo racing scene with their two-stroke machines, there were many who sought to improve on both their engines and frames, with names like

Maurice Cann leaving Governors Bridge heading for victory in the 1948 Lightweight TT.

Seeley, Spondon, etc, convinced that they could turn out a better racing bike with a Yamaha engine than the factory could. And whenever factory support of racing dwindles (it goes in cycles) there are always private tuners around ready to continue development and offer their services to the competitor who is prepared to pay to have a quicker than standard bike.

Nowadays most TT racers are based upon production machines and there seems little scope for the 'lesser lights' to challenge the big names. However, back in 1993 a machine that 'Motorcycle News' described as *'a backyard special'* proved that a home designed and built racer could still mount a credible challenge for TT honours. New Zealander John Britten brought his highly unconventional twin to the races and it shocked the established teams with its speed. It also grabbed the attention of spectators on account of its individualty. With its special engine note and striking colour scheme, it drew lots of attention away from the rows of look-a-like Hondas. It also bristled with Britten's innovative technical ideas with a chassis of kevlar and carbon-fibre that used the engine as a stressed member. Unconventional suspension and relatively light weight plus its liquid-cooled, eight-valve, fuel injected V-twin engine with belt-driven dohc, meant that the 150 bhp unit offered plenty of speed for the power-hungry TT Course.

The TT did its usual trick of revealing minor problems with the Britten that had not shown in lesser races, and although the team returned in 1994, the bike did not really live up to its promise at the very highest level, despite a win at Daytona earlier in the year. Sadly, John Britten died in 1995.

Shaun Harris and the New Zealand-built Britten racer leaves Parliament Square, Ramsey en route to a finish in the 1996 Senior TT. Two lengthy pit stops dropped the v-twin from a potential leader board finish to 33rd place.

LIGHT PEDAL ASSISTANCE

Light Pedal Assistance (sometimes abbreviated to LPA) is a term that has come down from the pioneer days of motorcycling. A number of the fairly primitive machines in the first TT of 1907 still showed their push-bike heritage by retaining pedalling gear. The race regulations recognised this situation but specified: *'Pedalling will only be allowed for the purpose of starting or restarting, or in traffic, or at sharp bends on stiff gradients. Excessive pedalling will disqualify'.* The climb out of Glen Helen was a problem for most of those early competitors, and as speed fell away riders of some of the single-speed bikes that lacked pedals were forced to jump off and run alongside their flagging machines to prevent them stalling. Those with pedals used them with vigour, bringing claims by those without pedals of *'excessive pedalling'* in contravention of the rules.

It is understandable that some of those without pedals in 1907 complained, particularly after they had run up Creg Willey's alongside their bikes on each of the 10 laps in thick tweed or leather riding gear. Reports tell that the Collier brothers both pedalled, although Dent, Silver and Martin did not, but Smyth was one of those who dismounted and ran alongside his machine. Jack Marshall rode a Triumph without pedals and told how he nursed his engine from Ballacraine on each lap in an attempt to keep it cool, then: *'on reaching Glen Helen I would open up, scrape round Creg Willies corner and get as far as I could up the hill, running the last few yards'.*

The single gear ratio available to early riders had to be a compromise between being high enough to make good progress on the flat, without being too high to allow the ascent of hills. Noted authority on Riley products, Dr David Styles, tells how the 3½ hp Riley that Robert Ayton used in the 1907 event had a 5 inch pulley on the engine and a 17 inch drive rim on the rear wheel, giving a ratio of 3.4:1. That sounds a high gear and a report of the time made mention of Ayton *'being geared too high'.* The Riley's pedalling gear comprised a 52 tooth chainwheel driving a 14 tooth freewheel sprocket, so providing a slightly lower 3.7:1 gear than the driven ratio. Robert Ayton was a private entrant and, even though we may think of 1907 as still the dawn of the motorcycle, Riley dropped motorcycles in 1906 and moved on to tri-cars.

With the organisers keen to push the development of touring motorcycles, it was no surprise to find that in revised race regulations for 1908 pedals were banned, so taking away the claimed advantage of LPA.

When the ACU moved the TT to the very much more demanding Mountain Course in 1911, they also introduced a Junior race open to single-cylinder machines of up to 300cc and twins up to 340cc. Showing a lack of confidence in the Mountain-climbing abilities of their smaller products, several manufacturers asked that pedalling gear should be allowed on Junior machines but the ACU resisted such calls. The switch to the Mountain Course did not only worry the Junior entries. With many bikes still belt driven their riders feared that if it rained, the subsequent risk of belt/pulley slip would pose major problems on the uphill sections. Such fears came true in 1912 when the Junior was held in pouring rain. Only 11 riders completed the Course and the winner, Harry Bashall (Douglas), stopped eight times during the race to make adjustments.

The move of the TT races to the Mountain and the problems that it presented to belt-driven, single-speed machines served as a spur to the development and adoption of chain-drive and multiple gears for all racing bikes over the next few years, so making thoughts of LPA a thing of the past.

LOTTERY DREAMS

Nowadays many British riders harbour a dream of winning the National Lottery and thus being in a position to fund their TT racing efforts on a no-expenses-spared basis. Some have even been known to buy a ticket! Thirty years before the British Government introduced the National Lottery, the Manx Hospitals Society created a Lottery to be run in connection with the TT and MGP races. First introduced on the approach to the 1965 MGP, the payout was based around the results of the Senior race. It was initially a big success, with reports that ticket-counterfoils and cash was pouring into the Island and that 20 members of staff were working overtime at the

Post Office to deal with them.

Tickets were drawn after the MGP prize-giving ceremony by the winning riders. First prize was £25,000, second was £15,000 and third £10,000. That was big money for the day and would have funded a nicely set-up race team. As well as making payouts to the lucky ticket winners (and to Manx Hospitals) it was claimed that some of the Lottery income would go to a scheme for the design of a British world-beating racing motorcycle - something that the country was badly in need of at the time, for its racing fortunes were at a low ebb. Japanese and Italian manufacturers were dominant in world racing (Norton, Matchless and AJS had ceased production of their trusty single-cylinder racers) but it has to be said that most people were highly sceptical about the chances of a revival of Britain's racing fortunes coming as a result of the Manx Hospitals Lottery. Nevertheless, invitations went out for the submission of designs to create a world-beater but, as predicted, nothing serious came of them.

MAD SUNDAY

The busy Sunday before race-week that everyone now knows as Mad Sunday was, from 1914, known as Sad Sunday. (Some called it Dead Sunday.) This was because in their efforts to get the Course in the 'best' condition for racing, (and, probably more importantly, to appease the many Manx people who sought a quiet Sabbath), the authorities prohibited ordinary users from travelling on it for the day. It was a restriction that only lasted for a short time.

There are plenty of TT fans who spend their time on the Island seeking to emulate the racers over the Mountain Course and, with a major influx of speed-hungry fans occurring on the day before, the Sunday prior to race-week is particularly busy. Recognising the problems that occurred (visitors found it difficult to resist taking the racing line on those sweeping Mountain bends) in about 1964 the authorities introduced a one-way flow of traffic over the Mountain from Ramsey to the outskirts of Douglas for part of Sunday. That, allied to the Island's lack of an overall speed limit, now allows the ordinary rider an opportunity to play racer over the 11 mile stretch and gives even greater credence to the title of Mad Sunday.

The opportunity offered of riding at speed over closed roads is seized by many, and they spend the whole day riding the one-way stretch, returning to Ramsey by other roads and riding it again, and again! Conspicuous by their absence from the Course on Mad Sunday are the actual race competitors. As one well-known racer put it: *'We racing motorcyclists have learned to avoid the roads on Mad Sunday'*. But locals are out in force (a relatively high proportion of the Manx population have bikes), some on the latest sports bikes, others on much older machines, but the 'oldies' are often the ones to be wary of. There can be much experience of the Manx roads tucked under those staid crash helmets and well-used leathers. Such riders may be conspicuous by their lack of back protectors, knee-sliders, jazzy helmets, £500 after-market exhaust cans and other such 'essentials' to fast riding, but there is many a visitor who gets a lesson on how to go quickly from following one.

Regrettably, some of those who set out to emulate the racers find that they are not up to the

A Mad Sunday shot at the Gooseneck with riders free to use all the road. There are almost as many spectators as on a race-day.

job, and whilst most will be lucky enough to get away with no more than a fright or two, others will overdo it and need the support of the rescue services. It happens every year, and police and ambulances are positioned at points around the Course to deal with the inevitable.

Mention has been made of locals showing visitors a *'clean pair of wheels'* across the Mountain, but they can also get caught up in the high-octane atmosphere and throw it away. Manxman and TT winner Richard 'Milky' Quayle tells of doing multiple laps one Mad Sunday during his younger days. On a bike of dubious road legality, (and relatively small capacity), 'Milky' left everything in his wake as he wore a groove in the road from Ramsey to Douglas. Treating it as his own personal race-track, he admits that, with all the associated traffic, he was an accident waiting to happen. On a fast and tricky bend before the Bungalow he lost the bike in a big way, and machine and rider slithered and bounced down the road doing damage to both. The bike was unrideable and 'Milky' could barely walk. Pushing it off the road, and praying that it would not be spotted by a passing police-car, he hitched a lift home and, with considerable difficulty due to increasingly swollen feet and ankles, managed to drive his van back to the scene of the accident, enlist aid in loading the bike into it, then, belatedly, made a visit to hospital.

Participation in the madder aspects of Mad Sunday is not compulsory! Visitors find many other attractions available on the same day, including a vintage rally, displays of racing machinery, an off-road Trial, meetings of one-make clubs, etc.

MANX RADIO

That the introduction of Manx Radio's commentaries on the TT and MGP races in 1964 has kept spectators better informed and entertained is indisputable, what is not quite so certain, but is strongly suspected, is that the information on lap times, race positions and time gaps between riders, has been instrumental in affecting the outcome of several races. The increase in the amount of detailed information broadcast by Manx Radio has allowed support crews to keep their riders much better informed of their race positions at pit-stops and at signalling points around the Course, and the biggest plus point is that it has been accurate and up-to-the-minute. Indeed, with the recent introduction of transponder timing relayed to the commentators' computers, it can now be up-to-the-second.

Where Manx Radio started in 1964.

One problem for Manx Radio in broadcasting so much detailed information on the races is that they must ensure that it is totally accurate. The mistakes they make are few and far between, but once made they are long remembered. Early in the 1971 Lightweight MGP, Charlie Williams already had a respectable lead of just under a minute on his rivals. But Manx Radio's timekeeper feeding information to Geoff Cannell at his commentary point on Ballaugh Bridge managed to add a minute to Charlie's elapsed time. This information was broadcast, picked up by Charlies support team and passed to him at his next signalling station. Being told that he was a few seconds down rather than almost a minute up caused Charlie a bit of concern before he increased the pace, broke the lap record and came home victorious - with three minutes to spare! Post-race consideration of the lap times showed that Charlie had not really shown his true hand in practice, even though he had got close to the existing lap record of 92.40 mph. On the first lap of the race he smashed the record with 95.55 from a standing start, and then, after the mistaken call to raise the pace he produced even more speed to achieve a staggering 97.09 mph lap (also beating the Junior 350cc lap record).

Spectators have come to rely on Manx Radio to keep them fully informed on all matters relating to the races, but most go equipped with the official Programme and Race Guide to use during and between the races.

The bulky Race Programme (above) offers useful reading material in the intervals between races, while the Race Guide comprises the list of entries with which to identify and record the progress of riders during a race. These versions date back to 1980, but today's follow a similar pattern.

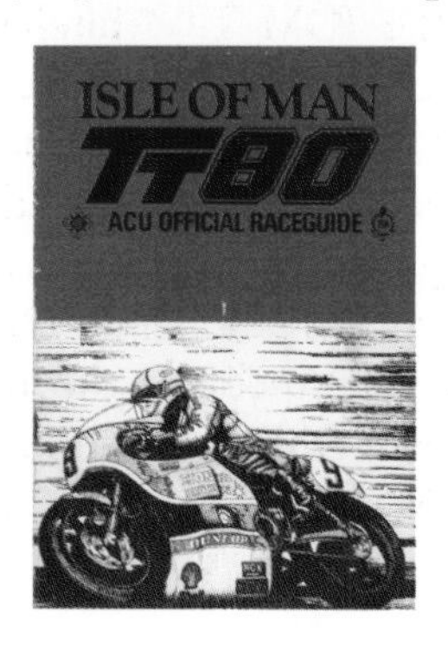

Although the duties are shared between commentators located at the Grandstand, Glen Helen, and one at the Start/Finish with a roving mike, the odd technical difficulty has seen individual commentators having to keep chatting for longer than expected. Formally known as 'the voice of the TT', the late Peter Kneale was anchor-man in the Grandstand from the outset of Manx Radio's broadcasts and recalled one occasion when contact with the commentators around the Course was lost and he had to keep talking for some 20 minutes. He must have used a fortnight's notes up in one session. With many fans (and an increasing number of competitors) from the continent at each TT, Manx Radio provides summaries of race positions in German and French.

Peter Kneale was succeeded as 'anchor-man' by Geoff Cannell who had done many years commentating from points around the Course, plus several years in the Pits with the roving mike. It was with disbelief that many TT and MGP fans heard that he was to be replaced by a 'TT unknown', Charlie Lambert, for the 2004 event.

A practice week shot of Geoff Cannell. Armed with camera, pen, paper and a talent for picking up the latest information, Geoff was doing his homework before beginning the task of keeping listeners informed on-air during race-week.

Whatever developments take place in TT racing it is likely that radio broadcasts will continue to develop alongside them. Today's output of TT news is certainly a vast improvement over the one man with a megaphone who was employed to convey information to just the fortunate few in the main Grandstand in the early 1920s.

MARSHALLING THE COURSE

Without marshals there would be no racing - that familiar dictum is trotted out at regular intervals by race organisers, and it is absolutely true. A full grid of riders for a race at the TT might total 80 and perhaps be nearer 100 at the MGP. To enable them to race, a veritable army of 1200 support personnel will be on duty around the Mountain Course. Some will have specialist jobs in Race Control and the Start area, other specialists like doctors, paramedics, radio-operators, etc, will be at various locations around the Course, as will the remainder of the 1200 who go under the general title of marshals.

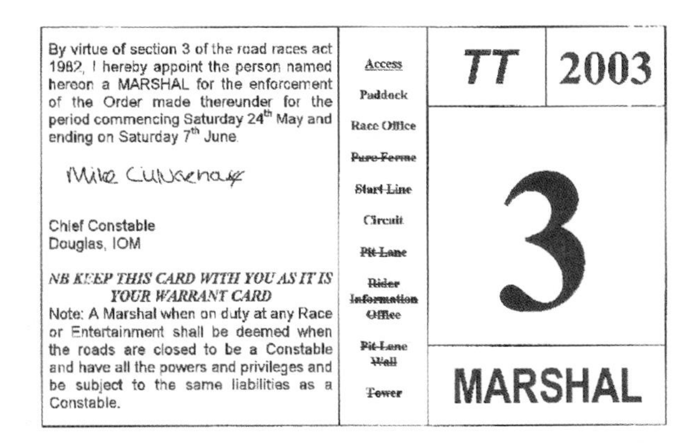

By virtue of section 3 of the road races act 1982, I hereby appoint the person named hereon a MARSHAL for the enforcement of the Order made thereunder for the period commencing Saturday 24th May and ending on Saturday 7th June.

Mike Culverhouse

Chief Constable
Douglas, IOM

NB KEEP THIS CARD WITH YOU AS IT IS YOUR WARRANT CARD

Note: A Marshal when on duty at any Race or Entertainment shall be deemed when the roads are closed to be a Constable and have all the powers and privileges and be subject to the same liabilities as a Constable.

Access
Paddock
Race Office
~~Parc Ferme~~
~~Start Line~~
Circuit
~~Pit Lane~~
~~Rider Information Office~~
~~Pit Lane Wall~~
~~Tower~~

TT 2003

3

MARSHAL

An example of the Warrant Card issued to each marshal.

Inevitably, matters have become more complicated in marshalling the Course since the earliest days when it was recorded of the 1908 TT: *'Police Sergeant Corkhill, of St John's, was in charge of a considerable force of regular and special constables who were employed in keeping the course. These worked with a will and the result was that the competitors were never for a moment hampered, while all elements of danger to spectators were eliminated'.* With the move to the longer Mountain Course in 1911 more marshals (who are all sworn-in as special constables) were needed, but they were thinly distributed, for very few would have had their own motorised transport, and getting to somewhere like Windy Corner in time for early morning practice could involve considerable effort.

The Isle of Man TT Marshals Association issues a booklet of advice to all its members.

With today's large numbers there has to be an organisational structure for marshals. Co-ordinated by the IOM TT Marshals Association Ltd, the Course is divided into sectors and top of the pile are the twelve Chief Sector Marshals who are each responsible for a defined stretch. They appoint Deputy Sector Marshals to assist them and each sector also has a number of white-coated Flag Marshals. The remainder of the orange-jacketed marshalling force will be stationed at potential trouble spots. As well as their general duties, each will be given specific duties at their allotted stations, for in the case of an incident it is vital that everyone knows what is expected of them and that all anticipated problems are covered. If a rider falls then, dependent on the number of marshals available, two will be charged with dealing with the rider, two with the bike and debris, one brings a stretcher and another telephones or radios Race Control to advise them of the situation and ask them to call out the rescue-helicopter, if required. In addition to the above, all marshals are looking for fire hazards, keeping possible well-meaning spectators off the Course and using their skills and training to assess and take action on the individual (and often unplannable) aspects of the incident. Incidentally, whoever is in charge will have ensured that the Flagman was warning riders of the problem before any marshals were allowed to set foot on the Course and the same person will continue to monitor passing traffic and the safety of the marshals.

For any incident involving a fallen rider, Race Control will despatch a Travelling Marshal to assess the situation, and, if necessary, he will take control and then report back to them in the Control Tower at the Grandstand.

Travelling Marshal Chris Fargher flies his Honda VTR1000 over Ballaugh Bridge as he speeds to a race incident.

If the helicopter is called out to take an injured rider to hospital, a whole new set of procedures come into force to ensure the safety of all concerned. Marshalling the Mountain Course can never be quite the exact science that organisers try to make it at conventional short circuits, but the Island's race organisers run many incident management courses to raise awareness and skills. Those are the occasions when established marshals, medics, etc, inform newcomers on well-tried procedures of first-aid, helicopter support, use of flags, communications and associated matters. They attempt to pass on some of their long experience of race procedures, so improving the service and safety aspects of Island racing.

So, after the countless hours spent on duty both before and during races, do the marshals deliver the goods? One man who thought so was Steve Hislop. He had a good safety record on the Island, but when he fell from his 250 Honda at Quarry Bends in 1989 he was travelling at some 140 mph, and rider, bike and resultant debris were scattered over a considerable distance. In Steve's words: *'I was very impressed by the efficiency of the marshalling. By the time I was able to say "What Happened?", they had me and all the debris cleared from the course, and within minutes the helicopter was hovering overhead, having been alerted by the marshals the moment I slid off*. A rider who created rather more than his share of work for the marshalling service was MGP and TT winner Nick Jefferies (five helicopter rides at the last count). Recalling a 120 mph spill whilst ascending Creg Willeys during a wet Senior, Nick described the seconds after his spill with: *'Silence! Running feet, shouts, radio messages, the world was spinning round. Lying on the pavement I knew I needed help, quickly. Within a matter of seconds the helicopter had been summoned, I had been made comfortable, the bike (what was left of it) had been swept up and the road cleared, the wall had been rebuilt, etc, etc. It was incredible how much had*

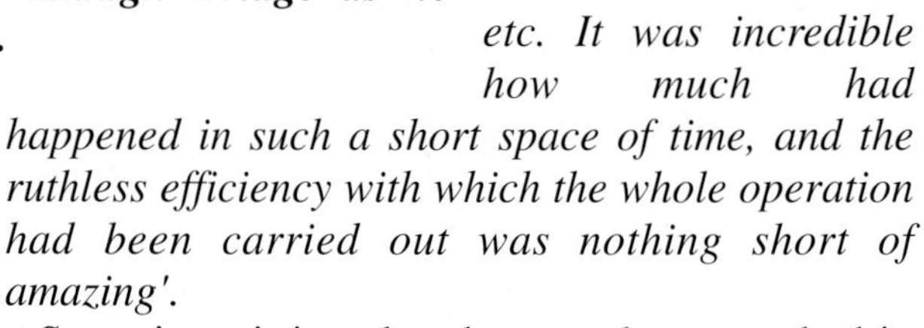

happened in such a short space of time, and the ruthless efficiency with which the whole operation had been carried out was nothing short of amazing'.

Sometimes it is only when good turns to bad in motorcycle racing that riders truly realise the value of efficient marshalling and support services.

MASSED STARTS

From the very first TT riders have been despatched singly, or in pairs, at defined intervals, and that has become one of the features that distinguishes the TT from other races. However, there have been occasional mass starts. The first was the 1924 Ultra-Lightweight (175cc) race when, amidst prophecies of chaos at the foot of Bray Hill, 17 competitors were sent off together.

No incidents were reported in 1924 and, although used again for the 175s the following year, the massed start did not catch on and it was to be 1948 before it was used again. That time it was for the Lightweight 250 race, and the process was repeated in 1949 and 1953.

When the Clypse Course was brought into use in 1954 the Ultra-Lightweights (125cc) and Sidecars were the first to use it, and their races had massed starts.

The Clypse Course avoided the plunge down Bray Hill by turning right at St Ninians crossroads to head across through Willaston to Cronk ny Mona. The Lightweight (250cc) and Clubman's classes later used the Clypse for their races (some with massed starts) until the Course was abandoned after the 1959 TT.

Production racing came to the TT in 1967 with one race that combined classes for 750, 500 and 250cc machines. Run on the Saturday before normal race-week, it featured a Le Mans type mass start for each class. The 750s went first, followed

Massed-start of the 1924 Ultra-Lightweight race. The front row is (left to right): Alec Bennett (Diamond) 9th, Geoff Davidson (Levis) 4th and Jock Porter (New Gerrard), the winner

A mixture of BMW and Norton sidecar outfits leave the start of the 1958 Sidecar TT.

five minutes later by the 500s and five minutes after them went the 250s, all over three laps. There had been some opposition to the introduction of the Production race, but spectators were kept on their toes by an event that was full of incidents and fine riding performances. John Hartle took victory in the 750 class on a Triumph Bonneville, Neil Kelly was first 500 on a Velocette Venom, and Bill Smith took the 250 class on a Bultaco Metralla.

At the 1970 TT the organisers planned to despatch riders in groups of 9 at 90 second intervals. However, although the new system was tried once in the Thursday afternoon practice, negative feedback from riders caused the method to be abandoned before race-week. Since then, all TT and MGP races have employed an interval start, with TT riders now being sent off singly and runners in the MGP despatched in pairs.

A busy first lap at Quarter Bridge in the 1966 50cc race. The Suzuki mounted quartet shown here of Tommy Robb, Hugh Anderson. Ernst Degner and Hans George Anscheidt have already been dropped by the conquering Honda twins of Ralph Bryans and Luigi Taveri!

MECHANICAL DEVELOPMENTS

From the TT's earliest days manufacturers entered the event to gain publicity for their motorcycles, to help speed development and, in many cases, to satisfy their own competitive instincts and show that they could produce as good (or better) motorcycles as the next man. It is not possible to chart all of the mechanical developments that can be linked directly to the TT, but there is little doubt that competing in the event served as a spur to each entrant to improve his product and that many lessons learned in racing filtered down to be used in road-going machines.

In the first races the single-speed, belt-driven machinery of the time found the 'Short Course' to be demanding and the lack of gears and reduction in power resulting from the overheating of their all-iron engines, meant that even modest hills were a challenge. It is widely accepted that the TT served to widen the use of variable gears, particularly after its move to the Mountain Course in 1911. Indeed, by 1912 there was only one single-speeder entered, the remainder being fitted with two-speed countershaft boxes, two and three-speed epicyclic hubs, and multi-gear arrangements via variable drive-pulley sizes.

AJS won the Junior TT again in 1921. This time with Eric Williams.

The First World War was responsible for rapid development of the internal combustion engine for aviation purposes, but motorcycle design stagnated. The result was that there were few technical advances in racing motorcycles in the period 1914-1920. AJS was one of the motorcycle companies that had been heavily involved in war-time aero-engine work and they were one of the few firms who produced a new engine in 1920. Fitted to their Junior machines the new ohv unit had valves set at an angle of 90 degrees, revved to 6,000 rpm and also enjoyed the advantage of four-speeds (achieved by way of two primary drives that could be coupled to the gearbox by a sliding dog on the engine shaft, a system first fitted to their 1914 TT bikes). The new AJS should have swept aside the outdated opposition, but the AJS team riders got involved in personal feuds and although way ahead of the field, they suffered mechanical failure and crashes. Only surviving rider for AJS, Cyril Williams, saved the day for them by pushing and coasting from Keppel Gate to take first place - and he still finished 10 minutes ahead of the runner-up.

Sunbeam concentrated their efforts in 1920 on the production of specialist racing bikes for the event. Although of modest specification by today's standards, they did, in the words of Graham Walker: *'finish for ever the chances of the semi-private owner on a super-tuned job'*, and also gave a lesson to other manufacturers on what was required to win the Senior TT.

By 1922 there had been some worthwhile advances on the mechanical side of motorcycles produced for racing. In his book 'Racing Round The Island', Bob Holliday describes how *'Nortons had produced their first ohv model; Rudges introduced their four-speed gearboxes; Barr and Stroud sleeve-valve engines appeared; the new big port AJS made much use of aluminium and aluminium-bronze. And the most exciting innovation was a two-port overhead camshaft 350cc JAP engine, designed by Val Page, in Bert le Vack's New Imperial. It was the first ohc unit seen in the TT'.* Many of such developments were also taken up by other manufacturers .

At the end of the 1920s overhead camshaft engines were in more general use and the victories of Rudge in the Junior and Senior events of 1930 were the last in those classes by push-rod machines. Purpose-built race machines were by then the only ones capable of winning a TT (not converted roadsters) and they made full use of the improved materials available. In 1934 AJS Junior and Senior models had the by then fairly common aluminium-bronze cylinder heads, with one exception. In what was described as *'a veritable marvel of metallurgy'* one was fitted with an all-aluminium head. Another report gave an indication of the compression ratios that the cylinder-heads of the mid-1930s were required to withstand, they being: Lightweights 9 to 9.25:1, Junior 8 to 8.5:1, Senior 7.5 to 8:1, with machines running on a 50/50, petrol/benzole mixture.

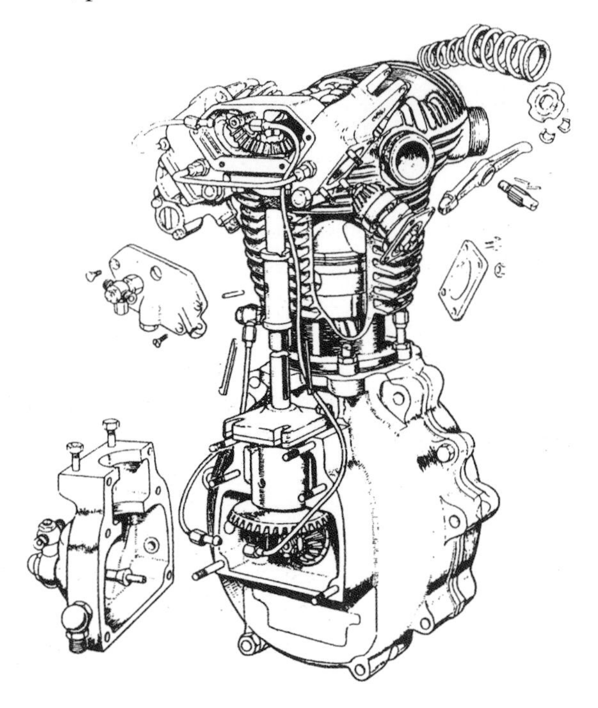

The 350cc ohc engine produced for New Imperial by JAP that led the 1922 Junior for more than half the race.

The successful use of sprung frames in the mid 1930s by Moto Guzzi and Vincent HRD persuaded firms like Norton and Velocette to use them on their TT machines, and in looking at the benefits to road machines from race activity, 'Motor Cycling' claimed in early 1936 that it *'held the view unswervingly that eventually the spring frame will come'*.

There had been four-cylinder machines at the TT prior to the Second World War (including British efforts), but in the post-war period the 'fours' of MV Agusta and Gilera were looked at with awe by many British competitors, despite the fact that in

Three stages in the development of the front suspension of MV Agusta racers in the 1950s

early appearances the big MVs sported a basic torsion bar and friction damped form of rear suspension, plus pressed metal front fork blades. Renowned for speed but not for handling, they then progressed to swinging fork rear suspension and telescopic forks at the front, before temporarily adopting Earles type leading-link front forks.

In the early 1950s Norton's out-dated single-cylinder powered machines continued to stay ahead of the more powerful Italian machinery by virtue of their better handling. This was mainly due to Norton's use of the Featherbed frame, but it was a situation that could not last. Eventually swept aside by the Italian fours, the singles were later humbled by Japanese machines, both large and small, despite continuing to make up the majority of the entries. Then the increased speeds of the large capacity Japanese two-strokes of the early 1970s saw them outstripping the performance of tyres, frames, chains, etc. However, as in previous years, the demands of racing served to spur development, resulting in improvements in tyres, brakes, ignition, carburation, water-cooling, etc, so that, eventually, Japanese machines were not only taking all the TT and MGP victories, but they were also dominating the entry lists in the manner that British machines had done before.

Swiftly consigned to history and Classic racing were features such as featherbed frames, air-cooled engines, drum brakes, spoked wheels and swinging fork rear suspension; having been left behind by the introduction of cantilever suspension, to be followed by twin alloy spar frames with single-shock rear suspension, disc brakes, cast alloy wheels, etc, with ever more powerful four-stroke power units gradually ousting the two-strokes.

This single-sided swinging-arm of the Honda RC30 also shows the mono-shock suspension and disc-brakes that were fitted as standard equipment by the late 1980s.

Increases in performance generated by better engines, suspension and brakes, were able to be used to the full by corresponding development of new materials, compounds, shapes and methods of construction of tyres for both race and road use.

Avon claimed a big break-through in the 1960s with the development of their 'cling' rubber. Tyres have provided a major contribution to the increase in lap speeds down the years, with some of today's

Yamaha's RD56 air-cooled, parallel twin 250 of 1963 (left) and their water-cooled, vee-twin of 1988 show the changes brought about by 25 years of development. Both used fairings when raced.

tyres being more than three times the width of the earliest versions.

With all the development and progress came a change of emphasis in the machines raced and, rather than producing no-expense-spared racers for use at the TT, today's race-winning bikes can clearly be seen to be derived from road-going machines. Honda always considered TT victory important enough to field their most expensive bikes until the end of the 20th century, but after David Jefferies stormed to victory on his V&M Yamaha R1 in 1999, 'Motorcycle News' rubbed salt into Honda's wounds with the headline: *'A £20,000 Proddie bike Shouldn't Humble £500,000 Honda RC45s'.* Honda have now gone down the same route as Yamaha, etc, by up-grading their road bikes for racing, and such a situation can be seen as a return to early TT racing principles.

MECHANICAL MISHAPS

The Norton that Rem Fowler rode to class victory in the very first TT in 1907 was a relatively primitive machine and, as was customary at the time, he had to cope with several problems in his winning ride. Among them was the need to change sparking plugs several times, repair a front-wheel puncture, fix a loose mudguard and tighten his drive-belt on two occasions. He also fell off twice during the race.

It is something of a cliché that running a bike at the TT will reveal weaknesses that have not shown up before - but it is true. From its earliest days the TT developed a reputation for dashing the hopes of the complacent who arrived with poorly prepared or inadequately developed machinery. BSA were amongst the biggest motorcycle manufacturers in

A tired photograph of Howard Riddell with the sloper BSA. Promising much, it turned out to lack the essential reliability required to cover six laps and 226½ miles of the Mountain course.

the early 1920s when they decided to produce a new bike specifically to contest the TT. Seemingly taking the matter seriously, they made 18 sets of components, assembled 12 race machines, tested at Brooklands where the bikes were clocked at 76 mph, and made 6 entries in the 1921 Senior race of their new single-cylinder 500. Rumours abounded that the new inclined-cylinder machines were the lightest and fastest in the race, but at the weigh-in they were found to be the heaviest (310 lbs) and, as BSA found to their cost, speed is nothing at the TT without reliability, for they had under-estimated the demands of the Mountain Course and none of their bikes finished the race. This was a loss to both BSA and the TT for, as Britain's largest motorcycle manufacturer, they turned their back on the Island races and sought future publicity by competing in off-road events.

Manufacturers soon recognised the demands imposed by the TT and realised that they could usefully use the races to test and develop their products. One man who found this out to his cost was Robin Bownass when riding his NUT in the 1922 event. Speeding round on his second lap, his front (girder) forks broke, throwing him from the bike. Fortunately he escaped injury, but it is hoped that NUT, or their fork suppliers, went back to the drawing board with that design. A man to have fork problems in 1923 was Geoff Davison, winner of the previous year's Lightweight TT. Geoff had to be content with the award of a replica in 1923 for, not only did he have fork problems but, in his words, *'my hand-built race engine was not completed until two days after the race!'*. Using his practice engine he did not have the pace to challenge for the lead and, potentially more serious, he broke a bottom fork link and *'I rode the last lap with the front wheel meandering away from the machine, expecting at any moment to be decanted on my chin in the roadway'*. Five years on and Maurice Davenport had the bottom spindle of his Webb forks shear as he was travelling flat-out past The Highlander. A long slide on his back left Maurice badly shaken, and he turned his back on the TT and continued his almost invincible sprinting career at home and abroad.

All component breakages are a cause for concern when they happen on the Mountain Course but when handlebars and clip-ons break at speed the potential consequences hardly bear thinking about. A man who had a double dose of this trouble was Bert Kershaw at the 1921 TT. On his Lightweight New Imperial his handlebars broke at Signpost Corner during practice. Fortunately, it was not one of the fastest parts of the Course, but it was still a shock for Bert when they failed. In the Lightweight race he was going well until, towards the end of the third lap, his bars broke again at Signpost Corner. Although such breakages were rare, they continued to occur. Multi-TT winner Charlie Williams remembers the 1981 TT for the fact that, fully committed to cranking the bike over for the ultra-fast 33rd Milestone, his right clip-on snapped. A similar fate befell Ray Knight the same year, but both riders survived their dramatic high-speed moments without crashing.

The purpose of the extensive practice period allowed before the races is to allow entrants to bring their machines up to race pitch. Rarely is there enough time to do so to everyone's satisfaction, even though in the early days practice was spread over two weeks. This was later reduced to about 10 days and today it is a week and a bit.

Reg Armstrong has the chain of his Norton break as he takes the chequered flag to win the 1952 Senior TT.

At the end of the practice period, the interval before the first race should really be used for a final check-over of machinery but, in pursuit of the infinitesimal improvement that is the goal of every racer, many succumb to the temptation to change components and settings. In 1928 AJS changed the make of valve springs used on its 350 engine just prior to the race. Five of its six entries retired with broken valve springs. Vincent HRD were newcomers to the TT in 1934 and made use of JAP engines. Between the end of practice and Senior race-day, their engine suppliers, J.A.Prestwich (JAP), persuaded Philip Vincent to change the cam followers on his three bikes, with the result that two of them retired from the race due to failure of those modified cam followers.

After all the intense effort involved in preparing and practising for a TT or MGP, to breakdown during a race can be extremely frustrating. During the 1935 Senior race 'Ginger' Wood's New Imperial failed him and he coasted to a standstill. In his frustration he lifted the bike up over the roadside bank and deposited it in a field. When the race was over, he found that he could barely lift the front end of the bike off the ground, let alone lift it back over the bank!

TT winner Henry Tyrell Smith worked on the development of Triumphs in the late 1940s and said: 'a run of 5 hours at full throttle, at the revs at which maximum bhp is attained, will prove an engine to be capable of finishing a TT without trouble'. MGP winner Robin Sherry's first Island ride happened to be on a Triumph in the 1949 Clubman's TT where he finished in eighth place. Taking the Triumph on to that year's MGP, its engine cried enough, when, in Robin's words: *'a conrod broke and cut the engine in half. It happened on those fast bends after Handley's - no warning, bang! All the crankcase was chopped off, bits were swinging in the wind against my legs. It was a horrible sight . . '.*

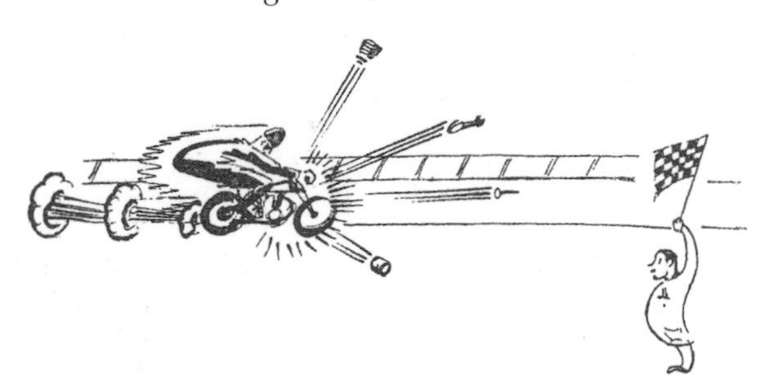

Whatever the output and duration figures from an engine's test-bed performance, the real test comes when it goes on to the track and is used under race conditions. The aim of a tuner at an event like the TT is not only to get a machine to deliver maximum performance, but also to get it to last the full race distance. It is a delicate balancing act and several TT winning bikes have suffered mechanical failure at the moment they crossed the finishing line. One of the most famous photographs in TT history is the one showing Reg Armstong's broken chain falling from his Norton as he took the chequered flag as victor of the 1952 Senior race.

Not so obvious to the watching crowds was the major failure suffered by the valve-gear of Stanley Woods winning Moto Guzzi at the end of the 1935 Lightweight, and few knew of the bevel-drive problem in Mike Hailwood's Ducati that ruined the engine as the chequered flag fell on his triumphant TT come-back victory in the 1978 Senior.

Honda four-cylinder engines of the 1960s had a reputation for reliability at the TT. This is a 350 version of 1963.

The two-strokes that challenged for the top spot in motorcycle racing of the 1960s were fast but often temperamental. This was particularly so at the TT where even the change in altitude from sea-level to 1400 feet was enough to affect their carburation, and the major swings in the weather between morning/evening practice and race-days was also upsetting. If the carburation was not correct the two-strokes were at risk of seizing and it was

Aussie Jack Ahearn who nicknamed Suzuki's particularly temperamental four-cylinder 250 racer *'Whispering Death'.* The Suzuki's handling also left a lot to be desired, so much so that one of their other riders, Frank Perris, offered to redesign the frame. When told that was not possible as the frame had been designed by a computer, Frank's immediate response was: *'Then let the b . . . .y computer ride it'.*

Yamaha were also top two-stroke runners (before going on to four-strokes) and Tommy Robb joined Phil Read and Mike Duff to ride 'works' bikes at the 1964 TT. Suffering from chronic plug trouble through most of practice, Tommy recalled in his book 'From TT to Tokyo': *'Things got really rough on one early morning practice when I stopped and ran out of plugs on the mountain - and believe me there is no lonelier place in the world at that time of the day! I had used my half dozen plugs and had begun to despair, when I spotted an old tractor in a field. I raced across with my plug spanner, took a rusty plug out of the tractor, put my Yamaha plug in its place, tried the bike; it fired first time, and was off again. The plug carried me back to the start, much to my relief'.* Clearly expecting problems, the Yamahas carried spare plugs inside their fairings.

It was a mechanical problem that caused the crash that brought the racing career of Italian ace Tarquinio Provini to an end. It happened on the sweeping bends approaching Ballaugh and although it seemed to be accepted at the time that the crash was caused by his being dazzled by the low morning sun, twenty-five years later Provini told 'Classic Bike' magazine of the scarcely believable mechanical bodge that was carried out on his 350cc four-cylinder Benelli. In his words *'The engine had broken on the Wednesday evening, and rather than stripping it completely, the mechanic removed one piston so that it could run as a three and we could do more laps the next day. A con-rod was sawn through just above its big-end. We ran the engine, and it seemed okay. But the remaining metal around the big-end eventually exploded, and a lump shot into the gearbox, locking the rear wheel'.*

The sustained ability of the Mountain Course to discover faults in design, materials and

George O'Dell and Kenny Arthur after their record-breaking victory in the 1977 Sidecar TT on their Yamaha outfit On the right are second placemen Dick Greasley and Mick Skeels and on the left third placed Rolf Steinhausen and Wolfgang Kalauch.

workmanship are well documented. George O'Dell was a hard-charger on a sidecar outfit who eventually finished up with a TT win and a World Championship to his credit.

In his second year at the TT (1971) O'Dell suffered a serious crash at Greeba Bridge when the front-wheel of his outfit broke-up, due to the pounding it had received. George was annoyed that this had finished his sidecar race and doubly annoyed that, due to having broken two fingers, his right foot and his nose in the sidecar incident, he was not permitted to take up his entry and start in the solo Production race - something he very much wanted to do, having set excellent times in practice. George later broke a leg when he crashed at the Bungalow in the 1978 Sidecar TT, a break that he repeated in a crash at Ginger Hall in 1979.

Mick Grant's ride in the Classic race at the 1982 TT comes to an end at Ballacraine on lap 4 with mechanical failure of his big Suzuki.

Riders know that the Mountain Course is dangerous but they are prepared to pit their skills against the harsh challenge that it offers, because they believe that they can remain in control of their machines by skilled use of throttle, brakes, clutch, etc. What all riders dread is having control taken away by serious mechanical failure. That was a fate that befell Robert Dunlop when the rear-wheel of his Honda collapsed just after Ballaugh Bridge in the Formula 1 race at the 1994 TT. Sustaining injuries that would have taken a lesser man out of racing for good, Robert had a long struggle to get back to race fitness. A past podium finisher at the TT on all capacities of bikes, the effect of his Ballaugh injuries limited him to racing in the small capacity classes with specially adapted controls.

Robert Dunlop shows the effects of a day's hard racing. His racing career on the Mountain Course spanned the period 1983 to 2004. Starting with a win in the Newcomers MGP he finished with a second place in the last ever Ultra-Lightweight 125 race.

Although the engines used in many of today's race bikes come from production machines, they have a generally good reliability record. But not all hang together when thrashed around the Mountain Course. Andy Lovett was given special permission to practice out of class towards the end of practice week at the 2003 MGP to get in the lap he required to qualify. He was pleased to arrive back to the Grandstand without trouble on what was his fourth (he thought - or maybe it was his fifth) 600 Yamaha engine of the week. It was a second-hand purchase on the Island, after he had blown three engines, plus one that he had built up from the damaged ones. Sidecar racing puts even greater demands on power units, and Steven Coombes and Gary Partridge were said to be on their 8th Kawasaki engine of the 2004 TT period, when they finally managed to keep things together and finish 30th in the second three-wheeler race.

CHAPTER 6

TALES OF . . .

MISCELLANEOUS

In the early years of the TT almost all machines were fitted with belt final drive, but they were not of the endless variety fitted to some modern-day machines. Although belts could be obtained in a single length (that required a metal fastening device), many were comprised of pieces of stout leather about 2" long that were held together with various patented fixing devices.

Typical early belt-drive.

The flexibility of the leather belts meant that they were capable of absorbing some of the shocks imposed by the single-speed, low revving bikes of the time, but they were subject to two main problems: slip and stretch. Belt slip was often experienced when riding in wet conditions and was also brought on by oil leaks and by the belt stretching. This stretching was a continual process that was sometimes bad enough to cause a TT runner to stop part way through a race and remove a leather link from the belt to shorten it, or to change the belt for the spare one that some riders carried. Cyril Pullin was an experienced TT rider who won the Senior TT on a Rudge in 1914 (his was the last belt-drive victory). Just as present-day riders 'bed-in' their chains by running them for a lap of practice to stretch them before a race, so Cyril Pullin would do the same with his leather drive belt. He would then remove it and hang it with a 56lb weight attached to preserve the stretch until just before the start of the race.

*

The Forward Motor Co were just one of the many small concerns making motorcycles in the early 1900s and they were represented in the TT from 1911-13.

Start of the 1911 TT was on the flat after the bottom of Bray Hill and a Forward machine (no.10) waits for the 'off'.

Forward also made drive belt fasteners called the 'King Hook' and the 'Forward' and announced in 1912: *'for the past three years in succession the first single-cylinder machines in the Senior TT fitted Forward belt-fasteners'*. Indeed, the Company found the manufacture of belt-fasteners and sparking plugs to be their most profitable activities and so dropped the manufacture of motorcycles.

*

Although the use of pedals was banned at the TT from 1908, many manufacturers continued to fit them on their road-going bikes. But, seeing an opportunity to publicise their slightly more sporting versions, from about 1911-12 makers began to make use of the title 'TT model' and it was not long before the term became accepted in the motorcycle world as denoting a machine that was not fitted with pedalling gear. However, the 4th edition of 'Hints And Tips For Motorcyclists' published in 1913 sounded a note of caution to would-be buyers about such models, saying: *'So-called "T.T." machines are really semi-racers, and not to be recommended for the inexpert'.*

*

It was not long before the dangers of the many twists and turns of the TT Course revealed themselves to over-enthusiastic riders. From the earliest events the organisers erected warning arrows on the approach to difficult bends, and it was not long before they began to put rudimentary protection in place. A report of the 1923 Lightweight race tells: *'R.V.Cranford took Creg ny Baa too fast, and hit the wall, but the mattresses saved him and he was soon away again'.* The organisers themselves were in no doubt that the Course could be dangerous, but as one pithy piece of advice in a MGP Programme said: *'providing we remember it is dangerous, then it is usually quite safe'.* In the 1930s a yellow line was painted on the road between the Gooseneck and Creg ny Baa to offer riders guidance in fog, and Harold Daniell wrote in respect of the fog-bound 1932 MGP: *'there were flares on the mountain road to guide competitors'.*

George Brown pushed in to finish after running out of fuel when leading the 1948 Clubman's TT - totally exhausted, he receives sustenance from officials.

*

The TT Course has been responsible for a huge number of mechanical breakdowns, particularly on the demanding climb of the Mountain. There is a myth that a rider who reaches Brandywell (the highest point on the Course) but then breaks down, has only to pull the clutch in to be able to coast home to the finishing line. That, as anyone who has tried it will tell you, is not true. If an engine fails at speed and the rider can knock it out of gear without losing much momentum then he might, with a following wind, get a fair way to the finish, but the climb at Cronk ny Mona is steep and will usually bring a bike to a halt. Signpost Corner soon follows and although it is easy enough to coast from there to Governor's Bridge, getting out of the dip at Governor's robs a bike of all speed and if pushing out of the dip leaves a rider with any energy, the long upgrade of the Glencrutchery Road will see him arrive at the Finish totally exhausted. Spectators in the Grandstand have given many a brave rider a generous round of applause for pushing in, but it is a rarer sight nowadays, for marshals will, on safety grounds, usually seek to dissuade a rider from pushing on the Course.

But not everyone bothers to push in after a break-down. In the 1928 Amateur race (predecessor of the MGP) Tim Hunt started the last lap with a 2½ minute lead over local rider Harry Meageen. Plunging down to the Creg on the last lap Tim's Levis suffered valve failure, whereon he pulled in and retired to the bar of the Keppel Hotel (as it was then known). Not for him the attempt to coast and push in for a possible leader-board place, even though he had over 14 minutes in hand on the man who eventually finished third.

*

In its TT number for 1927, the magazine 'Motor Cycling' wrote: *'In the fullness of time, when television becomes a practical proposition, one of the greatest uses in the sporting world will be to enable spectators in the Isle of Man to watch riders all round the 37¾ mile TT course'.* Well, perhaps unsurprisingly, spectators are still waiting, but those who pay to sit in the Grandstand probably feel that a few big screens showing competitors at other points on the Course would not go amiss; and they could be on their way.

*

The Lightweight machines of the 1930s spent most of their time with the throttle against the stop at the TT, for they were not troubled by an excess of power. This led to riders adapting a canny riding style to minimise wind resistance. Sid Gleave (Excelsior) won the 1933 Lightweight and it was said in the race report that Sid: *'scientifically utilises hedges and walls as shelter from the wind'.*

*

A visit to the TT allows riders and spectators to concentrate on motorcycle racing to the exclusion of worldly affairs, and that is the way that it has always been. Back in 1935 'The Motor Cycle' wrote: *'Who cares what Hitler says, or whether there has been another coup in the Balkans? This week we don't read the national papers - we live, dream and read motorcycles'.* However, some could not escape their political masters, for after the 1937 Lightweight TT 'The TT Special' reported that news of Omobono Tenni's victory on his Moto Guzzi *'was cabled to Mussolini, The Italian Dictator, by Signor Parodi . . . who is on the Island in charge of the Guzzi machines'.*

The T.T. Special

THE T.T.'s OWN NEWSPAPER

ELEVENTH YEAR OF PUBLICATION

WEDNESDAY, JUNE 16, 1937.

*

In an attempt to publicise their event and gain a few more entries, officials of the Manx MCC attended a Clubman's meeting at Donington Park in the summer of 1939 and offered free MGP entries to two of the race winners, Lesley Parsons and Stanley Barnett, but neither were able to take up the offer at the time. Although the 1939 MGP was all organised and set to run, the outbreak of war caused its last minute cancellation. With the coming of peace the Manx MCC were the first to get their event up an running, and at the MGP of 1946 two of the competitors were Messrs Parsons and Barnett. They had written to the organisers asking if the pre-war offer of free entries still stood and, perhaps admiring their cheek, the organisers said 'yes'. Lesley Parsons showed that six years absence from motorcycle racing had not blunted his talents, and won the Lightweight event of 1946 on a Rudge.

*

Apart from interruptions caused by wars, the TT races ran every year from 1907. However, there were a couple of instances when they were threatened and one of those was 1935. The first arrivals for practice found themselves caught by the tail-end of a General Strike on the Island. Porters were amongst those on strike so everyone had to carry their own bags, electricity was off, and an air of uncertainty prevailed. Fortunately, matters cleared up quickly, and practice and racing went ahead as planned.

These riders carry their bags from the boat on arrival in Douglas in 1935.

*

There were virtually no new racing machines available in the immediate post-war years, but Norton had left a cache of new racing spares on the Island after the 1939 TT, with the idea that they would be used a few months later at the MGP. Those spares were still intact after the war and they contributed to the construction of several new racing machines, although they had to be detuned slightly to run on the 72 octane 'Pool' petrol which was the only one available.

In 1966 the TT was affected by a seamens' strike and the month of June was a strange one, for no TT races were run. As a result, the Island was bereft of the thousands of visitors who customarily made their annual pilgrimage to what they regarded as motorcycling heaven in the middle of the Irish Sea. The decision to postpone the races was delayed for as long as possible, but was finally made on the 1st June, in the week before practice was due to start. That was time enough to allow most people to cancel their travel arrangements but too late to prevent a team of Yamaha mechanics flying in from distant Japan. Apart from its adverse effect on the Island and its tourist industry, the postponement of the races posed a serious problem to the top riders and factories because the TT was a major event in the World Championship programme. By juggling with the dates of the MGP, time was found for the TT to be run at the end of August, just after the Ulster GP. Revised race days were Sunday 28th August, Wednesday 31st August and Friday 2nd September. The first race day had to be on a Sunday to allow many of the riders to make a quick dash by specially chartered boat to honour commitments at a major UK meeting at Oulton Park on the Bank Holiday Monday. New legislation had to be passed by Tynwald, the Manx Parliament, to allow Sunday racing.

Newcomers to the MGP wear orange waistcoats during practice. Here Tommy Clucas goes through a debriefing at his first MGP in 2002.

*

Taking part in a TT or MGP has always required a big commitment from competitors in terms of time and expense, and some do it all just to take part in a single race. In the past that meant that there was a 6 lap 'blast' to look forward to, but that has now been reduced to 4 laps in some classes, (3 laps for sidecars, but they do get two races). However, the actual race is only part of the TT experience, for competitors also have practice to look forward to. Indeed, some of them believe they do their best racing in practice! Perhaps a little explanation is called for. A TT race sees riders started singly at 10 second intervals (at the MGP they are despatched in pairs at 10 second intervals) and that can often result in a fairly lonely 4 or 6 lap ride, with competitors racing against the clock and seeing little of the opposition. It is not always like that, but it is a factor of Island racing that the opportunity for fairing to fairing jousting with the opposition can be limited. But that is not the case during practice. The time available for each practice session is restricted (but generous compared to short circuits) and, although there is some separation of classes, it is a fact that several classes will be out together and riders will be far denser on the Course than in a race. This means plenty of close action and, although now a thing of the past (because the class has been dropped at the TT), spectators used to watch in delight as good riders on 125s dived over, under and around Newcomers on 600s. The 125s would then be zapped on the straight, but they would be snapping at the 600s' heels at the next series of bends. A similar situation still prevails at the MGP where 125s still race and where experienced riders of Classic Manx Nortons and G50s are out with Newcomers on modern machinery. Not only do the 'old' riders know their way around but they are also most reluctant to shut off for bends, with resultant embarrassment of those who are still learning the way on their up-to-the-minute race bikes.

So, although a rider may only be entered for one race of 4 laps (150 miles) he can, during practice, indulge in 2 lap 'races' every day for over a week, which means that the number of racing miles that he will put in during a TT or MGP fortnight will probably exceed the total of what he does for the rest of the season on short circuits.

John Goodall won the first Classic Senior MGP held in 1983. Over twenty years later he is still taking podium places. This is a photograph from practice in 2002, for John has the white waistcoat worn by riders of Classics during practice sessions.

*

After over 50 years of attendance at the TT as a professional photographer, Don Morley has many tales to tell about the riders and racing (and quite a few that he dare not tell). He recalls: *'It was back in 1990 when Joey Dunlop advised me to visit and photograph from a certain spot where he reckoned he plus his big Honda were taking off whilst flat out in top gear and literally flying over 70 yards in mid-air. Did I get my picture? Did I heck, principally due to my being far too busy diving for safety, and sod's law landing right amidst a very large patch of nettles. Joey would of course known I would have taken the bait and been there, and as often happens very probably hammed it up a bit more for my camera, but as mentioned it proved a wasted effort, and though he won't admit it I rather suspect that he overdid things somewhat and frightened himself as much as I was, certainly he never jumped nearly as far or high again'.*

*

Honda's strong showings in the Formula 1 races of the 1990s guaranteed that many of the lesser runners bought and entered Hondas in an attempt to emulate the winning of riders like Joey Dunlop, Steve Hislop and Phillip McCallen, with the result that entries were almost monopolised by Honda. Then in the early years of 2000 it was Yamaha and Suzuki that were doing the winning and in 2003, out of 66 starters in the F1 race, only 5 were on Hondas. The worse news for Honda was that buyers of street bikes were following the same course of action. It was proof, if it was needed, that success in racing boosts sales of roadsters.

*

Kiwi, Shaun Harris, was a consistently good rider at recent TTs. Often appearing as a last-minute entry, he gave his sponsors good value for money, both in his riding and during the media interviews when he never failed to mention everyone who supported him. However, getting his TT racing deals together from half a world away, and sometimes at the last minute, meant that things did not always go right for Shaun on the Island and he acquired a reputation as a bit of a whinger during some of his radio interviews. But in 2003 he had the ideal TT set-up with sponsorship from Kevin Stephens Racing and, showing a nice line in self-depreciation, an obviously happy Shaun made the pre-race comment: *'People think I'm always moaning, but this year I'm not flinching from saying "I'm content"!'* Race results showed that he had good reason to be, for it turned into the year that he gained his first TT victories, taking the 600 and 1000 cc Production races. But 2004 saw Shaun with a change of major sponsor and his big bikes were supplied by Des Collins. Both Shaun and Des were strong-minded (and spoken) individuals and, recognising the fact, they came to a pre-TT agreement that any disparaging comments made during the pressure of practice or the tensions of race-week, would be mutually forgotten in the post-TT period.

*

When top-runner John McGuiness found himself without a 400cc machine for the 2003 Lightweight TT, he took unusual steps to locate one. Digging out some back numbers of 'Motorcycle News', he scanned the British short-circuit results of the previous couple of months to see who had been doing the winning in the 400 class. Spotting that Steve Tomes was the 'man of the moment' on a 400, he approached Steve's sponsor, who readily agreed to let John run the bike at the TT. The result was beneficial to both, as John took the little Honda to victory after a minimum of practice, a feat that he repeated in 2004.

*

The Manx Motor Cycle Club's Guest of Honour at the 2003 MGP was Murray Walker, who was known for his TT commentaries long before he moved over to talk about F1 four-wheeled racers. Now Murray did the customary tasks of shaking hands all round and starting the races in 2003, but he went one better than the usual Guest of Honour and did post-race radio interviews of several of the race winners.

Guest of Honour at the 2003 MGP was Murray Walker. He is accompanied at the Start area by former rider and Clerk of the Course at both the TT and MGP Jack Wood (left) and Geoff Karran (right) President of the Manx Motor Cycle Club at the time.

MIST ON THE MOUNTAIN

Manx legend has it that the great sea god Manannan Mac Lir rules and protects the Isle of Man and that he has the power to throw a mantle of mist over the Island as if to make it disappear. But quite why he should choose to use that power so often at TT time is a question that has been asked by countless thousands of frustrated riders and spectators down the years. The Island actually experiences an above average amount of sunshine for the British Isles, but it also seems to suffer more than its fair share of 'Mist on the Mountain' during some race fortnights. What makes this particularly frustrating is that while small sections of the Mountain can be blanketed in cloud, other parts of the Course can be basking in sunshine.

Archer (New Imperial) : "I may be the "Aldershot Flyer," but I haven't got my blind flying certificate yet"

'Aldershot Flyer' Les Archer (New Imperial) is shown in the misty 1935 Lightweight race, as he struggles to find his way across the Mountain.

Up to 1934 no practice session or race was postponed or cancelled, even though the weather was no better than today and speeds had risen rapidly down the years. In a tragic incident in the 1934 Lightweight race, seasoned competitor Syd Crabtree crashed his Excelsior on the Mountain and was killed. The race was run in thick fog and nobody saw or heard the accident, with the result that Crabtree lay undiscovered for approximately 40 minutes. (It was the organiser's system of logging every rider at defined points on the Course that revealed Crabtree was missing and brought about the search that found him.) Such a state of affairs could not be permitted and it brought about the introduction of the Travelling Marshal service, whereby motorcycle-mounted marshals could be sent on to the Course during a practice or race to search for a missing rider. Those experienced Travelling Marshals were all former racers, and they could make on the spot assessments of the weather on the Mountain. Indeed, one year later such an assessment brought about the first ever postponement of a TT, the 1935 Senior.

FRIDAY DAWNS IN A THICK MIST : THE STEWARDS CONFER—START POSTPONED

How 'The Motor Cycle' headlined the first ever postponement of a TT race.

Other postponements followed in later years, but races were still run in conditions that would not be acceptable today. Riders of the 1970s and even the 1980s speak of riding through mist over the Mountain and realising that they were gaining on another rider by catching the smell of the exhaust of the machine ahead, long before they sighted it.

The length and mixed terrain of the Mountain Course means that it is quite common for riders to meet with wide variations in weather conditions in just one lap. During an early morning practice period for the Clubman's races in 1953 there was a strong wind and patches of mist on the Mountain, then heavy rain in Douglas, while at Sulby it was dry and windless but low sunshine was dazzling the riders.

With growing speeds, ever increasing safety awareness and today's need for the rescue-helicopter to be able to land at any part of the Course, the number of practice and race sessions affected by Mist on the Mountain has increased to the point that rarely does a TT or MGP escape a postponed session. Only one race has ever been totally lost due to adverse weather (the 1987 Production Class A & C - due to be run together) but postponements and reductions of race distance have become more frequent. Things have reached such a pitch that experienced TT runners sometimes try to anticipate the organisers thinking with regard to races held in wet weather. One such was Joey Dunlop, who came to the 1998 TT with injuries received earlier in the season at Tandragee and limited himself to racing in the Lightweight classes. Really suffering from his injuries, Joey barely scraped on to the top-twelve leaderboard during practice and had thoughts of scratching from the 125 and 250 races. However, he was on the line for the Lightweight (250) race in what were deplorably wet and misty racing conditions. Gaining advantage from the wet (reduced speeds meant less high-speed wrestling with the bike), Joey also used his many years of experience of the TT to second-guess the organisers. Like most other riders, he was due to stop for fuel after just one lap of the already shortened from four to three-lap race, but Joey decided to go straight through, gambling that with the weather deteriorating the race would be stopped after two laps. It was, he was at the head of the field and he took what was perhaps the least expected of his many TT victories.

Joey Dunlop (Honda) splashes his way to victory in the 1998 Lightweight TT.

Although the cancellation of a race or practice can cause frustration for thousands of spectators and riders, spare a thought for the men who make such decisions, the race organisers. Housed in the Control Tower above the Grandstand, they have but a distant view of the Mountain. Juggling information on weather conditions from around the Course, they are also in constant touch with the weather-men at Ronaldsway Airport and their Travelling Marshals, as they attempt to judge what the next few hours will bring. With one eye on the clock and the other on the race programme, it is their unenviable job to decide on delayed starts or postponements. Sometimes that decision can be quite clearcut (30 yards visibility from the Gooseneck to Creg ny Baa means no racing) at others it can be marginal. Take the case of the Junior MGP of 1999. Former MGP racer Keith Trubshaw was the Travelling Marshal on duty at the Bungalow when, with a sense of horror, he saw thick mist descend on just a few hundred yards of the Course on the second lap of the race. In radio contact with Clerk of the Course Neil Hanson in the Control Tower, Keith could see things from both sides - that of an experienced rider and as the organiser's representative. The incident had overtones of the Syd Crabtree incident from many years before. There were few course-marshals around, riders were disappearing into the mist where they could not be seen and could barely be heard. With the danger increasing with every second, Keith took the decision to recommend to Race Control that the race be stopped. The Clerk of the Course supported his recommendation, and the chequered flag was hung out at the end of the second lap. It was a bold call, and Keith was pleased to hear the top finishers agree with his decision when they were interviewed after the race.

Whilst everyone on the Island knows that Mist on the Mountain will eventually blow away and a race be run, they know equally well that it will return another day - whenever Manannan Mac Lir decides.

MISTAKEN IDENTITIES

Beneath all-enveloping leathers, boots, gloves, full-face helmets and tinted visors, is everything what it seems in respect of rider identity when one of them wheels a bike to the line to start a lap of the Mountain Course? Rumour has it that it has not always been so.

In the earliest races when competitors wore little more than leather hats, their facial features were easily seen, and then for many years the colour of a rider's helmet, the cut of his leathers, his riding style and, of course, machine and number, all served to help organisers and spectators in the task of recognition, either while stationary or at speed. Some riders worked hard to highlight their identities, usually with conspicuous helmets like those of Albert Moule (black and blue rings), Phil Read (black and white tapering stripes), Giacomo Agostini (red, white and green panels of the Italian

Albert Moule retained this conspicuous helmet design during his long racing career.

flag), Charlie Williams (with initials CW inscribed) and Joey Dunlop (yellow Arai).

Today's riders sometimes seem to be trying to hide their identities, for not only are their helmets a mish-mash of colours but, in an attempt to please sponsors they change leathers from race to race so confusing their fans. It is strange that in an age where top riders strive to promote themselves in so many ways, they sometimes hide their identities on the track. In the Formula 1 race at the 2003 TT, the need to jump in and out of different coloured leathers actually caused top-runner Bruce Anstey to retire from the race. The shiny new leathers of his sponsor turned out to be too tight and they interfered so much with his riding that he just had to pull out.

Richard 'Milky' Quayle (Molnar Manx Norton) in one of his many different sets of riding leathers and helmet colours.

But what about the rumours of mistaken identity, impersonation, misrepresentation by riders - call it what you will. These are difficult to pin down, but one described by former rider Alan Brodrick as 'a credible rumour' circulated in the early 1950s. The organisers had resisted the demands from women to race at the TT for many years, but when the Clubman's races were created in 1947 the requests increased in number for here, surely, was the ideal event for them to compete in - the answer was still no. It was against such a background that the word began to go around that, taking advantage of the sleepy timekeepers in the just breaking dawn of an early morning practice, one girl borrowed her competitor boy-friend's riding gear and race bike, stood in line with the other racers, moved up to the Start and, upon a casual wave of the timekeeper's hand, was sent on her way for a lap in official practice at a MGP meeting. Was it true? Riders of the time seemed to accept that it was quite possible. What would the boy-friend's attitude have been? Whether top-man or a mere rabbit, every rider is jealous of his lap times, for they are published for everyone to see and assess him by. With due respect to our mystery lady rider, her first lap of the Mountain Course could be expected to be on the slow side and thus not good for the boy-friend's reputation. But perhaps he was prepared to cover up with talk of a mysterious mechanical ailment.

A couple of years before that rumour went around, 'Ixion', a long-standing columnist for 'The Motor Cycle', wrote one of the fictional pieces that he did for each TT and it was on the theme of a mystery lady rider. His story was a good bit more fanciful than the rumour, with all being dramatically revealed at the prize-giving ceremony when the rider concerned - who had supposedly won a Replica in the race - was called up to receive it and then announced to the crowds that she was a lady and thus, under the rules of the race, was unable to accept the award. A definite piece of fiction that one.

And what about the MGP entrant under the christian name of Phillip in the 1970s, is it true that the organisers discovered the name on the entry form should have been Phillippa? Whatever, 'Pip' did not get to race.

Riders sometimes find themselves under intense pressure during the practice period. This is usually because, with sessions slipping away, mechanical problems prevent them putting in the number of laps required to qualify for the race. There is little that they can do about this except, if really lucky, borrow another bike, fit their own numbers, and hope that it will prove reliable and keep going. But there are other scenarios with regard to difficulty in qualifying. The standards set for qualifying lap times are not too difficult to meet for a competent rider, though it may not look that way to a total newcomer whose first few practice sessions take place in damp and misty conditions. Is it possible that an experienced rider might be persuaded to put in the one lap that is required to be achieved under the qualifying time on behalf of a worried newcomer? Inducements might be offered, leathers and helmet loaned - a quick excursion over 37¾ miles lasting about 20 minutes and the job is done! It is certainly possible, but not proven.

One known case of unauthorised rider substitution did occur in the case of an entry for a Production race. (Names have been withheld to protect the guilty.) The rider concerned fell in the first practice session and injured himself. As further sessions slipped away, he became increasingly desperate to get out and do the two further laps that he needed to qualify, particularly as his injury was healing and he felt that he would be fit to ride by race-day. Taking the bike up to the last early morning practice session, he had it scrutineered, left it ready to go and then tackled the problem of getting into his leathers. He knew that his injury would make it difficult, but it proved impossible. In desperation, he managed to talk an off-duty Travelling Marshal (a former competitor) with whom he was well acquainted, into putting on the leathers that he had failed to get into, and going out and doing the two necessary qualifying laps on his behalf. The impostor recalls his worries as he wheeled the bike past officials and friends to the grid, for even with his visor pulled down and deliberately steamed-up he felt that he must be recognised. However, as he gradually worked his way to the front of the queue of riders waiting to start, his confidence grew, all went well and at last he was away on what proved to be two enjoyable laps that were completed well within the qualifying time. But then the worries started again as he and other riders were flagged off and made their ways back into the Paddock. Over the last few miles of riding he had made plans to disappear into the back of the rider's van and get the incriminating riding gear off as quickly as possible. Just as he stopped by the van another rider pulled up alongside him, tapped him on the shoulder, stared deep into his visor and said: *'I knew you weren't 'X' because you haven't got any hair hanging out of the bottom of your helmet'.* Fortunately his secret was safe with that rider, but one or two whispers did go around the Paddock.

So, plenty of rumours but few facts to support them. However, considering some of the other rule-bending that riders have indulged in, it is not difficult to believe that there have been a few impostors over the past 100 years.

NAMES REMEMBERED

Most locations on the Mountain Course carry long-established Manx names, but since the TT races started using its 37¾ miles there are places that, for varied reasons, have become known after the names of TT riders. Taking a quick trip around the course, it is just past the bottom of Bray Hill that we reach Ago's Leap. The hump in the road that used to cause Giacomo Agostini's front wheel to reach for the sky in such spectacular fashion has been much flattened, but it is still an exciting spot. About 8 miles from the Start is the sweeping left-hand bend after Ballig Bridge that is today called Doran's Bend. This is named after top rider of his day Bill Doran, who fell and broke a leg there in 1950. Some 3 miles on from Doran's is the relatively little known Drinkwater's Bridge located among the sweeping bends after the 11th Milestone and named in memory of the unfortunate Ben Drinkwater who lost his life there in the 1949 Junior.

Giacomo Agostini (MV Agusta) shows how the rise after the bottom of Bray Hill got its name of Ago's Leap.

Soon after the 11th Milestone comes Handley's Corner where first double-TT winner (in a week), Wal Handley, took a heavy fall in the 1932 Senior race but lived to ride another day. Less fortunate was Archie Birkin, and it was recorded earlier how, in 1927, he met his end in a traffic accident just outside Kirk Michael when the roads were still open to ordinary traffic as the racers practised. That spot is now called Birkin's Bend.

Not until after Ramsey do we come to the next rider-named place on the Course. That is the bend named Joey's which is located in the early stages of the Mountain ascent near the 26th Milestone. It is an appropriate spot to commemorate the 26 TT-win career of Joey Dunlop who lost his life whilst racing in Estonia in 2000.

'Joey's', the bend at the 26th Milestone named in honour of Joey Dunlop and his 26 TT victories.

Another famous rider to lose his life away from the TT Course was six times TT winner Jimmy Guthrie who was killed while racing in Germany in 1937. He is commemorated at the Guthrie Memorial, a stone cairn located in a tricky sequence of uphill bends between the 26th and 27th Milestones at the spot where he retired in his last Senior TT.

After completing most of the Mountain climb the Course levels out for the spectacular run around the Verandah, and it is just after the Verandah that the Graham Memorial is located on the right-hand side of the Course. Erected in memory of World Champion and TT winner Les Graham, it is a tribute to a man who would surely have gone on to more TT wins had he not had a fatal crash on the 500cc MV Agusta, just after the bottom of Bray Hill during the Senior TT of 1953, the day after winning the 125 race. Although most of the 1400 feet of Mountain ascent is complete by the Verandah, there is another gradient shortly after. Running from the Bungalow to the highest point on the Course at Brandywell, it is known as Hailwood Rise and leads to Hailwood's Height, named in memory of 14 times TT winner Mike Hailwood.

As the Course begins to run downhill from Brandywell, riders come to the tricky series of left-hand bends at the 32nd Milestone that in 2003 was officially named Duke's in honour of the great Geoff Duke. From there to the Finish, the last point on the Course to carry the identity of a rider was, in fact, the first to be named. Located between Creg ny Baa and Hillberry, the fast left-hand sweep of Brandish Corner leaves little room for mistakes, being enclosed by banks on both sides. Walter Brandish did not get it quite right during practice in 1923, hit the outside bank on his Triumph, broke his leg, and is remembered more for that episode than for his fine riding performances, which included second place in the Senior TT of 1922.

Walter Brandish (Rover) is shown here in 1921, two years before the big crash that ended his TT career. The photograph is taken when the pits were located on the Glencrutchery Road, much closer to St Ninian's Church (in background) than they are today.

Several other points on the Mountain were known by riders' names for a few years, usually after those involved parted company with their machines in the vicinity, but the names did not endure or, like George's Folly (after Alex George), did not really catch on and are remembered by only a few.

Although he took a record-breaking 10 TT wins (all pre-1939), the name of Stanley Woods now comes into the category of 'legend' rather than being a direct memory to most spectators, and he is officially remembered by the clock opposite the Grandstand. Amongst the most respected TT riders within the memory of most current fans are Mike Hailwood and Joey Dunlop. They not only have points on the Course named after them, but both are the subject of commemorative plaques sited opposite the Start-line.

In addition to the plaques, etc., behind the Pits is a building known as 'The Mike Hailwood Riders Centre', and an organisation called The Mike Hailwood Foundation gives financial assistance to the organisers in encouraging new riders to the Island races.

Ambitious fund-raising efforts efforts are in progress for a Joey Dunlop Injured Riders Centre to be located nearby near the Start area, and Joey is also remembered by a life-size statue sited adjacent to the former Motorcycle Museum at The Bungalow. It is exactly the same as one that occupies a place in a memorial garden to Joey in his home town of Ballymoney in Northern Ireland and, fittingly, shows him Honda mounted.

It is not just by way of points on the Course that riders are remembered. The Joey Dunlop Trophy plus a cash award of £10,000, is now awarded annually to the competitor with the fastest aggregate time in the Formula 1 and Senior races. Many other famous TT names are remembered by the award of Trophies that bear their names, including Jimmy Simpson, Fred W Dixon, John Hartle, John Williams, Jock Taylor, Norman Brown and others.

NEAR MISSES

Every competitor has had a near miss whilst taking part in the TT or MGP (as have quite a few spectators engaged in their unofficial versions of the races). For competitors it is all down to the demanding nature of the circuit, to the lack of run-

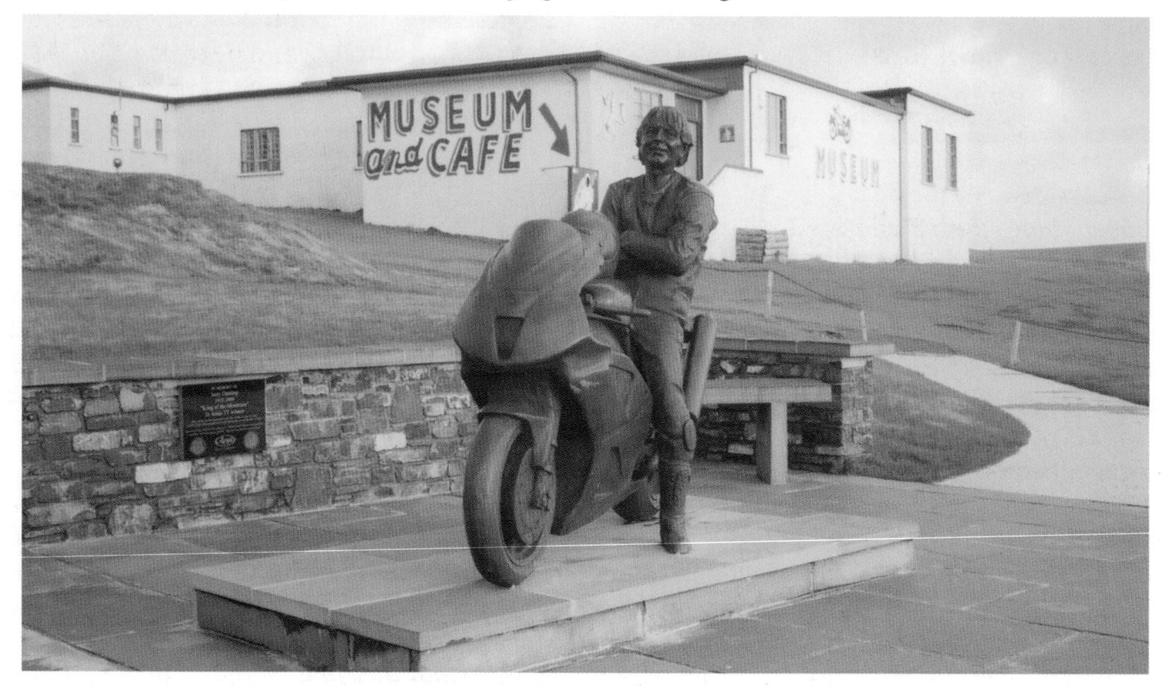

Joey Dunlop statue in the grounds of the former Murray's Motorcycle Museum at The Bungalow.

Tim Hunt nearly got away with this big slide at Quarter Bridge in the 1930 Junior TT, but the back continued to go around and brought him off. Unhurt, he remounted to finish in 9th place.

off space, to the prevailing high-octane atmosphere, and to the very reason why they are there with powerful motorcycles; to ride them close to their limits. Nobody can expect to get every one of its 264 bends absolutely right on each lap of practice and racing, and so there are incidents.

Much has been written and said down the years to the effect that *'the throttle works both ways'* and that competitors only ride at 90% in Island races, but all that has to be taken with a pinch of salt. There have been many very determined competitors who have been prepared to risk all for the glory and reward of a TT or MGP win. When Stanley Woods won his first TT over the badly surfaced roads of 1923, 'The Motor Cycle' wrote: *'The sliding wheels of Woods Cotton threw up a bow-wave of dirt and stones'* at Hillberry. That does not sound like a rider who was taking it easy. A man who never looked as though he was taking it easy was eleven-times TT winner Phillip McCallen, who explained: *'People talk about riding the TT at 90 or 95%, but those riders don't win, it's 100% or nothing . . .'.* It is hardly surprising that Phillip had a couple of 'offs' and his share of near misses on the Mountain Course.

Wal Handley was looked upon as one of the great TT riders of the 1920s and 1930s, justifiably so, as he took four outright wins and many other leaderboard places on a variety of machinery. Whilst he had his share of triumphs, Wal also had one truly frightening incident that almost turned into a tragedy. It was in 1932 when, after finishing third in the Junior, he was holding third place in the Senior until a heavy spill at the spot now known as Handley's Corner left him lying immobile in the road with a damaged spine. His concern at being hit by a following rider was matched by the horror he experienced to see petrol flowing all over the bike that lay alongside him with its engine revving. With petrol also soaking into his leathers he knew that a stray spark could send bike and rider up in flames. Fortunately, help arrived in time and he was carried to a nearby cottage. It was certainly a near miss, but Wal was soon sitting up in hospital and, as TT riders do, was laughing at the incident with visitors.

Wal Handley (Rudge) on his way to victory in the 1930 Senior TT. It was the year that Rudge took the first two places in the Senior and first three places in the Junior.

A rider does not have to be going quickly to have a near miss, but speed usually adds to the excitement. The AJS 7R was introduced in 1948 and quickly became a favourite. Nicknamed the Boy's Racer it was close to the Manx Norton in performance and cheaper to buy. G.W. Robinson brought his to the 1948 MGP and explained his claim to Island racing fame with words to make one shudder:

'Unfortunately, the Junior ended when the Boy Racer and I parted company at Barregarroo at full song in top after a fracas with a slow rider with engine trouble. This resulted in us

making the longest slide mark in the Isle of Man'.

It is doubtful if Robinson's record for the longest slide still holds, for there have been many other high-speed get-offs on the Mountain Course and a couple of worthy challenges came from none other than multi-TT winners Steve Hislop and Phillip McCallen. A win in the Lightweight 250 TT eluded both Steve and Phillip, although it was not for want of trying, indeed, perhaps they tried too hard, for both parted company with their 250s at something like 140 mph, both did it at Quarry Bends, both slid an awfully long way and both walked away without serious injury. Steve's 'off' was in 1989 and Phillip's in 1997 and in each case their spills prevented them from achieving four TT victories in one week - although Phillip had achieved that record-breaking distinction the year before. Two days after his big spill on the 250, Phillip was back riding the Course in the Junior race and tells how he was particularly cautious through Quarry Bends. Quite understandable, because he could still see the tyre and scrape marks on the road from his earlier spill.

Stuart Graham was a TT winner of the 1960s whilst a 'works' rider for Honda and Suzuki, and he told Christopher Hilton in 'Honda - Conquerors of the Track' of a near miss on one of the tricky bends near Laurel Bank: '. . . *the back end jumped away. I was pitched against the wall and the sole of my riding boot was torn off. I bounced away from the wall across the road into the wall at the other side, bounced off that all the way back - amazingly I was still on the bike but sitting on the fuel tank - and I regained control'.*

Stuart Graham charges for the line to win the 1967 50cc TT.

Near misses are not confined to solos, for over the relatively narrow Manx roads things can be especially exciting for sidecars. Multiple-winner Dave Saville told how he always took the right-hand bend at the end of the Cronk y Voddy straight with the merest feathering of the throttle on his Formula 2 machines. With a bumpy approach, such a high-speed passage required extremely accurate placement of the outfit, but *'In 1989 I clipped the kerb on the right-hand side. Fortunately I always use strong fittings for the fairing and it was this that brushed along the kerb. If the fairing had been a fraction higher and gone over the kerb God only knows what would have happened! That's an incident that I never told anyone about at the time'.* Dave recalled another fright when he attempted to pass an outfit on the Sulby Straight: *'It was when it was really bumpy, the machine went into a tank-slapper, everything was a blur and I just hung on and hoped'.*

One of the most serious, perhaps notorious, near misses, was that of Jim Moodie who was involved in the aftermath of David Jefferies fatal crash at Crosby during Thursday afternoon practice at the 2003 TT. David's crash brought down a roadside telegraph pole and left wires trailing over the road. Jim, who was later criticised for not taking sufficient heed of waved yellow warning flags, came upon the incident and became entangled in the trailing wires. The resultant photographs showing the grooves that the wire cut all the way around his neck, revealed that Jim had a very near miss. Tough fellow that he is, he made a quick return to practising in later sessions.

Not all near misses on the Island relate to crashes and incidents, for there have been many near misses in relation to race results. Brian Reid's performances had him threatening to win a TT several times in the early 1980s and, after setting a new lap record in the Junior race, it looked as though 1985 would be his year. But it was not to be, for just two miles from the finish he ran out of fuel at Hillberry and so handed victory to Joey Dunlop. What made it worse for Brian was that he had been forced to drop out of the Formula 2 race earlier in the week whilst in the lead. An even worse fate befell Mick Boddice and Chas Birks in the first Sidecar race that year. Leading for the entire 113 miles of the three lap race, the chequered flag was in sight when, 200 yards from the finishing line their drive chain jumped the sprocket and they could only limp over the line, thus handing victory to Dave Hallam and John Gibbard by 9 seconds.

'NO LIMIT'

Huge numbers of TT fans have seen the film 'No Limit' and indeed, for many a repeat viewing at each TT was a traditional part of their visits. Starring George Formby on his home-brewed 'Shuttleworth Snap' (based on a 1920s AJS), the ramifications of the film's plot saw gormless George eventually riding a 'Rainbow' (based on a 1934 Ariel) to TT victory. It was filmed on the Island at the time of the 1935 event and used the crowds in the Grandstand and locations around the Course to capture the right atmosphere. It was an expensive film for its day, and the makers enlisted local riders such as Jack Cannell (father of long-time race commentator Geoff Cannell), plus Harold and Bertie Rowell (both top-flight MGP runners), to supplement some of the work carried out by professional stunt riders.

George Formby on the Shuttleworth Snap.

George Formby was a big-name in the entertainment world in the pre and post-Second World War years and was sometimes on the Island doing shows at TT time. He had a genuine interest in motorcycles, owning a Norton International, Vincent Rapide and other models. Indeed, there is a reliable tale that George was spirited out of his room at the Castle Mona Hotel by other motorcycle enthusiasts early one morning in 1947, taken up to the Mountain Road, given an overcoat and goggles and allowed to blast up and down the Mountain Mile on one of the new Vincent twins - something that the 'minders' of this high-earning entertainer would certainly not have permitted.

'No Limit' must have given a strange impression of the TT to non-motorcyclists down the years, but it is still shown occasionally on the Island at TT time and still has its fans. One of those is local MGP and TT winner, Richard 'Milky' Quayle. Indeed, he has gone as far as to convert his vintage Raleigh into an imitation of the 'Shuttleworth Snap'. Appearing at local charity events in black leathers and pudding-basin, Richard uses the 'Snap' to raise money for charity.

Richard 'Milky' Quayle with his version of the Shuttleworth Snap. The fine body of men behind are members of the Isle of Man Section of the Vintage Motor Cycle Club, with the smiling fellow fourth from the right being Jack Ward who, as a very young boy, appeared as an extra in 'No Limit'.

OVERSIZE ENGINES

There have been a number of known instances of competitors using engines of greater than permitted capacity in Island events and, probably, an even greater number that have remained unknown. In most cases, making use of a 'bandit' motor is done with the deliberate intention of deceiving the organisers and gaining an advantage over other competitors but, occasionally, there have been occurrences of less serious intent. Manliff Barrington told that at his first TT in 1934, where he had a Lightweight entry, he suffered major problems with his Rudge 250 in practice. Being a newcomer and wanting to take advantage of every practice session, he borrowed a friend's 500 Rudge, put his own number plates on it, and went off and did several more laps while his own bike was being repaired.

No one was more surprised than newcomer Manliff when his name later appeared on the practice leader-board for the Lightweight class. It did not take the organisers long to find out what he had been up to. He was given a mild ticking-off and had his 'over-sized' practice times scrubbed.

The first Clubman's TT races were run in 1947, catering for machines in classes up to 1,000cc, up to 500cc and up to 250cc that were, essentially, road-going models. Bill McVeigh was a

Manliff Barrington with his 'correct-capacity' Rudge at the 1934 TT.

comfortable winner of the Lightweight Clubman's race on a well-used Triumph from the late 1930s, but when his machine was subjected to the obligatory post-race measuring of its engine, it was found to be fractionally oversize and he was disqualified. McVeigh submitted a protest against this decision of the organisers on the grounds that the engine had received a minimum rebore and, going through various appeal processes that took months to resolve, he was eventually reinstated as the winner. In a contrasting incident, Alan Westfield had an entry in the Junior class of the 1949 Clubman's TT on a 3T Triumph. The engine had been sent to Francis Beart prior to the race for tuning and, although a newcomer, Alan put up some respectable times in practice. He bumped into Francis towards the end of practice and remarked that the bike was going well, to which Francis replied: *'You know that it was bored?'*. Alan did not and felt that he should withdraw from the race. As with all Clubman's competitors, he had been entered by his local motorcycle

Alan Westfield with the 'stretched' 3TA Triumph chats to a group of enthusiasts after early morning practice.

club (North Lincs MC) and he was persuaded to ride *'for experience'*. A couple of last lap retirements saw him finish in a surprisingly high sixth place. The race regulations prescribed that *'motorcycles placed first, second and third, and that which has set up or broken a lap record, will be liable to be examined'*. Alan's sixth place would normally have been sufficiently far down the order to have avoided any risk of having to have his engine measured but, perhaps the word had gone around - as it does, and a cover-all provision in the regulations stating that any machine could be examined was enforced. The organisers asked to measure his engine, it was slightly over-size, and he was disqualified.

Not everyone could afford 350cc and 500cc machines in the post-war period, but many riders sought to get two rides at the TT by entering a 350 in both the Junior and Senior classes. However, in 1951 the race regulations specified that machines for the Senior race had to be from 351-500cc. This resulted in a rash of entries of 352cc bikes, and amongst them was Bill Beevers. Bill had trouble in the Senior race on his '352' but eventually reached the finish, only to be challenged by Scrutineer Vic Anstice over the true engine size of his Norton. Admitting that it was only 346cc he was disqualified for having too small an engine. Bill was not impressed with this show of officialdom but consoled himself with the fact that he had at least managed to achieve his sought after second ride.

Bill Beevers with his 'small' Norton

Fred Launchbury was a regular and popular Lightweight competitor for many years. In the Lightweight 125 race of 1969 he looked like achieving his best ever finish when he came in third, a position that brought automatic measurement of his Bultaco's engine. To everyones dismay this yielded a figure just fractionally over 125cc. No one wanted to rob Fred of his hard-earned podium place, but rules were rules. So small an element was it oversize that the organisers allowed the barrel to be immersed in cold water for an hour and then remeasured. Result - still a smidgeon over. With time to ponder the problem of his *'oversize'* engine, Fred put it down to the fact that because it had nipped-up several times during practice, he had run a honing brush (in an electric drill) down the bore after each of those partial seizures and such mild action had, seemingly, been enough to take the engine fractionally oversize.

After the first Sidecar race during one TT of the 1980s, the scrutineers were left with suspicions about the engine size of a bike that did much better lap times during the race than it had achieved in practice. Although it had finished off the leader-board it could still have robbed someone with a standard engine of their rightful place, so Chief Scrutineer of the time, Alan Verity, managed to get his wife to casually mention to the rider's wife between the two sidecar races that any finishers engine could be selected for stripping and measurement. In Alan's words: *'My spies tell me that he was up all night before race two and, funnily enough his lap times were a lot slower'*.

In some cases of running oversize engines the offence is of a technical nature (such as a minimum rebore), in others it involves a rather more serious infringement. In the 400cc class of the Lightweight race at the 2000 TT Geoff McMullan rode to victory over Brett Richmond. Come the post-race measuring of engines and Geoff's was oversize. Not the couple of cubic centimetres that might have come from a rebore but a full 200cc. He had used a 600cc motor in a 400cc race. Despite his protests of innocence (he must have thought that 400 to have been a flier!), he was disqualified and the race was awarded to Brett

Richmond. There was an irony about Brett eventually receiving first place, for due to crankshaft problems his bike ran much of the race on three-cylinders. Was he using an under-sized engine?

PIT SIGNALS

Nowadays a rider expects not only to receive signals when he passes his Pit (plus information when he stops to refuel) but also from boards displayed at pre-arranged points around the Course. Such procedures were barely known at the first TT, although Rem Fowler is supposed to have been shown a board with the word 'OIL' on it in 1907, as a reminder for him to make good use of the hand-operated oil pump mounted on the side of his petrol tank. Jack Marshall rode in the same event and had a man located on the steep Creg Willeys hill to advise him on his race position and that of other leading contenders. When asked some years later what information was displayed to him on his signalling board, he said: *'There was no need for that sort of thing. As I came up Creg Willeys my chap ran alongside me and just shouted'*. Geoff Davison also recalled that his Pit signal at the 1921 TT lacked sophistication. It consisted of his Pit-attendant *'furiously waving a petrol tin which meant go flat out - and a bit faster if possible'*.

The man who brought a little sophistication to race signalling was one who always applied an above average amount of thinking to the job of motorcycle racing, and that was Stanley Woods. He knew that conventional pit signals were of limited value, because, with a near 40 mile lap, much of the information that could be passed to a rider at the pits was often a lap old. In addition, the frightening flat-out descent of Bray Hill that followed the Pits was not the best place for a rider to attempt to mentally juggle information on how far he was behind the rider in front and how close his challengers were behind. So, in the early 1930s, Stanley devised a scheme that provided him with information on the race at a point roughly half-way around the Course.

For his personal signalling system Stanley stationed an assistant in a public telephone box on the Sulby Straight, enlisted the help of a friendly householder with a telephone close to the Start and, in his words, *'blarnied the telephonists in the local exchange to give the calls priority'* (it was before the introduction of direct dialling, all calls went via an operator, and it was 60 years before the use of mobile phones). Not only did his system allow him to outwit the opposition, but on a couple of occasions when Norton wanted his fellow teamsters to win races, Stanley, by using the information gained from his private signalling station, realised that Norton's pit signal for him to slow the pace was not because he had an enormous lead, but because they wanted someone else to make up enough time to win the race. The Norton team soon copied his system with the use of a phone at Ramsey.

Today's top competitors rely very much on their signals and ride their races in accordance with the information they are given. That information is much more than was available to Stanley Woods in the 1930s and comes from sources like Manx radio, machine-mounted transponders, helpers with mobile phones, and blackboard-toting signallers located at several points around the Course. Some riders even complain about information overload, especially when well-meaning people start flashing information to them outside their normal signalling stations.

Perhaps it is only a matter of time before riders receive radio messages direct from their Pits. As well as providing race positions and advice on strategy, such a means of communication would avoid the sort of embarrassing incident experienced by Phillip McCallen. It was during the

Riders rely on receiving information out on the Course, as well as at their Pit. Here Mark Parrett's helpers have the board prepared and strive to spot their rider approaching at maximum speed down the Sulby Straight.

Spotting their man, the board is held out as he brakes heavily for the right-angled turn of Sulby Bridge.

Mark flashes past still under heavy braking, having received the information that he is 6 seconds behind the rider in second place and 6 seconds ahead of the rider in fourth place. An experienced Island rider and former MGP winner, Mark held his third position to the finish.

133

1993 Junior TT that the Honda 'works' rider was due to bring his 250 into the Pits to refuel at the end of the second lap. The only problem was that Phillip's attention was distracted by the need to put a slower rider behind him on the Glencrutchery Road and he steamed past his waiting Pit-crew at 140+ mph. Packing their gear away, the crew knew that their services would not be needed and, sure enough, the Honda spluttered to a stop at Quarry Bends. It happened right in front of a film-crew who, seizing the opportunity for an interview, opened with the embarrassing question *'what's up Phillip?'*.

Determined that there should be no mistake about which lap he was due to re-fuel, this is the board that Honda hung out for Phillip McCallen after his problems in 1993.

Multiple Formula 2 class sidecar winner Dave Saville recalled that he had *'a signalling station on the exit from Governor's Bridge onto the Glencrutchery Road instead of the Pits which you go past too fast to be able to note anything'*. Sidecars do not normally refuel but, had they done so, Dave's signalling crew at Governor's Bridge could have given him a timely reminder. This was something that Honda realised after McCallen's error, and in the next race they had a man with an extra large sign stationed at Governor's.

POSTPONEMENTS

From the very first TT in 1907 through to race-week in 1935, every practice period and race was run to schedule. As the weather was no better in those days than it is today, it is not difficult to imagine that some of the sessions must have been ridden in atrocious conditions.

This rider in the 1928 Amateur race shows just how miserable conditions can be.

With ever growing speeds, racing in fog and rain became increasingly dangerous and after several years of bad weather (considered to have contributed to several fatal accidents), the year of

1935 saw the first race postponement. It was the Friday Senior event that was called off and rearranged for Saturday. The Island had no contingency arrangements to cope with the aftermath of a postponement and a degree of chaos prevailed. As the Steam Packet Company had brought 11,000 visitors over just for the day, the majority of them had to return on Friday evening without having seen any action. Several riders who had weekend commitments to ride on the continent also had to leave, resulting in just 28 starters coming to the line for the Senior race on Saturday. The only bright spot was that some race fans from England who had not been able to get Friday off work to join the day-trippers, were able to come over to see the Saturday race.

The pursuit of motorcycle racing is inherently an unsafe one, but today's TT organisers are very careful not to do anything to add to the danger. The introduction of the rescue-helicopter in 1963 was a big step forward in getting prompt medical attention to anyone unfortunate enough to fall off. However, the helicopter has become such a vital part of the race organisation that it is now unacceptable to run a practice or race without the airborne rescue facility being operational. Due to fickle weather conditions this can sometimes mean that although the weather at ground level may be acceptable for riders to be out practising or racing, low-hanging cloud or mist can be enough to prevent the helicopter from seeing some of its nominated rescue sites with sufficient clarity to land. Frustratingly, this can result in the postponement of a race or practice session.

The biggest ever TT postponement occurred in 1966 when, as a result of a long-running seamen's strike, the entire event had to be put off and rearranged for later in the year. It eventually ran just before MGP, so giving Island residents, officials and marshals, four weeks of solid race activity.

Postponements are no longer uncommon in Island racing. The weather was particularly bad for the start of racing in 1986 and the opening Formula 1 race was first postponed to Sunday then to Monday, when a shortened race of 4 laps was run. Almost as bad as a postponement is the increasingly frequent action of the organisers of delaying the start of races in the hope that weather conditions will improve. A declared delay of a couple of hours can, grudgingly, be accepted by riders and the thousands of spectators gathered around the Course, but it is the practice of delaying the start by a quarter of an hour, followed by another quarter of an hour, then another ... that really gets people grumbling in the organisers direction. But the last thing that the organisers want to do is to postpone one of their events. Such an action not only affects riders and spectators, because it has ramifications for many other aspects of the Island's day to day life, not the least of which is that a few yards from the Startline is the main entrance to Douglas Cemetery where cremations and interments normally take place every day.

Not all delays to race starts are due to the weather. Incidents such as cars parked on the Course and wandering animals, have all forced the organisers to interrupt their carefully programme of racing. With roads being used by ordinary traffic there is always the chance that a normal traffic incident can affect the scheduled start time of a practice session or race.

The only thing worse than a postponement is cancellation, and that was the fate of Island racing in 2001. Desperate to protect the Island's farming industry from the potential ravages of foot and mouth disease that swept other areas of Britain, the organisers took the only reasonable course and cancelled both the TT and MGP.

The Manx Organisation for Motorsport Medical Officers and Paramedics (Motorsport Medical Services) were one of many concerns who hoped that the 2001 TT would go ahead. It did not, and their early printing of stationery for 'the TT that never was' turned into wasted effort.

QUALIFYING

Sensational newcomer to the TT in 2004 was Guy Martin, who found no difficulty in meeting the qualifying standards set by the race organisers.

Soon after the TT races moved to the Mountain Course in 1911 the organisers introduced qualifying standards that every rider had to reach during practice, before they were allowed to race. As well as serving as an indicator of a rider's competence, the ability to lap in a respectable time meant organisers knew that riders accepted to race would be able to complete the event within a specified overall time limit. That was an important factor, for the Manx roads were only available for racing for the limited periods specified in the official Road Closing Orders issued for the races. The 1911 winner took 4 hours to complete his race, and lesser lights took considerably longer.

The basis for qualifying to race has remained the same down the years. The organisers stipulate that each rider must complete a required minimum number of timed practice laps, of which at least one must be within the specified qualifying time. In 1914 riders had to do at least 6 laps and one of those had to be in under 70 minutes (Junior) or 60 minutes (Senior). Those times have been progressively reduced down the years and by 1925 they were 50 minutes (Junior), 45 minutes (Senior). By the time of the Diamond Jubilee TT in 1967 they were 30 minutes (Junior), 29 minutes (Senior), 37 minutes (Sidecar), 35 minutes (Lightweight 125), 33 minutes (Lightweight 250), 45 minutes (50cc). Riders were by then required to do three timed laps of practice, with at least one lap being within the qualifying time.

An indication of how close the performance of today's Production bikes are to their racing counterparts is shown in the mere ½ minute difference in their qualifying times.

Solo Newcomers are now required to do a minimum of 6 practice laps (5 for previous participants) and Sidecar Newcomers must do 4 laps (3 for those who have ridden previously). Riders with entries on more than one machine must do at least 2 laps on each of them. Similar procedures exists at the MGP, although the qualifying times are more generous than at the TT. Some riders struggle to meet the qualifying standards, whilst others do it with ease. Guy Martin was a sensation in his first TT in 2004, completing his first ever lap of the Course on closed roads at 114 mph and finishing the fortnight with a fastest lap at 122 mph in the Senior race where he finished in 7th position on his GSX-R 1000 Suzuki.

In the early days of TT racing, riders were allowed two weeks of practice, although some would arrive a week or more before the start of official practice.

The lap times required to qualify for the 2004 TT races were:

Formula 1 and Senior
21 minutes = 107.80 mph
(Newcomers are allowed 22½ minutes).
Sidecars
24½ minutes = 92.40 mph
Junior
21½ minutes = 105.29 mph

Ultra Lightweight 125 & Lightwheit 400
23 minutes = 98.43 mph
Production 600
22 minutes = 102.90 mph
Production 1000
21½ minutes = 105.29 mph

Ossie Wade inspects the barrel of son John's 500cc HRD in between practice sessions for the 1926 TT. They stayed at the Nursery Hotel, Onchan, making use of its garaging.

Shown in the photograph above, father and son Ossie and John Wade were on the Island for a month in connection with the 1926 races. Although all looks very relaxed in this posed photograph, preparation for the event was still a rush for many and it was not unknown for a manufacturer to bring his latest model to the TT without having had chance to test it beforehand. He would rely on the extensive practice period to allow him to test and bring the new model up to race pitch, although it was quite common for him to have to telephone back to the factory and ask for modified parts to be made and despatched to the Island. 'The Motor Cycle' was critical of such a way of dealing with the event and wrote in 1928: *'There are thousands of pounds sinfully wasted by clumsy TT policies every year; and a little ingenuity spent on specially devised bench tests during the winter would send teams to the Island with engines almost guaranteed to stand up to seven laps'.*

Sidecar drivers and passengers are required to qualify in the same general manner as riders of solos but, at the time when sidecars could be fitted on the left (usual for British entries) or on the right (favoured by most Continentals), a passenger who qualified on a machine fitted with a left-hand sidecar was not considered qualified to race in a right-hand chair until he had done a further set of practice laps. A slightly different problem was faced by Dave Saville who swapped from the passenger platform to the driver's seat at the 1968 TT. Over to race as passenger with driver Fred Brindley, the pair qualified before Fred fell ill with pneumonia. In Dave's words: *'As I had course experience Fred suggested that I should take over the ride. The ACU agreed to the change, I grabbed a spare passenger and qualified myself as driver'.* Dave finished a creditable 10th and embarked on a TT career of over 20 years that saw him come to dominate the F2 class that was run with the main sidecar races.

Experienced TT sidecar passenger Dave Corlett decided after many years of keeping a third-wheel down that he would switch to two-wheels and so he entered the 2002 MGP. In a 'rules are rules' situation he found that his 20 years of three-wheeled race experience over the Mountain Course counted for nothing, and that even being a Manxman did not help. Rules were not to be bent and the organisers decreed that he had to do the obligatory instructional lap in a coach and then, when eventually allowed on the Course, wear the customary Newcomers orange jacket as he sought to qualify in the usual way.

The need to qualify puts pressure on a rider from the very first session. Many desperate tales can be told of the troubles that riders have experienced in qualifying. Most of those who consider themselves good enough to ride in the TT can meet the qualifying time, it is getting machines to hold together long enough to complete the required number of laps that can be the problem. Even with today's more reliable machinery and with practice still extending to just over a week, riders can find it difficult to qualify. This is particularly so for those competing in several classes, because they are required to qualify in each class. Failure to qualify usually means no race, but riders are allowed to appeal to the Clerk of the Course and such appeals to race are occasionally granted.

John McGuiness entered six races at the 2003 TT and managed to qualify all his machines. Here he is putting in a lap on his 600cc Triumph in practice for the Junior race.

CHAPTER 7

TALES OF . . .

RACE REGULATIONS

The regulations covering the Tourist Trophy races have been the subject of 100 years of evolution. For the first few years there were two races (one for singles and one for multi-cylinder machines) that ran concurrently, and the only restriction on engine size was that the capacity of each cylinder should not exceed 500cc. Then two races were created, Junior and Senior, specific engine capacity limits were introduced which varied between singles and twins in the same race and the races gradually grew in number. Those races have seen wide variation in the distance covered, with the first 50 years seeing the number of laps gradually increase to a maximum of 8, whilst the last 50 years has seen a decrease, with 4 laps now regarded as the standard distance and 6 laps being the maximum for any race.

Constantly changing, the TT rules have seen the banning of pedalling gear, the allowing of straight-through exhausts, removal of the requirement to carry tools, banning of alcohol fuels, minimum and maximum weight limits, control of tyre sizes, etc. The period of the late 1930s saw a growth in use of supercharged machines, with examples from AJS, BMW, Velocette and Vincent HRD (the latter two using theirs only in practice), but when racing restarted after the war, regulations were changed and the FIM banned supercharging, so several interesting machines that were on the drawing-board never made it to the Island.

Pre-war MGP competitor Allan Jefferies came second in the Senior Clubman's TT in 1947 on this Triumph. Father to TT winners Tony and Nick, and grandfather of David Jefferies, Allan remained involved in the TT as an official after retiring from racing.

Introducing a Clubman's TT in 1947 for almost standard machines, the organisers found themselves with regulations that sounded straightforward but that proved difficult to police, a situation that was repeated some years later when races for Production machines were included at the TT.

The 1960s was a highly competive era in racing, with manufacturers producing ever more complex and expensive machinery in their attempts to achieve racing success. One, two, three, four, five, six and eight-cylinder racers were amongst those produced by Honda, Suzuki, Yamaha, MZ, Benelli, Moto Guzzi and MV Agusta with, in the smaller classes, gearboxes containing eleven (Yamaha) and fourteen (Suzuki) gears. The expense created by such high levels of activity was enormous and, as a result, several manufacturers made the decision to drop out of racing in the late 1960s, and the FIM belatedly stepped in with new rules designed to reduce costs. 50cc machines were limited to one-cylinder, 125 and 250 machines to two-cylinders, and 350 and 500cc to four-cylinders. All classes were restricted to a maximum of six gears.

The Supplementary Regulations illustrated were issued by the organisers to deal with rules that were specific to the 1967 TT. It was of modest A5 size and ran to 16 pages. The FIM also issued its own substantial Rule Book that laid down the general regulations under which all races were run. Juggling with the regulations at the TT and MGP continues, covering alterations to machine specifications and stating what riders may or may not do in the interest of safety and the races. In 2004 the Isle of Man Government took a 20 year licence from the ACU (who had controlled the TT since its inception in1907) that permitted them to organise and run the races. The Government then appointed the Manx Motor Cycle Club Limited (tried and tested organisers of the MGP) to run the races on its behalf, and it falls to the Manx MCC to administer the rather more complex regulations that cover the running of the TT today.

RACING AND MANXFOLK

This is a topic that almost justifies a book in itself, for with motorcycles racing over their normal day-to-day roads for so long, there is no way that the Manx people can ignore the TT and MGP meetings. Indeed, very few try to ignore them, because whilst the racing has a very considerable effect on their lives, they have also had a huge influence on the races and all the aspects that surround them. That is not to say that everyone on the Island supports the races, indeed, soon after they moved to the Mountain Course a small and vocal element of the Manx population expressed their opposition by claiming that riders were *'desecrating the peace of Mona with these dangerous nuisances'*. Now, only the most blinkered supporters would claim that motorcycle racing does not bring noise and danger, but that is the attraction for many, both residents and visitors, and people flocked to see those early events, with a local newspaper reporting in respect of a race-day: *'The Island indulged itself in a National Holiday'*. So frequent did this indulgence become amongst the Manx people that the authorities eventually declared Senior race-day to be a Bank Holiday on the Island, as it is today.

With the passage of time the TT and MGP have become even more deeply ingrained with the local inhabitants, because for the current generation the races have always been there - four weeks of every year - and they are an inseparable part of Manx life. To give a few 'for instances': the Island's Honda Dealer, Tommy Leonard, talks of one of his first childhood memories as being wheeled down to the Course in his pram to see the race action. Long-time Manx Radio commentator Geoff Cannell recalls his father competing in early post-war events and his life has been bound-up with the races ever since. Clerk of the Course for both the TT and MGP, Neil Hanson, remembers when his father was Clerk of the Course for the MGP and Neil, like so many who hold high-office in the race organisation, has come up through the ranks doing many jobs on his way to the top. Amongst the many Manxfolk whose activities take them out on the Course, Lightweight 400 TT winner of 2002, Richard 'Milky' Quayle, said that from his youngest years: *'all I ever wanted to do was win a TT race'*. Amongst the many people helping riders to race are vitally important local sponsors like the Kelly brothers of Mannin Collections, Martin Bullock, Des Collins, and many others who help out on a smaller scale.

SUPPLEMENTARY REGULATIONS
for the
AUTO CYCLE UNION
TT
1907-1967
DIAMOND JUBILEE
ISLE OF MAN
12th, 14th and 16th JUNE 1967
Held under the International Sporting Code of the FIM, the General Competition Rules of the ACU and these Supplementary Regulations.
An International Classic event counting for the "World Championships" of the FIM.
IMN No. 1/4
Promoted by the
AUTO-CYCLE UNION
31 BELGRAVE SQUARE
LONDON SW1
Telegrams:
Auto-Cycle London SW1
Telephone:
BELgravia 7636

This is the cover of the Supplementary Regulations issued to cover the Diamond Jubilee races in 1967.

Lloyds TSB have sponsored riders in the TT and MGP for several years in conjunction with Mannin Collections. Here Norman Kneen rounds Signpost Corner on his way to 3rd place in the 1999 Ultra-Lightweight MGP.

It is not every Branch of Lloyds Bank that sponsors riders in the TT and MGP, but as Island Director Andy Webb explained: *'To outsiders, it may seem strange to see a bank sponsoring motorcycle racing. The reality is that racing is at the heart of the Manx community'.*

The majority of those who marshal the races are Manx residents, including veterans like Jack Ward who did the job for almost 60 years. Jack and three generations of the Ward family have given immeasurable amounts of time to the races.

Jack Ward (left) keeps an eye on the racing with the Flagman at the sweeping bends of the 11th Milestone, where he spent many years as a marshal.

Most of the local people involved in the events are unpaid, and they include several members of the House of Keys (part of the Island's Parliament, Tynwald). However, despite the fact that both the TT and MGP are run mostly through the efforts of unpaid volunteers, there is undoubtedly a large and important commercial aspect to the events. Timetabled to extend the beginning and end of what was the traditional Manx summer tourist season, the races are also commercially important to the participating motorcycle manufacturers who seek Island success to help promote their products world-wide. At the TT professional riders get the chance to earn good prize-money, and up and coming riders get to perform on an International stage where a good showing can attract offers of sponsorship and machinery that will help them up the rungs of the road-racing ladder.

The Island's Lieutenant Governor in 1904, Lord Raglan, was instrumental in getting the roads closed for competition use and successive holders of the post have maintained varying degrees of interest in the racing. Sir Laurence New was Lieutenant Governor from 1985 to 1990 and here, with Lady New, he enjoys a pre-Classic MGP chat with multi-winner Bill Swallow in 2002.

The benefits derived by the Manx economy from the races are many and varied. All sorts of figures are bandied about in terms of the amount of money the events bring to the Island, but whatever those figures may be, no one will dispute that TT and MGP fortnights are the busiest tourist periods of the year. It is not all one-way traffic, for the Island has to continually invest in the races. As just one example, the near £400,000 of prize-money on offer at the TT is certainly not covered by riders entry fees. Strange as it may seem, as race fans are flocking to the Island, those Manx residents who do not like the event are departing on 'get-away-from-the-TT' holidays organised by enterprising local travel agents - it is all TT-related business!

'Escape the TT' holidays for Manx residents!

Although the off-Island image of the events is that the TT and MGP occupy 4 weeks of the year, they are 52 week topics on the Island. Rarely does a week pass without reference to some aspect of the meetings in the local papers or on the radio, and the permanently positioned corner marker-boards serve as a constant reminder to local drivers that they are on the Course. Like it or not, the TT and MGP are all-permeating in Island life. One spin off is that the Isle of Man must have the greatest number of motorcyclists per head of population in the world. Their activities range across the full range of recognised disciplines like road and circuit racing, Moto Cross, Super Moto, Trials, Enduros, road-riding, vintage, etc, and they also include one previously unknown form of motorcycling - that performed by the notorious Purple Helmets.

Not all motorcycling on the Isle of Man is taken seriously.

Garages large and small are at a premium in Douglas during race fortnights, for they are sought after as working space by race competitors. Most are provided free of charge, often with endless cups of tea and minor support services. The enthusiasm for racing of some of those garage owners is very apparent but looking at other owners, who are patently not racing types, competitors must wonder why they put themselves to the inconvenience of turning out the family car and lawnmower and making space available to a bunch of visitors who often work all hours of the day and much of the night. This is where the races being engrained into the Manx way of life comes into play. These people do not consider their actions to be out of the ordinary and they are happy doing their bit for the events. Maybe their parents made their own garages available or, perhaps years ago, they were asked to help someone who was 'garageless' - it is now a part of their lives. TT and MGP rider Chris McGaghan explained that: *'The average race fan probably doesn't realise what a warm welcome is given by the Manx people to competitors, both at the TT and MGP. They open up their homes for 24 hours a day supplying tea, sandwiches and encouragement. Without this help, many riders would not be able to compete in the world's greatest motor cycle road race'.*

Once riders find a garage they like, they tend to go back year after year. In one such case a regular race-time occupant departed after TT with a mutual exchange of *'see you next year'*. Accordingly, as next year's race time approached, our racer made a quick telephone call and was told *'all OK, look forward to seeing you'*. Coming off the boat and making his way to the familiar location in Onchan, he was not surprised to find no one was at home, so went around the back, let himself in and was soon sitting down with a nice cup of tea. It was at that moment that a complete stranger walked in the back door and said: *'who are you?'*. Our racer duly explained, to be told that the gentleman in front of him was the new owner and that the previous owner had moved six months ago. Despite the precautionary telephone call, the previous owner had forgotten to mention the all-important fact that he had moved house and garage. In most cases where owners move house a rider will move with them to use their new garage. It is something that can happen several times over a long TT career!

A similar situation to the one that exists with garages prevails with regard to somewhere to stay, for both riders and spectators. With the Island's traditional bucket-and-spade tourist trade much diminished there are less bed-spaces than before. Each TT sees an appeal from the Tourist Board for private householders to open their doors and provide a bed under the 'Homestay' scheme. It is a chance for a little income, but most house-owners do it to help the races rather than themselves. Many hotels and guest-houses support the races by providing free or discounted accommodation to a rider. This again is primarily for the benefit of the events, for the Hotelier is unlikely to receive much commercial profit from seeing the name of his establishment on the fairing of the rider who finishes in 52nd place in the Senior MGP.

Many of the large Douglas hotels of the 1930s to 1970s whose accommodation and garaging was used by factory teams and by members of the Trade are no more. But they used to advertise the presence of the racers as an attraction to draw in the ordinary spectator. Breakfast in such hotels would certainly be more interesting than in an ordinary establishment if you could eavesdrop on the conversation of a couple of top riders at the next table.

Not only has the Isle of Man provided the motorcycle racing world with the unique Mountain Course, but Manx riders have had their share of race glory from its events. Three riders have won solo TT races (Tom Sheard, Neil Kelly and Richard Quayle), one has been a multiple winner of the Sidecar TT (Dave Molyneux) and 2005 winners Nick Crowe and Darren Hope are also locals. Manxmen have fared even better at the MGP, taking many victories since Cumbrian born but Manx adopted Harry Meageen came home first in the 350 Amateur race (predecessor of the MGP) in 1928.

There are some Manx residents who would like the Island to remain a backwater, and others who have their own highly personal views on what image the Island should project to the modern world (not all think that it should include the TT). But for 100 years the spectacle of motorcycles racing over its roads has gripped the imagination and attention of a world-wide audience. The attraction of the unique TT and MGP racing still holds good and with same-day transmission of race action to an audience of countless millions by way of satellite television, the Island's name (and that of race sponsors) continues to be spread across the globe. Money just cannot buy the sort of coverage that has been built on a century of racing heritage.

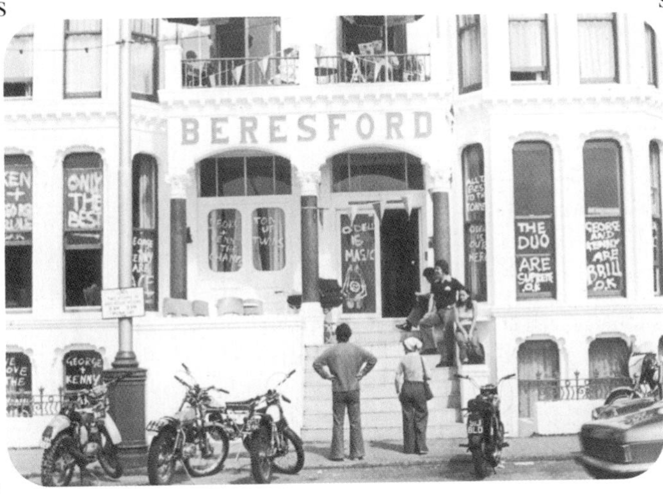

To have a TT winner staying on your premises can be reason for celebration. This is the scene at the 'Beresford' after George O'Dell's sidecar victory in 1977.

So, when Manx residents see the first Course-side bales going into place each April, they know the TT is on its way again for another year. Roadworks increase as race-time draws near, there are occasional sightings of visitors on high-powered motorcycles who come to gain, or to refresh their Course knowledge for racing. As the event gets ever closer, kerbs get a fresh coat of black and white paint, hedges and verges are trimmed, warning notices erected, barriers and road- sealing equipment put ready for use, marshals are sworn in, road-sweeping lorries are out in force, big race transporters arrive in the week before practice and, once again, the Island begins to hum as it prepares itself for its annual explosion of noise, colour and speed.

John Watterson was on the spot to catch this sensational shot of Carl Fogarty, Nick Jefferies and Steve Hislop bursting over the top of Lambfell on their Castrol Hondas in 1991. And look at the old gentleman on the footpath - how many great TT riders had he watched at the spot down the years? Although it would probably have been too early for him to have seen the first race over the Mountain Course in 1911, he would be aware that some of the pioneer TT riders had to push their single-speed machines over the top of the hill at this point.

RACING COME-BACKS

Much has been written over the years about the 'TT Bug', and plenty of it has come as direct quotes from riders. Seems that participation in a TT or MGP race plants something in riders' systems that they find difficult to get rid of and, as many motorcyclists know, a similar complaint can affect race spectators. There are many things that can prevent a rider from racing: lack of money, lack of machinery, injury, family/work considerations can all, in the worst cases, bring a rider's career to a halt, but most live in hope of making a come-back.

There are some interruptions to racing that are beyond everyone's control. The first to hit the TT was the First World War that stopped racing from 1915 to 1919. Sadly, many former riders lost their lives in that conflict, including third-place man in the singles class of 1908, Captain Sir R.K. Arbuthnot (an Admiral at the time of his death), and the winner of the 1911 Senior, Oliver Godfrey, who was reputed to have been killed in aerial combat with the Red Baron's squadron.

Captain Sir R.K. Arbuthnot with his Triumph at the 1908 TT. After his death in the First World War the Arbuthnot Trophy was created and it is still competed for, although not at the TT.

Many of those who did return counted themselves lucky to be racing again. This was certainly the case with joint second-place man in the 1914 TT, Howard Davies, for his war-time experiences included being shot-down whilst flying with the RFC. Believed to have been killed, the magazine 'Motor Cycling' published an obituary of this fine rider. However, reports of his death were premature and Howard (who afterwards carried the obituary in his wallet) returned to contest the 1920 TT on AJS machinery. Out of luck in the first year of his racing come-back, he achieved TT immortality in 1921 when, after taking second-place in the Junior, he took victory in the Senior TT on his Junior machine - the one and only time this has been achieved. For good measure, he gained another Senior victory in 1925. A few other former riders did return in 1920 but without doing any winning, and most victories in the post-First World War period went to a new generation of young men.

It was a different story after the Second World War where race victories in the first post-war TT meeting (1947) went to established pre-war runners Harold Daniell (Senior), Bob Foster (Junior) and Manliff Barrington (Lightweight). Each may have had eight years taken out of their racing careers, but each was good enough to come back and win. This situation continued for several years and the average age of the podium finishers across the three recognised TT classes in 1949 was 36.

Pre-war TT winner Bob Foster (Velocette) took second place behind another man who started his TT racing career in the 1930s, Freddie Frith (Velocette), in the 1948 Junior race. With him are sponsor Dickie Wilkins, Jimmy Simpson and Ken Bills who retired his Velocette.

A major threat to those established runners came in 1949 when 25 years old Geoff Duke took his first Island victory with a win in the Senior Clubman's TT. Moving on to the MGP three months later, he won the Senior and came second in the Junior. Everyone knew that there was a star in the making and few were surprised when he took a TT victory the following year.

A come-back that certainly made the headlines in 1977 was the return to the Island of multiple World Champion Phil Read and, of even more importance, the return of Honda with 'works' machines for him to ride. Read was one of the most voluble of the top riders who boycotted the TT after 1972, but he then had to stand aside for the next few years and watch as the TT's prize-money soared far beyond that paid at any of the conventional World Championship meetings he contested. As Read's world title efforts went seriously off the boil in 1976 compared to his early Yamaha successes and those of his MV glory days of 1974 and 1975, he decided that it was time to return for another TT pay-day. In explaining his almost unbelievable about face, he claimed that because from 1977 the TT was no longer a round of the World Championship, he was no longer forced to chase for championship points and so the event was once again acceptable to him. However, that did not mean that he was acceptable to a large number of TT fans, to marshals, or to many Manx people. Fans expressed their opinions of what they saw as a purely money-orientated return in letters to the press, some static marshals tried to persuade their colleagues to strike while others made clear that if he fell in front of them they would not pick him up. Phil also tells of backlash from the Manx public in the form of being refused petrol at filling stations and the like. For all the genuinely strong feelings raised by Phil Read's return and the accompanying hot-air that it generated, it was actually good for the TT to have him back, and it was even better to have Honda back.

With 1977 having been a good year for TT fans, 1978 was an even better one, for it saw the triumphant return of Mike Hailwood. The details of Mike's come-back are covered elsewhere in this book (see 'Hailwood's Return') but he received a tremendous reception, for he was still respected by the fans. They knew that he had not turned his back on the TT and then returned to make money, for he had been forced to leave by Honda's withdrawal from racing at the end of 1967. Mike's wins in 1978 and 79 have gone down into TT history and represent the most successful TT comeback of all time.

Joey Dunlop was forced to miss the TT through injuries sustained at Brands Hatch in 1989 and

with young guns like Steve Hislop and Carl Fogarty taking victories in his absence, there were some who started to write-off Joey's TT career. Making a comeback to the event in 1990, Joey was still not fully fit and concentrated his efforts on the smaller classes, but, with fitness regained for later years, he confounded the doubters by getting back to winning ways across all classes and upping his total number of TT victories to an unsurpassed 26.

Suzuki first entered the TT in 1960 and in 2000 they celebrated 40 years of TT involvement with a special display in the 'Suzuki Village' near the Grandstand.

Despite their many TT wins, Suzuki were not particularly heavily involved with the actual racing in 2000, but in 2002 with David Jefferies and Ian Lougher they put more effort into their racing and having linked with TAS (Temple Auto Salvage), they got back to their TT winning ways.

In 2002 the target for the top sidecar crews was to put in a lap at under 20 minutes and one of the favourites to do it was local man Dave Molyneux. But sidecar racing is a team affair and Dave's passenger was the man with whom he won his first TT back in 1989, Colin Hardman.

Colin's comeback to sidecar racing was spoilt when he was knocked off a road bike a few days before the first race. Talk of a wrist injury was enough to tell 'Moly' that the pair were unlikely to achieve a sub-20 minute lap in 2002. More worrying were Colin's additional injuries that were not made public. Hardman he was by name and by nature at that 2002 TT for, riding in a lot of pain, the pair still managed a 4th place in one of the races. It was an impressive comeback under the circumstances.

RACING FAMILIES

For many riders, taking part in the TT is a family affair and they bring wives, children, fathers, uncles, etc, to the Island in June. Sometimes these family members come just for the holiday but in most cases they are actively involved with race preparation and support of the rider. A popular expression amongst motorcyclists down the years is that *'racing gets into the blood'* and there have

Dave Molyneux and Colin Hardman on the way to their first TT victory in 1989.

been plenty of instances where families have shown this to be the case. Sons have followed fathers into the TT, brothers have raced together, wives have passengered their husbands in sidecars, and there have been a couple of solo races where husband and wife rode against each other.

From the first TT race in 1907 through to 1914, talented brothers Harry Collier and Charlie Collier competed together on the Matchless models that they produced. Although they suffered several retirements, neither finished in lower than fourth place in the nine races in which they were classed as finishers and Charlie took two wins (1907 & 1910) to Harry's one (1909).

Brothers Charlie (left) and Harry Collier whose names are amongst the earliest to appear on the Tourist Trophy.

There have been other successful combinations of brothers such as the Twemlows who each rode the TT from 1924-1930, with Ken taking one win and Eric taking two; the Pike brothers in the pre and early post-war years, and the Simmonds in the 1960s on predominantly Japanese machinery that included Tohatsus and early Kawasakis. The 1969 MGP was unusual in having three sets of brothers entered, the Dowies, Kirwans and Bilsborrows, whilst twins Peter and Ron Hardy formed a sidecar crew at the 1970 TT. Particularly successful brotherly riders in recent years have been the Jacksons.

Probably the most successful family racing relationship of all was that of Joey and Robert Dunlop, who shared an incredible 32 TT wins between them.

Many sons have followed their fathers into TT racing and in some instances they have competed against each other. 'Pa' Applebee was riding in the Senior TT of 1912 that was won by his son Frank on a Scott. George Cowley (Senior and Junior) both rode in the same races in the early 1920s, as did John and Ossie Wade in 1926. Les Archer was a well-known competitor in pre-war years and in the early post-war period his son, also Les, joined him in the Island races before going off to become European Moto-cross Champion. The 1960s saw sidecar racers Bill Boddice and Mick Boddice in the same event, whilst in later years Mick and his son Mick Boddice Jnr raced against each other at the TT. Father Fred Hanks and sons Norman and Roy were also sidecar racing in the same era (Roy still is) and on several occasions all three were in the same race. Other members of the Hanks family have since joined in the racing on three-wheels.

In a few cases, particularly talented fathers and sons have both achieved TT wins. Les and Stuart Graham did so, as did Tony and Michael Rutter, Bill and Ian Simpson, plus Tony and David Jefferies. The Jefferies family, almost a dynasty, is amongst the most successful of TT families. Patriarch Alan Jefferies was a talented all-round motorcyclist who rode in the MGP in the 1930s and in the first Clubman's TT of 1947. His eldest son Tony started his TT career in 1969 and, riding in various classes, he took victory in the 1971 Junior on a Yamsel and the 1971 F750 on a Triumph. Brother Nick started his Island racing career in the MGP of 1975 and rode to four third places before winning the Senior MGP of 1983 and moving on to the TT. Thereafter he was a consistent leaderboard finisher and, in his best ever ride, won the Formula 1 race at the 1993 TT. Even greater TT glory was to come the way of the

David Jefferies

Jefferies family with the representative from their third generation, David. The brilliant riding of David Jefferies, son of Tony, surpassed that of other members of his family and put him on a par with the TT greats.

Amongst other honourable TT family names are Jack and Peter Williams, plus George and Carl Fogarty. There have been TT/MGP father and son riders like George and Tony Brown, father and son MGP winners like Roger and Ralph Sutcliffe and, uniquely, father, mother and daughter competitors over the Mountain Course in John, Hilary and Gail Musson. And then, in what sometimes seemed like an attempted take-over of the MGP, five Kneen brothers competed in the event through the 1980s to 2000s, with wins going to twins, Mike and Norman - a unique occurrence.

Many husband and wife combinations have taken to the Course to ride together and work as a team, but the husband and wife combination of Peter and Sandra Barnett were in opposition, for they were riding solo Yamaha R1s in the 2000 Production TT. With Sandra being the fastest lady around the TT Course at the time, few were surprised when she finished ahead of Peter.

RECORD LAPS

It is lap speeds that grab the attention of most visitors to Island racing, for they provide the easiest image of what people are there to do, which is to ride or watch the host of high-speed activities available to them. A hundred years ago Rem Fowler set the fastest lap at the first TT. Many years later he was still able to quote his lap speed of 42.91 mph, because one of the biggest delights that the TT offered to those early racers was the freedom to exceed 20 mph on public roads without fear of prosecution. Rem had a much harder job to remember the time it took to do his fastest lap - 22 minutes 6 seconds.

That first TT was held on the 'Short Course' starting at St John's, and although it was only used for four years, lap speeds had climbed to 53.15 mph before the races moved to the Mountain Course in 1911, where the fastest lap in that first year was 50.11 mph by Frank Phillipp (Scott) in the Senior race, whilst P. J. Evans (Humber) set the fastest lap in the Junior race at 42.00 mph.

The concentration on lap speeds has continued down the years with Jimmy Simpson being much feted for being the first rider to lap at 60, 70 and 80 mph in a TT race. When Freddie Frith (Norton) lapped at 90.27 mph in winning the Senior TT of 1937, press and public asked themselves just how much faster the Mountain Course could be lapped, and the verdicts seemed to be - not much. But twenty years later they were celebrating the breaking of the 100 mph barrier by the great Bob McIntyre (Gilera) in a race that was extended to eight laps (300 miles) to recognise the 50th anniversary of the TT. It was fitting that it was during the Golden Jubilee that the first 100 mph lap was achieved, but it also highlighted that in just 50 years lap speeds had more than doubled. With celebrations of 100 years of TT racing to hand, it is perhaps fortunate that the growth in lap speeds has slowed during the event's second 50 years.

Bob McIntyre was a popular winner of the 1957 Jubilee TT on his 500 Gilera. Breaking the 100 mph barrier four times during his ride, Bob is here surrounded by well-wishers after the race.

For many years the 100 mph barrier was the target for would-be TT racers. Prior to the 1950 TT, 'Motor Cycling' ran an article *'How Much Longer Till That 100 MPH Lap?'*. It predicted record speeds and explained: '. . . *records we must have, for everybody's heart is set on them'*. The average spectator wanted higher speeds and all the race excitement they would bring, and 'Motor Cycling' added: *'there is nothing like a few records to bring satisfaction all round and a happy feeling that progress is maintaining itself and generally doing its stuff'*. However, a 100 mph lap was not expected in 1950, for the writer felt that considerable advances in design were required before that target was reached. He pinned his hopes for 1950 on the fact that with the fuel available increased from 72 to 80 octane, Harold Daniell's 1938 outright lap record of 91.00 mph would be broken. It was broken, indeed, it was 'smashed' by a young Geoff Duke who took his new featherbed-framed Norton around at 93.33 mph. But was it the better fuel, the better-handling frame, or the talents of Geoff Duke that was responsible for the new record lap speed? It was probably the combination of all three, for such things are never totally clearcut.

The 100 mph lap remained an almost magical speed figure long after Bob McIntyre's record-breaking victory in 1957, and it continued to dominate the consciousness of racers for many years. But if one of those aspirants to breaking the 'ton' had been told that they had lapped in 22 minutes 37 seconds, the reaction would probably have been 'so what?', even though that time represented a speed of just over the dream target speed of 100 mph. It was lap speeds that dominated the thoughts of the majority, not lap times, and it was only the deeper thinking riders and mechanics who were more interested in times than speeds. This was particularly the case amongst those looking for signs of performance improvement after the carrying out of adjustments or fitting of new parts to a bike. Seeing a reduction of a few seconds on lap times meant far more to them than the resulting lap speed.

The Roll of Honour of those setting fastest race laps contains all the great names of TT racing. Gary Hocking (MV Agusta) lifted the Junior 350 class into the 100 mph bracket in 1962 and Jim Redman (Honda) did the same for the 250s in 1965. The incredible Bill Ivy (Yamaha) did it on a 125 in 1968 and sidecars first broke through the 100 mph barrier in 1977, Dick Greasely (Yamaha) being the first to do it in a race. Records have gone ever upwards, with the 100 mph lap being left far behind, and the record lap for what was the smallest class at the TT, the 125s, reached just over110 mph with Chris Palmer (Honda), before the class was dropped after 2004.

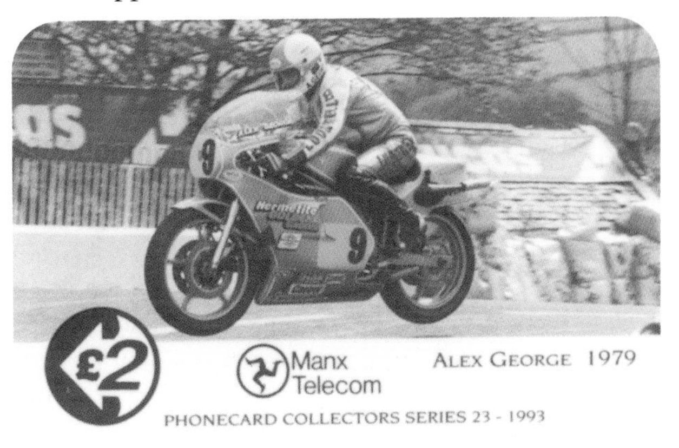

Alex George's ride on a Suzuki 500 in the 1979 Senior TT is commemorated in this Manx Telecom's Phonecard, but it was also the year that he won the Formula 1 race on a Honda with a record-breaking lap of 112.94 mph.

Although the breaking of the 110 and 120 mph barriers were eagerly awaited in the big bike classes and fairly quickly breached (even by the Production class), the 125 mph lap figure remained tantalisingly out of reach for some 11 years after 120 was reached. It eventually fell to David Jefferies (Yamaha) to lift the outright lap record over the 125 mph barrier in the millennium year of 2000. In a stunning display of committed riding he averaged 125.69 mph. It was a figure that he was to lift even higher before his untimely death in 2003 and, by doing so, showed that a 130 mph lap is within reach.

REFUELLING

The draft regulations for the first TT stipulated that each machine had to have a fuel tank of at least 2 gallons capacity. There was immediate opposition to this as hardly any of the prospective entries were fitted with a tank that would hold that amount, (although Norton advertised that their's did). The regulation was amended to a minimum tank size of 1¼ gallons and thus, from the very first race, it was necessary to make provision for machines to be refuelled. Race fuel was provided by the organisers in 1907, and each rider received a specified allowance which he paid for at 1/3d per gallon. Part of the allowance went into the fuel tank and that was then sealed. The remainder was handed to the rider in a sealed can for use at his compulsory mid-race stop. Seals were not allowed to be broken until the refuelling stop, where riders were supposed to arrive with the seals on their petrol tanks intact. The petrol allocation in 1907 was based on single-cylinder machines being required to average a minimum of 90 mpg and multi-cylinders limited to 75 mpg. Although there was pre-race talk that some riders might have to ride at less than full throttle to achieve those figures, come the race and there were no major problems over fuel consumption. Perhaps winner of the single-cylinder class, Charlie Collier (Matchless), cut it a bit fine at 94½ mpg, but second place man, Jack Marshall (Triumph), still had plenty in his tank after returning 114 mpg. Limitations on the amount of fuel that could be used during a race were abandoned in 1909.

Even when restrictions on the amount of petrol that could be used were removed, competitors were only permitted to refuel at officially designated points. For the first three years of racing on the Mountain Course those points were at Braddan Church and Ramsey. Thereafter refuelling could only take place at the Douglas Pits, where each rider was allowed an Attendant to help with the job. Taking on fuel at other than the designated location meant exclusion from a race.

There is so much detail in this photograph that it repays careful study. It was still a few years before the organisers provided each pit with a post-mounted fuel containers and Geoff's Pit Attendant is using the traditional funnel and can to top up the Levis. But look at Geoff Davison's riding gear, in his words it comprised: *'Dance pumps, light stockings, drill breeches (held in by garters to reduce windage), cricket sweater, wash-leather gloves and a crash hat'*. It was part of his attempt to reduce all-up weight of machine and rider to give his little two-stroke Levis the best possible chance over the 5 laps (189 miles) of the TT Course that even he, the winner, took 3¾ hours to complete.

The Pits were on the Glencrutchery Road when Geoff Davison brought his Levis in to refuel at the 1922 TT. The little Levis two-stroke had a top speed of only 63 mph, yet he rode it to victory at a race average speed of 50 mph.

Initially, a fuel-stop was compulsory but this was later dropped. However, riders almost always did stop because the size of their petrol tanks dictated that they had to do so. To have fitted a tank of sufficient size to last a seven lap race would have meant a substantial increase in weight that might well cause a deterioration in handling and braking performance. There was a time in the late 1950s when several riders decided that the advantages to be gained from a non-stop race outweighed the disadvantages, so they fitted pannier tanks within the sides of their fairings and went the entire distance without stopping. In later years the regulations specified a maximum size for petrol tanks (currently 24 litres/5.28 gallons) and this now means that competitors need to refuel after two laps of racing.

In the mid-1920s the race organisers arranged for the provision of identical gravity-fed fuel fillers for all competitors. Although all the refuelling rigs were supposedly the same, the Velocette camp got a sight of the fillers intended for the Norton pits at the 1938 TT and noticed *'that the normally rough brass castings of the nozzles had been smoothed and internally streamlined to hasten the flow of liquid through them'*.

Every TT rider used to be contracted to use a particular petrol company's product. For many years this was a relatively straightforward business, because after the use of alcohol fuels was banned at the TT from 1925 the majority of competitors used similar petrol-benzole mixtures, with only the occasional demand from a two-stroke such as DKW to complicate matters. With the post-war growth in use of highly-tuned racing two-strokes, the provision of fuel became something of a nightmare for the petrol companies. Most two-strokes required pre-mixed petrol and oil, and each maker wanted it supplied to their very exact specification.

The petrol allowances and consumptions at the first TT races are quoted above and 50 years later, riders of Manx Nortons allowed themselves 9 pints of petrol per lap with actual consumption being about 35 mpg, a figure that could be affected by the gearing used, weather conditions and riding style. Four-strokes have always been regarded as more economical than two-strokes and singles more economical than multi-cylindered machines. Some thirty-five years ago, Alan Barnett was said to have averaged 50 mpg when lapping at almost 100 mph on his single-cylinder 350 Aermacchi in pursuit of Giacomo Agostini's four-cylinder MV Agusta, that gave him 20 mpg and lapped at nearly 105 mph. Todays 'fours' are considered to be doing well if they give 15 mpg and some struggle to do 2 laps on a tankful.

This is the impressive line of refuelling rigs mounted above the Pits that are used for todays races.

For all the pre-race concentration on having the best bike, rider, support team, tyres, etc, etc, mid-race refuelling can be the stuff of nightmares and can ruin the performance of the most highly rated team. Sometimes this can result from errors in fuel consumption calculations and a rider runs out before reaching the Pits, in others a full tank may only just allow a rider to complete two full laps - nail-biting stuff. At the actual refuelling stop it is always difficult to be sure that the tank is filled correctly. Too little and the rider might run out, too much and it can spill onto a rider's leathers and gloves which can be uncomfortable and dangerous. Even failure to get the fuel cap back on properly has been responsible for the loss of at least two TT races and has involved a considerable degree of panic in a few others.

The tale is told under 'Pit Signals' of how Phillip McCallen lost a Lightweight victory by missing a Pit-stop, but in 1997 he pulled in on schedule for his second stop in the Senior race. Phillip was leading on his Honda RC45 and took a quick drink whilst his team went through their normal procedures. The only snag was that the refuelling nozzle was in the tank for 20 seconds before anyone realised that no petrol was getting through. Although the mechanic had squeezed the trigger on the release nozzle the team had forgotten that (due to earlier problems with a leak) the main valve on the refuelling container was still in the OFF position. In the ensuing panic the tank was not properly filled. Phillip sensed rather than saw this and with careful riding he held onto his lead, won the race by 8.7 seconds, and finished with no more than an egg-cupful of fuel in the tank. Amongst those whose race hopes have been dashed by botched refuelling stops are some who would like the race rules changed to permit them swap a near empty petrol tank for a full one at their stop. However, this is not allowed, for the regulations state: *'In the interests of safety, the use of ready fuelled replacement tanks in the Pit will not be permitted'*.

Refuelling may often be a serious and race-deciding business, but there is the occasional lighter moment. One rider had his Laverda run out of petrol at Hillberry during an evening practice in the 1970s. Unable to borrow any on the spot, he hitched a lift via side-roads and managed to get back to the Paddock. Grabbing a can of petrol, he then managed to get a lift back to Hillberry, refuelled the Laverda and completed his lap in a time that was published as well over one hour. It probably had the timekeepers scratching their heads

This Moto Guzzi would not be every riders choice to ride the Mountain Course in the Production TT but Ashley Law showed spectators something different from the usual Japanese machinery when he rode it in 2002.

and wondering if he had actually done two laps and they had missed him on one of them.

In 1996 Production bikes returned to race at the TT. They were a new generation of machines and there were several question marks as to how they would perform over the Mountain Course. It is interesting that amongst various pre-race claims, one centred on the fact that some of the top runners might have to back-off the throttle to save fuel during the race. That sounded like just the same sort of 'kidology' that was used by a few of the riders in the first TT of 1907, when they tried to lull the opposition with similar claims.

RESCUE HELICOPTER

The rescue helicopter that takes medical support to any incident on the Course before conveying injured riders to hospital, is nowadays an indispensable part of the race support services. Indeed, neither practice sessions nor races will run without a helicopter being available and there are two in use on race-days. The 'chopper' represents the serious side of motorcycle racing and when the sound of one in flight is heard during practice or a race, it does, for a few moments at least, take the attention of spectators away from the exciting spectacle of motorcycles racing before them and creates thoughts of what might have resulted from similar high-speed action somewhere else on the 37¾ miles of the Mountain Course.

In the early years of the TT an injured rider could sometimes have a long wait at the side of the road before receiving medical attention. Nowadays, if there is not a doctor or paramedic stationed at the point where the incident occurs, medical support will arrive by helicopter within a few minutes of marshals making a call for assistance. Chief Medical Officer for the TT and MGP races, Dr David Stevens, MBE, operates the helicopter on the 'scoop and run' principle, believing that it is better to get casualties to the specialist care available in hospital as quickly as possible, rather than spend too much time treating them at the site of the incident. From time of call-out to a rider arriving in hospital rarely exceeds 20 minutes, which, in Dr Stevens words: *'is faster than most mainland short circuits can get a casualty off the track into a First Aid centre never mind to a fully-equipped Hospital trauma unit'.*

A generous donation from Honda towards the cost of providing the rescue-helicopter in 1990.

Provision of the rescue-helicopter service is an expensive and serious business, but it is not without its humorous side. Pilots have to be aware of the multitude of landing sites available at the edge of the Course, including those that are less than perfect for the job. A level surface is particularly desirable, because a few degrees of slope can feel exaggerated to the occupants of the helicopter. On one occasion at a Course-side landing the Doctor was poised in the open doorway ready to jump out as it touched-down. Unfortunately there was a slight slope, it heeled over a few degrees, he was not hanging on and rolled out head first. Luckily he was not injured, but it is not the way that a Doctor likes to arrive.

Chief Travelling Marshal Allan 'Kipper' Killip was present at one accident in the early days of the helicopter service and assisted with loading an unconscious rider into the helicopter. Just as the door was about to be closed the rider opened his eyes and posed the classic question *'Where am I?'*, to which Kipper responded *'Don't worry boy, you're on your way to heaven'.* The only problem was that, by the look on the rider's face, he believed what Kipper had told him. In a similar incident, a first-time rider recovered consciousness in the helicopter and came out with the words: *'I've got to get to the ferry to the Isle of Man, I'm racing next week.'* How unfortunate that the bang on the head he received in his crash seemed to have blotted out what should have been one of the highlights of his racing career, his first full week of practice on the Mountain Course.

In another helicopter-related incident involving Kipper Killip and Deputy Chief Travelling Marshal at the time, Des Evans, the pair were taken up to get an airborne look at some of the tricky Course-side landing sites. Kipper made the mistake of asking the question *'What happens if the motor cuts?'*, to which the pilot replied *'You mean like this?'*, cutting the engine. The ensuing period without power was exciting and concerning, leaving Kipper (and Des) sorry that he had asked the question.

The most skilled of operators in any job can make mistakes, but helicopter pilots cannot afford to make too many. In an instance when a 'chopper' made an unexpected landing at a marshalling point, a first-aid box was thrust at the marshal who came forward, with the words *'here's the replacement you asked for'.* When the marshal replied *'did we?'*, the reply was *'this is the bottom of Barregarrow isn't it?'*, to which the marshal replied *'no, it's the top!'*. Fortunately, it was an instance when a mistake of a few hundred feet was of little consequence.

One helicopter pilot of the early 1980s who was particularly confident of his skills, had a special technique for flying casualties into Nobles Hospital (Douglas) that he reserved for warm sunny days. Switching from his usual approach, he would fly the length of the nearby Westmoreland Road at little more than tree-top height towards his landing-site adjacent to the five-storey Nurses Home next to the hospital. When almost there, he would rapidly gain height and then quickly lose speed to hover over the normally totally secluded and peep-free flat roof of the Nurses Home. If the flight strategy had worked, pilot and passengers would be greeted by the sight of sunbathing nurses hurriedly trying to recover previously discarded clothes, a task made doubly difficult, as the pilot well knew, by the considerable downwash and turbulence from the helicopter rotor blades.

The rescue-helicopter coming in to land at the Hospital in Douglas, with the Nurses home in the background.

Even when landed, the rescue helicopter keeps its rotors running, something which is permitted by the emergency procedures under which it operates but which requires vigilance by anyone in the vicinity, for part of the spinning rear rotor is well below head height. It was customary for a policeman to be on duty at the hospital landing site to stop traffic as the helicopter landed, and then to keep the unauthorised away from the scene. On one occasion the turbulence from the rotor of a just-landed helicopter blew the duty-policeman's pristine white summer helmet off his head and sent it bowling towards the back of the helicopter. Concerned for his precious helmet, the policeman set off towards the rear in pursuit and passed within a couple of feet of the spinning rotor. That was rather too close for comfort, as the pilot explained in a few blunt words.

Travelling Marshals play a leading role in coordinating helicopter landing, loading and take-off at the site of an incident and one of their number, Robin Sherry, attended a spill in the 1980s to which the helicopter was called to take the slightly injured rider to hospital. It is a requirement for the rider's helmet to go with him to hospital (for inspection in case he has banged his head) and, supervising the incident on the ground, Robin asked another marshal to ensure that this was done. After seeing the chopper away, he then prepared to mount his Travelling Marshals's Honda and ride on to the next 'station'. Only then was it realised that the other marshal had loaded Robin's helmet into the helicopter instead of the rider's.

Manxman 'Decca' Kelly enjoyed unusual sponsorship in the blue and yellow colours of Aeromega at a time when they provided the rescue-helicopter service at the TT and MGP.

Many of those who fall off are only slightly injured, some more so, but if they can walk they are always keen to get out in the next practice session. It is well known that motorcycle racers are a breed apart, and an injury that would keep Mr Average off work for a few weeks is not usually regarded by riders as sufficiently serious to keep them from going out in the next practice session and delivering another 120+ mph lap of the TT Course. The Chief Medical Officer knows all about rider attitudes to injury and, under a strictly policed system, requires fallers to prove to him that they are as fit to ride as they claim. Not for him the conventional consulting room, for riders have to visit him at the top of the Control Tower at the Grandstand. The seemingly never-ending steps to get there are a major deterrent to those with leg and ankle injuries, whilst for those that make it to the top, 'Doc' Stevens probing questions followed by a request to do a few press-ups, quickly shows any deficiencies in their fitness to race. It was Jamie Whitham (recalling his first Island race to Mac McDiarmid) who told that after injuring his shoulder, reporting to the Medical Officer and being asked to do ten press-ups: *'Quick as a flash, down I went. And couldn't move. In fact I had to get the Medical Officer to pick me up'.*

The camera mounted under the nose shows this 'chopper' to be on a filming mission.

It is not only the rescue-helicopters that can be seen in the Manx skies at TT time, for film crews have found them to be the ideal platform from which to capture the action around the Mountain Course.

It was David Jefferies who, showing astonishing awareness, would find time to give the filming helicopter a cheeky wave as he got into his stride going up the Mountain. With the throttle of his Suzuki nailed to the stop he would often leave the 'chopper' behind, even though it could cut the corners that he had to employ all his characteristic skill and bravery to ride en-route to a 127 mph lap. This happened more than once, leading 'DJ' to suggest that they got a faster machine; whilst the pilot plotted ways to 'ambush' him further up the Mountain.

RETURNING TO THE PADDOCK

The Mountain Course presents competitors with an extremely long lap and although good riders may whistle round in under 20 minutes during practice and racing, if they suffer a break-down it can be a time-consuming and awkward business getting back to the Paddock in Douglas. Many of today's competitors will have entries in more than one class and will often have planned to take two different machines out in the limited time offered by a practice session, but breaking-down at Sulby, Ramsey, or on the Mountain, can be enough to scupper those plans. Riders have often shown considerable resourcefulness in overcoming their difficulties and getting back to the Start.

After Geoff Davison and Howard Davies had machine troubles that caused their retirements from the 1923 Senior TT, they hired an open horse-drawn carriage and were driven back to the Paddock in style, still wearing their leathers and carrying their crash helmets. Other riders even used public transport to return to Douglas, for the Island had a network of railways and bus services. Norton 'works' rider Tim Hunt was one to do so. When his bike failed at Ramsey in the 1930 Senior, he bought himself a newspaper, a ticket for the Manx Electric Railway, and then enjoyed a scenic ride back to Douglas.

For many years it was acceptable for a stranded rider to get a lift on the back of another rider's bike during practice, although few machines had anything like acceptable pillion-carrying arrangements. Occasionally a Travelling Marshal would also give a rider a lift over the last few miles of the Course and, if a rider was very lucky (or famous), the Roads Opening car might even pick him up.

THE ISLE OF MAN RAILWAY
(The Unique Victorian Steam Railway)

ANNOUNCES THAT ON

TUESDAY, 3rd SEPTEMBER, and
THURSDAY, 5th SEPTEMBER, 1968

'A Grand Prix Special'

WILL DEPART FROM DOUGLAS STATION at 9.30 a.m.

Calling at . . .
Braddan, Union Mills, Crosby, St. John's
Kirk Michael, Ballaugh, Sulby Bridge
and Ramsey

Returning from Ramsey at . . .
3.45 p.m., on Tuesday, 3rd September
2.30 p.m., on Thursday, 5th September

Parts of the TT Course were close to the Island's Railways that could conveniently be used by those without their own transport.

Two-up through Schoolhouse Corner at Ramsey in this shot from a practice session of the 1920s.

The carrying of pillion passengers was eventually outlawed and the Roads Open car now travels too fast to stop - except for the most privileged, which usually means a star rider whom the organisers want to have brought back to Douglas so that he can take part in the next race of the day.

One star rider who was particularly privileged during a practice session in the 1970s was Mick Grant whose engine exploded at the 33rd Milestone. The unfortunate Klaus Klein was close behind and came off on the oil deposited by Mick's Suzuki. Klaus was seemingly unhurt, but the rescue-helicopter was nevertheless called up to take him away for a medical check-up. Meanwhile, unintentional perpetrator of the incident, Mick Grant, used his star status to hitch a ride in the helicopter back to Douglas, so that he could take another bike out in the same practice session. Another to make use of the chopper was Wayne Rollinson who fell at Westwood during practice for the 2003 MGP. Although helicoptered to hospital, he got himself discharged, returned to the Grandstand, obtained swift medical clearance and took another bike out in the same session.

Part of the process associated with gaining experience of Island racing is for a competitor to learn the roads inside and outside the Course. With that knowledge it is sometimes possible to get a member of his support crew out to collect him via the back-roads, or to enlist the assistance of a spectator to provide transport back to the Paddock and thus make the most of a practice session. Many riders now carry mobile phones in their leathers during practice to communicate with their team if forced to stop.

On occasions, riders still make use of public transport, and one who did was Joey Dunlop. With a lengthy Island racing career in which he sometimes raced in four or five events, Joey inevitably had his share of problems out on the Course during both practice and racing. At the 1984 TT he won the opening Formula 1 race and was all set for a good race-week. However, after setting a new absolute lap record of 118.48 mph in the Senior race (unusually held mid-week) he retired on the Mountain when out of fuel. After his retirement he took the Manx Electric Railway down from the Bungalow to Laxey where he was jokingly presented with a free train pass. Come the 250cc race and Joey had cause to use his new pass for, once again, he ran out of fuel on the Mountain.

In the 1995 Ultra-Lightweight race Joey retired

Joey Dunlop walks towards The Bungalow with Travelling Marshal Des Evans after his second retirement through lack of fuel in 1984.

at The Hawthorn some seven miles from the Start. Needing to get back to the Paddock for the afternoon's Lightweight race, he hitched a lift with the Course Inspection car that does a lap of the Course between races. It was something he was to regret for, never a good passenger, Joey later described it as a frightening experience, even though the driver remembered it as one of his slower laps.

Many more tales are told of 26 times TT winner Joey Dunlop, for he was an unconventional racer by today's standards. He was also a resourceful one whose total of TT wins would have been even greater if he had not lost several races by running out of fuel. He ran out again at the 2000 TT, but fortunately it was during practice that his 250 Honda spluttered to a halt at the Bungalow rather than during a race. As ever, busy Joey had another bike waiting in the Pits that he wanted to take out that morning, but how was he to get back to the Paddock? Finding a plastic cup at the side of the road, he used it to transfer petrol from Travelling Marshal Dick Cassidy's Honda. But as the 250 was a two-stroke, he needed oil to mix with the petrol. Borrowing a screwdriver, he removed the sealing plug from a fork leg of his racer, drained-off some oil, added the oil to the borrowed petrol in the tank and thus had an acceptable 'petroil' mixture that allowed him to ride back to the Paddock .

There are many Manx born riders who have contested the TT and MGP and, unsurprisingly, they have a few advantages over visiting racers in respect of getting back to the Paddock. One MGP winning Manxman who went on to contest the TT in the 1980s used this advantage to the full and showed particular ingenuity after his machine seized during practice. It was not the first time that it had seized and valuable time had been lost on earlier outings, with the result that he was in danger of failing to qualify. After the latest seizure he managed to grab the clutch and, taking advantage of a downhill stretch, coasted at high speed for almost a mile until he reached the spot that he was aiming for - the house just off the Course where a racing relative lived. This relative had been racing at the Jurby South race-meeting the previous week-end and, knowing where his bike was, our stricken TT rider wheeled it out of the garage (without waking anyone), checked it for fuel, pushed it away from the house, bump-started it and used it to ride the remaining 25 miles of the Course back to the Paddock where he had another bike waiting to take out.

Richard 'Milky' Quayle is a double MGP winner and one of only three Manxmen to have won a solo TT (the Lightweight 400 TT of 2002). Suffering a breakdown near The Bungalow early in one practice session, he persuaded a spectator to loan him his trail-bike, intending to take an off-road route towards civilisation and so get out on another race machine. But Richard had underestimated the wetness of the Manx uplands, even in summer. Struggling through mud, water and bogs, he was soon plastered with muck and physically shattered. What had seemed like a good idea had turned into a muddy nightmare. However, he made it to Brandywell, convinced a car driver of his need and managed to get through the tortuous roads of Injebreck and back to the Paddock, just in time to take another bike out before the session closed.

Riding his 380cc Greeves in Thursday afternoon practice for the 2004 Senior Classic MGP, Peel man Ian Rycroft had his primary drive belt snap at Ballacraine. Finding someone to drive him the three miles to his home, he collected a new belt, returned to Ballacraine, fitted the belt, got under way again and completed his lap in 63 minutes.

RIDER WELFARE

There is huge variation in the level of support that riders receive in their racing. Through TT and MGP history there have been individuals who, from choice or necessity, operated totally on their own. Dealing with their race entries, paying for their own bikes and spares, preparing and maintaining their machines, they often came to the Island without even an assistant for the Pits and had to recruit a stranger for race-day. But such people are the exception and most riders have a back-up team. Those 'teams' can vary from wife/girl-friend, a couple of mates, a well-organised sponsor and mechanic, or, for the select few, the services of a full 'works' team like Honda with its race-transporters of bikes, workshops, spares, hospitality, plus first call on the services of the Trade suppliers of tyres, chain, oil companies and the like. All the above is aimed at supporting a rider in his racing, and little thought is given to what will happen if things should go badly wrong.

When any TT or MGP competitor arrives on the Island he will, as a rider, be made to feel that bit special and receive extra help and attention, for the Manx people have a hundred years experience of his needs. The loner who has secured the use of a private householder's garage will find it clean and almost empty for his use. If he is a Newcomer he can be sure that the garage owner knows an experienced past competitor who will take him around the Course for a few instructional laps. Such a person will also prove an invaluable source of contacts if the rider needs a bit of emergency welding or the fabrication of a new part, for he will be able to direct him to firms who will give a competitor priority during race-fortnights.

Whilst TT riders with their International Race Licences and wide experience will usually be expected to 'know the ropes', the MGP organisers go out of their way to offer support to less experienced riders. Writing 60 years ago, the then President of the Manx MCC the Reverend Bertie Reid explained that: *'Everything humanly possible is done to ensure their safety and comfort. When they make their first appearance they will be assisted, guided, warned, encouraged and controlled, in such an easy, friendly way that they will unconsciously find themselves being smoothly absorbed into a wonderful sporting fraternity'.* No doubt the current MGP organisers would like to feel that those words hold true to this day.

All the above levels of support work well whilst things are going right, but what happens when they go wrong - in the worst scenario when a rider is badly injured or killed - does a similar level of support exist? Fortunately the answer is yes, for in amongst the slightly unreal and high-octane atmosphere of the fortnight of race-orientated activities that take place at each TT and MGP, there exists a member of the organisation whose feet remain firmly on the ground - the Welfare Officer. As many riders down the years have come to know, that position is filled by Wyn Evans. Based in the Control Tower at the Grandstand, she immediately gets to know when an incident occurs. In most cases it means a rider is hospitalised and, with each incident being different, Wyn is available to answer the many questions that such an occurrence generates, ranging from the position regarding on-Island hospital care, assisting with the bringing over of relatives, transport of vans and bikes back to the UK and, by making daily trips to the Hospital for as long as there are TT or MGP patients there, seeing that no rider feels that they are forgotten.

Such support services have to be financed and the Welfare Officer is fortunate to have access to several funds that assist her in this work where, for once, the racing of motorcycles is forced to take second place to more practical issues in life. The irony is that whilst riders who fall in practice may be confined to a hospital bed with injuries that will prevent them earning to support their families for months, their friends and fellow competitors continue to live out their fantasies for the rest of the fortnight with high-speed racing over the Mountain Course.

Much of the funding to support injured riders (support that can go on for years) comes from the ACU Benevolent Fund (BEN Fund). Many spectators will have bought the badges that the Fund bring out for each TT, for they recognise that it is a small way in which they can help the less fortunate members of not just the racing fraternity, but all motorcycling members of ACU Clubs who fall on hard times.

RIDERS VIEWS

The pre-eminence of the TT in the world of motorcycle racing for its first 65 years, saw barely a harsh word spoken against it in public. Riders, manufacturers (and spectators) knew it to be the greatest racing challenge with every good reason to participate, because a win at the TT was considered the supreme victory - nothing could better it.

All the great riders spoke of the personal satisfaction gained from a TT success, and all knew that an Island win guaranteed a boost to their racing careers and to their earnings. Even after the establishment of the World Championships in the late 1940s, riders still rated a TT win higher than becoming World Champion. Freddie Frith won the first ever 350cc World Championship in 1949 on a Velocette but said later: *'The TT was the Blue*

Riband of racing then, worth more than a World Championship to people in the sport'. Geoff Duke was a particularly successful TT rider and his views on the worth of Island racing have never wavered. After Clubman's and MGP successes, his first International win in the Senior TT of 1950 was followed by a Junior/Senior double in 1951, a year in which he also took 350 and 500 World Championships, was voted Britain's 'Sportsman of the Year' and awarded the RAC's coveted Segrave Trophy. At the very top of the sporting tree, Geoff summed up that tremendous year with: *'A personal satisfaction for me, though, was that I had scored an Isle of Man TT double'.*

Honours were heaped upon Geoff Duke in the early 1950s, but it was his TT wins that he held in the highest regard.

This recognition of the TT's importance continued into the 1960s, for racers of all nationalities. But then, with money suddenly tight through factory withdrawals from racing, the tone began to change and the organisers of the TT were slow to inject more cash to counter rider discontent with their expensive-to-compete-in race meeting. It is interesting to recall the views of some of the biggest of the names who changed their attitudes and fronted the anti-TT campaign of the early 1970s. Speaking of his first TT win (the 1961 Junior), Phil Read said: *'What a moment. Junior TT winner . . . no wonder I felt over the moon'.* Then as late as 1969 Giacomo Agostini said: *'For me there is something very special about the TT. It is, without doubt, the most testing circuit in the World Championship series. A victory on the Isle of Man has great prestige - like winning a world title'.*

Three years later Read and Agostini claimed that the TT was unacceptable to them, and criticised it in words that were almost unbelievable when compared to their early utterings. They backed their criticisms with a campaign to have the TT stripped of its World Championship status, something that happened in 1976. Then, just as unbelievably, in 1977 Phil Read was back at the TT, claiming that as there was no longer pressure to score World Championship points, the meeting was once again acceptable to him. Indeed, such was the apparent swing in his opinion that by 1982 he was saying: *'I don't want to knock the Grand Prix (World Championship) riders as they are a special breed on their own, but to ride and win a TT is the ultimate'.*

The races continued without the support of some of the star names, but, as ever, those who aspired to victory found that winning at the TT did not come easily, for it still required a lengthy apprenticeship for all but the most talented, with the prospect of harsh punishment of any riding error. Sidecar World Champion and TT winner in the 1970s, George O'Dell, summarised both points when he said: *'It's a long way round and concentration all the time is essential for survival'.*

Kiwi Graeme Crosby proved in the early 1980s that top World Championship contenders could mix both road and circuit racing. 'Croz' explained what he liked about the TT: *'the way the racing is spread out over ten days, the enthusiasm of the fans, dawn practice, hard partying on the days off, the history of the place . . . it's magic, really, but it's so hard to explain the place to people who've never been there'.* Some people felt that 'Croz' occasionally overdid the partying business, amongst them top photographer Don Morley, who, twenty years after the event, told that he *'still shuddered to recall Kiwi-Cros riding his paddock bike*

Graeme Crosby and mechanic wait for the start of the 1981 Classic TT.

somewhat drunkenly up and over my expensive new car, and me watching in horror as the panelling caved in!'. After three TT wins in the early 1980s, Graeme Crosby's TT riding career was brought to an end when a combination of circumstances forced him to join a race team run by none other than anti-TT man Giacomo Agostini.

Sharing the enthusiasm of Graeme Crosby for the Island event was TT and World Championship winning Scot on three-wheels, Jock Taylor, who said in 1982: *'It's without doubt the greatest feeling in the world winning a TT race. It's even better than winning a World Championship. I still regard the mountain circuit as the ultimate challenge and finishing a TT race alone is still one of the greatest achievements in sidecar racing'*. A man whose solo TT racing career ended at about the time that Jock was uttering his words was Charlie Williams. Speaking some 20 years later, Charlie, winner of 8 TT races - 9 if you include a shared win with Tom Herron in a two-man Production race - perhaps 8½ if you do not, said: *'I never rated myself as a TT specialist, I held a number of short circuit records at the same time. However, I don't think anything gave me the same satisfaction as riding on the Mountain Course'*. He was making the point that a rider did not have to specialise in just one of the polarising divisions of motorcycle racing - road or circuit, as other good riders of the time like Chas Mortimer and Mick Grant also proved by succeeding in both. Mick was quoted in Ronnie Mutch's book 'The Last of the Great Road Races' as saying of the TT: *'It's the finest race in the world. Unconditionally, the name of the game is road racing, not circuit'*.

As the TT moved through the 1980s into the 1990s, road racing specialists like Joey Dunlop tended to have the upper-hand on the Island, but young 'hot-shots' with names like Carl Fogarty and Steve Hislop both used the TT to boost their reputations and serve as a stepping-stone to racing at World Championship level.

Team-mates with Honda at the 1991 TT, Carl Fogarty (left) and Steve Hislop pose with some of their race machinery.

Unfortunately, both Carl

and Steve blew hot and cold on the TT in later years, responding to questions in a manner that lacked consistency and carelessly failing to mention what Island racing had done for their careers - and could do for others. But in 2001 Steve Hislop said, with perhaps a hint of nostalgia: *'I managed to get away from the TT, but there's always a little bit of it inside you . . .'* - that is hardly surprising if, like Steve, you recorded 11 victories on the Mountain Course and were recognised as one of the TT greats. Another man with 11 wins was Phillip McCallen with his all-or-nothing riding style. When asked his favourite circuit he said: *'It has to be the Isle of Man, six laps in the big races there, two hundred and twenty five miles at over 120 mph, that is the ultimate buzz, there really is nothing like it'*. The period through the 1990s to date has continued to see TT wins going to stars of British short circuit racing, with names like Iain Duffus, Jim Moodie, John McGuinness, Michael Rutter and David Jefferies showing that the two disciplines could still be mixed. Conflict with their short circuit obligations occasionally kept some of those riders away from the Island, and others had reservations about the level of commitment required for a win. Iain Duffus explained what was required: *'Do not listen to any top rider who says he doesn't ride the TT Course on the limit. I raced at 90% for years getting 3rds, 4ths, etc, now it's 110%'*.

Other winners have echoed Iain's words, and with big money at stake in today's TT races the top professional riders are determined to take home the major part of it - and that usually means going all out. But getting a good payday from the TT has not prevented some of those professionals from expressing elements of dis-satisfaction with the event. Jim Moodie said from the sidelines in 2002 (when he did not ride through injuries sustained elsewhere): *'They could definitely move with the times a bit more. They could probably do with a few younger people on the organisational side but other than that it's still pretty good you know'*. Others think better of the organisation, with 2003 winner Adrian Archibald saying: *'things run like clockwork'*, whilst multi-sidecar winner (and a man known to speak his mind) Dave Molyneux says: *'I don't think a lot of people realise how good the TT is, especially for sidecar racing'*. Unfortunately, Dave's complimentary remarks were followed by some stinging criticism of the TT after the 2005 event.

For all the tempting rewards available from TT success, the carefully considered words of the late and great David Jefferies make recommended reading to anyone contemplating riding the event. He said: *'The TT is dangerous there's no two ways about it, and anyone who says that I shouldn't say that is wrong: you have to be able to sit down, talk about the risks, and understand them before you go there'*. He went on: *'All you need to do is leave a little more room for error at the Isle of Man. The biggest thing at the Isle of Man is knowing your limits, and knowing that if you're a little unsure - you shut off. You don't keep the throttle on until you know where you're going. If you ride it like that, you're fine'*. Those were the words in 2003 of a man who had been raised in a world of TT racing. His grandfather took a second place, whilst his father and uncle each took a victory. He came into the TT and progressed sensibly up the ladder until multiple Island success was his, but then, on a disastrous Thursday afternoon practice lap in 2003, a combination of circumstances caused him to crash at high-speed in Crosby, and the most demanding of motorcycle race circuits claimed another victim.

To those who do not seek to race on it, the Mountain Course is *'Too dangerous . . . too difficult . . . too long . . . too expensive . . . too remote . . .'*, but for those of a different mind-set it is the very same multiplicity of challenges that constitute the attraction of Island racing. Irrepressible Kiwi, Graeme Crosby, was a star rider who approached the TT with the right attitude, but he was guilty of oversimplifying the challenge when he described racing over the Mountain Course as *'just like a swift blast home from the pub with your mates!'*.

Iain Duffus (Honda) is fully committed to clipping the apex at the Bungalow during his winning ride in the 1995 Junior TT.

CHAPTER 8

TALES OF . . .

RIDING NUMBERS

The regulations for the first TT specified that: *'every machine must have its competing numbers distinctly painted on the side of the tank in figures not less than 4 inches high and ¾ broad in every part'.* The policy of identifying machines and riders by numbers has been followed ever since, although at some TT meetings of the 1920s, riders without confirmed entries were allowed to practice as reserves and for such sessions they carried letters instead of numbers.

Panther riders at the 1925 T.T. Tommy Bullus (left) ready for practice on his Panther carrying a 'D' reserve plate.

Although the photograph above shows Tommy Bullus with a 'D' reserve plate, team-mate Oliver Langton crashed his Panther during practice and broke his collar-bone, so Tommy immediately moved up from reserve to take Oliver's place but then immediately wrote-off his bike by hitting the parapet of Sulby Bridge. Panther had one spare machine with them which they gave to Tommy, and he brought it home in 4th position. It was regarded as a very satisfactory finish, particularly as he broke the frame at the head lug when jumping Ballig Bridge on the third lap. Fortunately, the under-tank frame tubes were strong enough to allow him to finish the race.

At the 1937 MGP respected Manx runner Harold Rowell (Rudge) was asked to keep an eye in the last practice session on a fellow Lightweight Rudge runner, H. Knowles, who had still not qualified to race. When the session got underway, Harold tagged on behind Knowles until the latter's engine seized at the top of Creg Willeys hill. As the stricken bike would not restart, both machines were wheeled into a nearby farmyard where Harold removed the number from his bike, replaced it with the one from Knowles bike and quickly sent him off on it to qualify. Only after he had done his good deed did Harold begin to think about what would happen if it was found out that they had swapped machines part way through a lap. Knowles qualified, got his hoped for start, but retired from the race. Harold's action remained undiscovered, he had a fine ride and took second place in the Lightweight race on his Rudge.

It was the custom for many years that riders practised with only a front number-plate, adding side plates for the race. Plates were often a different colour (and sometimes a different shape) between practice and race.

The motorcycle-mounted numbers were supplemented by a tie-on waistcoat worn by each rider, which also carried his number. Tie-on waistcoats lost favour in the 1950s after riders progressed to one-piece leathers incorporating a panel in the back for the number to be sewn into. With the advent of fairings upon which to mount numbers, those on riders leathers were eventually dispensed with.

To achieve consistency and ensure that they were clear enough to be read by the timekeepers at speed, the TT and MGP organisers issued sets of official numbers to riders. In the early 1950s MGP riders had to pay £1 deposit on the set of bolt-on race numbers issued to them. This was a respectable sum at the time and as most riders finished the fortnight desperately short of cash, the numbers were almost always returned and deposits reclaimed.

For many years it was the custom at the TT for the previous year's race winner to be allocated number one, with the remaining numbers subject to ballot. An introduction in 1959 was that of 'seeding' the top riders in the Junior and Senior TT races and giving them early start numbers, something that Geoff Duke in his autobiography 'In Pursuit of Perfection' claimed to have been *'instrumental in persuading the ACU to bring in'.* The previous system of balloting for start numbers could see a top rider draw a 'late' number and so have the handicap of having to battle his way past many slow riders. This meant that he was not racing on equal terms with other top riders who may have drawn 'early' numbers and enjoyed relatively clear roads. From a spectator's point of view the new seeding system had the advantage of putting the top riders closer together on the road. This made it easier to measure the time intervals between them, so making it simpler (and more exciting) to follow the progress of the race. By 1960 the starting order of the 6 leading riders was decided by ballot, (by 1961 the leading 10 were balloted and by 1964 it was up to the best 20).

With as many as a hundred entries in some races, it can happen that an up-and-coming rider who has been allocated a number down in the 60s or 70s reveals such good form in practice that he deserves a higher starting number. As there are usually a few non-starters in every race, the organisers sometimes allocate such a 'dark-horse' a revised number, perhaps in the 20s.

In the early 2000s the organisers decided to allocate riding numbers for the Senior race in accordance with the fastest times achieved by the top 90 riders in practice. In 2003 the fastest rider was David Jefferies although, tragically, his death during the Thursday afternoon practice session meant that he never took his place on the grid with the number 1 plate. Next fastest was his TAS Suzuki team-mate Adrian Archibald and so he was allocated number 1. However, as he had not beaten the practice time of David Jefferies, Adrian declined the offfer of the number 1 plate and rode at number 0 in the Senior race; the first time that had happened.

Adrian Archibald rode to victory as No. 0 in the 2003 Senior TT on his TAS Suzuki.

ROADS OPENING CAR

There was a time in TT history when the roads comprising the Course were not closed to ordinary traffic during practice sessions. That changed after 1927 and a car was used to close the Course before riders were allowed out to practice or race. That procedure was dropped after the Second World War, and the roads are now reserved for racing activities by enforcement of the statutory Road Closing Orders that define the precise times that they are closed. The principal duty of the four-wheeler nowadays is to carry the 'Roads Open' plate and thus open the Course when practice or racing is finished, although it can also be seen with an 'Inspection' plate doing pre-race and between-race laps of inspection.

Early drivers provided their own cars, but during the 1930s firms like Austin, Morgan, Humber, Singer and SS Cars loaned vehicles for Road Opening duties. In the post-war period other makes were used, and they were organised through local firm, Mylchreest Motors. There have been many different car drivers, with usually two or three sharing the duties at each TT or MGP.

The need to hand the roads back for use by the Manx public with the minimum of delay after practising and racing has seen some spirited car-driving over the Mountain Course. Inevitably, this has resulted in the occasional clouting of a road-side bank, over-stressing of engines, etc, with consequent breakdowns and even a couple of fires. To reinforce the reliability of the Roads Opening ser-

Chief Travelling Marshal Peter Crebbin carries the 'Roads Open' plate on his Triumph at the 1956 TT. Others in the picture (from Peter's left) are Angus Herbert, Colin Broughton, Bob Foster and Jimmy Linskey on Triumphs that, for the first time, were fitted with radios

vice, the organisers arranged in the mid-1950s for a motorcycle mounted Travelling Marshal to follow immediately behind the car. The bike also carried a 'Roads Open' plate and could take over and complete the lap, if the car hit trouble. Such reinforcement is no longer felt to be necessary.

It has become the custom for major and minor celebrities attending the races to occupy the passenger seat of the Roads Open car and be taken on a rapid lap of the Course. Not everyone enjoys the experience, some finding it rather more rapid than they imagined it would be, particularly with today's cars getting around at close to 90 mph average lap speed. In a publicity stunt, ace rally driver of the time, Tony Pond, achieved a 100 mph lap of the TT Course on four-wheels in 1990, and he did it using a Rover Vitesse on closed roads. It was a flying lap and with a co-driver reading him pace notes, he got round in just under the magic target of 22 minutes 38 seconds.

Drivers have their share of tales to tell about experiences on Road Opening duties. Mike Kelly was a top MGP runner of the early 1960s and served as a Travelling Marshal for many years, so he had his share of excitement and high-speed activity over the Course on two wheels. Mike also drove the Roads Open car for a number of years and one particular four-wheel scare still has him shaking his head as he recalls it. At the end of one practice session he set out from St Ninians crossroads (the departure point for the Roads Open car) and was soon motoring well out of Union Mills and up the Ballahutchin. Taking a firm grip on the wheel, he set the car up at 110 mph for the demanding right-hander at Ballagarey, prior to the descent into Glen Vine. It was just after the corner as the road began to fall away downhill that, with gathering speed, he spotted the little grey saloon car tootling along at 30 mph - on closed roads! Fortunately, it was travelling in the same direction as Mike who had already begun to pull to the right-hand side for the stretch through Glen Vine, but it was still a scary moment that caused a flutter of the heart, an instant cold sweat and the acquisition of a few more grey hairs for our driver.

For most TT visitors, the passage of the Roads

Open Car after the last race of the week serves to indicate that their holidays are nearing an end and that there is almost a year to wait before they next watch racing over the Mountain Course - unless they are wise enough to return for the MGP.

Confirmation that the TT holiday is almost over comes with this familiar sign.

ROTARY NORTONS

The tale of the rotary-engined Nortons of the late 1980s and early 1990s is one of David and Goliath, for the once mighty Norton concern were by then almost a spent force in the world of motor-cycling and had negligible resources to devote to racing compared to the large Japanese manufactur-ers who held sway at the TT.

The rotaries had engines operating on the Wankel principle and, although some disputed the method of calculating their capacity, they quickly came to dominate British short-circuit racing after Brian Crichton converted a standard engine of the type used on police-machines into a potent racer.

The first Island appearance of the 'works' rotaries was at the 1988 TT, where they were ridden by Simon Buckmaster and Trevor Nation. Running at extremely high temperatures and spitting flames, the bikes were fast but they were found wanting by the demands of the TT Course, with niggling faults developing after a couple of fast laps.

Norton team boss Barry Symmons talks to Robert Dunlop about his practice times at the 1992 TT.

Trevor Nation on the way to second place in the 1990 Senior TT on his JPS Norton.

Robert Dunlop and Trevor Nation were Norton team-mates at the 1990 TT and there could hardly have been a greater contrast in rider physiques. Robert was 5ft 4ins in height and weighed 9 stone, whilst Trevor was 6ft 1in and weighed over 13 stone. But both were accom-plished riders and contributed to making the rotaries a major threat to the likes of Honda and Yamaha. With the bikes showing far greater reliability than in earlier years, Robert brought his Norton home to take third place in the Formula 1 race and Trevor came second in the Senior TT. Robert's abiding memory of riding the rotary was of the ease with which it would spin the rear wheel due to the combination of its awesome power and his light weight.

The rotary Norton's greatest glory came at the 1992 TT, where Steve Hislop chose to ride one in the Formula I and Senior races. Although a complicated funding arrangement saw his bike being leased and finished all in white, he enjoyed back-up from the Norton factory, as did the other Norton rider, Robert Dunlop. In charge of the Norton set-up was the highly experienced Barry Symmons.

Steve Hislop (Norton) on his way to victory in the Senior TT of 1992.

Steve Hislop spent the practice period getting used to riding the 150 bhp rotary-engined Norton, for with its almost total lack of engine-braking, its riding characteristics were very different to what he was used to. Fortunately, the Norton's use of a twin alloy spar frame, telescopic forks, single-shock rear suspension and radial tyres was fairly conventional for the class. Riding to second place in the week-opening Formula I race behind Phillip McCallen (after early leader Carl Fogarty on his Yamaha struck gearbox problems) showed that Steve learnt quickly, particularly as he lost time at his first pit-stop. This was because, for all the team's thorough preparation, as he pulled in for his first refuelling session, Steve confused the black and gold overalls worn by Johnny Rea's pit-crew with those of the similarly coloured Norton team and stopped at the wrong pit. Then, as a result of Robert Dunlop's early retirement at Kirk Michael with over-heating, he lost more time as his mechanics decided to strip off his front mudguard to allow more cooling air to the motor.

The Senior TT had recovered much of its former prestige by 1992 and was run as the last race of the week. Race-day dawned fine and with riders like Hislop, Fogarty, McCallen, Joey and Robert Dunlop all in with the chance of a win after their scorching practice times, fans knew they were in for a treat. They were not disappointed, for it turned into one of those races that would be talked about for years to come. Four seconds covered the first three (Fogarty, Hislop, Robert Dunlop) at the end of the first lap. Four seconds then covered the first two for the remaining five laps (apart from a bit of ebb and flow at pit-stops), and the lead changed five times between Fogarty (Yamaha) and Hislop (Norton). Manx Radio kept everyone up to date throughout the 226 mile battle in which the top two did not see each other, for the interval start kept them 2½ minutes apart (Fogarty rode at number 4, Hislop at 19). Informed only by signals from their support crews, it was down to each to ride his own race in a typical against-the-clock TT battle, whilst his opponent did the same elsewhere on the course. With both men pushing to the limit, Steve Hislop eventually triumphed over Carl Fogarty and his Yamaha, giving Norton their first Senior TT win since 1961. The evenly matched duo both entered the record books with Steve setting a new race record average speed of 121.28 mph, whilst Carl grabbed the outright lap record in his all or nothing last lap attempt to catch Steve, leaving it at 123.61 mph.

Steve Hislop's winning ride in 1992 on what became known as 'The White Charger' was undoubtedly the highlight of the rotary Norton's TT appearances. Thereafter, it was largely left to privateers to race the unique-sounding racers, and they were few and far between. The man who claims to have ridden the most rotary racing miles on the Mountain Course is Huw Hughes, for he campaigned his rotary Norton in the MGP from 1992 - 2002.

ROYAL CONNECTIONS

Whilst the TT has not been graced with quite as many royal visitors as events like the Derby and Wimbledon, it has had its share. During the 1930s the Duke of York (later to become King George

VI) was Patron of the ACU, but his brother the Duke of Kent is believed to have been the first royal visitor when he mingled with riders and officials on the start-line in 1932. The current Duke of Kent, came to open the new Grandstand in 1986 and his son, Prince Michael, not only attended the 1979 MGP but also donned riding kit and rode a lap of the Course on a Travelling Marshal's Honda that he borrowed for the purpose.

Chief Travelling Marshal 'Kipper' Killip briefs Prince Michael of Kent on the four-cylinder Honda that he rode on a lap of the Course in 1979.

Although an infrequent visitor in the period of more than 50 years that he has been Patron of the ACU, Prince Phillip the Duke of Edinburgh was present in 1949 and 1969, and the Earl of Snowdon was another to ride a lap on two-wheels when he paid a TT visit.

The latest royal visitor, and one who seems to have a genuine interest in bikes, is Prince William who visited the 2003 TT. Spotted spectating at several points around the Course, he was also taken for a lap in the Roads Opening car. A future Patron of the event, perhaps?

SCOREBOARD

A scoreboard has always been used at the Start and Finish area to record the progress of competitors in a TT race and, as their number increased, so the scoreboard had to be enlarged. Today it is a huge structure, for not only does it have to cope with a race entry of over 100 riders but there are actually two scoreboards facing the Grandstand, this duplication is so that spectators seated at both ends and riders' support teams in the Pits (that extend for the length of the Grandstand) can see the full race information.

The Start was at St Johns from 1907-1910 (on the 'Short Course'), and in 1908 it was reported that: *'The scoring board was placed opposite the Tynwald Inn . . . and the timing and scoring were both smartly accomplished so that the spectators in the vicinity were always in a position to gauge the positions of the various competitors'.*

An early version of the scoreboard, before the Start area was moved to the top of Bray Hill.

When the races moved to the Mountain Course in 1911 the Start was on the flat of Quarterbridge Road, a few hundred yards after the bottom of

The scoreboard scene has hardly changed from this 1920s shot.

Bray Hill. From there it moved to the top of Bray Hill in 1914 and to the Glencrutchery Road when the races returned in 1920. Both the Grandstand and the scoreboard were initially temporary structures that were erected for the race periods and dismantled after they were over.

At a time when so many calculating and recording processes are computerised, the race scoreboards are a fine example of tradition, although things have moved on of late. Computerisation and transponder timing have brought changes but timekeepers in their nearby 'box' still convey information on rider numbers, lap and accumulated race times to time auditors who then pass it to the Scouts who have been the mainstay of the scoreboard operation for so many years. (The use of clothes-pegs, drainpipes, multiple slips of paper and radios are involved in their Scoreboard activities.) Scouts eventually pass the information to white-overalled painters who, using gallons of white paint, transfer it to the scoreboards under each riders number in figures that are legible to those watching from the Grandstand and Pits.

The scoring system worked well from early days and reporting on the erection of a new Grandstand in 1926, the local press also mentioned that *'spectators at the Start are kept fully posted with information regarding the progress of the competitors around the course and incidents on the track, and the signalling system is the acme of perfection'*. In what was a classic example of not being able to leave well alone, the organisers attempted to improve on *'the acme of perfection'* by automating some aspects of the scoreboard operation in 1927. However, a report in 'The Motor Cycle' said: *'The new electrically operated scoreboard proved a failure and caused considerable confusion to those in the Grandstand'*. The manual system continued but there must surely have been problems in presenting all the information at the 1947 MGP, for the Lightweight and Junior classes ran concurrently with a total of 140 riders in the one race.

The introduction of round-the-Course commentaries went someway to keeping spectators in the Grandstand informed of what was going on in a race, however, such commentaries naturally tended to concentrate on the top riders and there was still a need for scoreboards to show information on the others. That information was vitally important to those in the Pits and one aspect, the 'clock' over each rider's name (introduced in 1920), was particularly helpful. As a rider passes certain named points on each lap (nowadays there are three) his pointer is moved on by the Scouts maintaining the scoreboard. Whilst it continues to move all is well, but if it stops then a worrying time can ensue for pit-crew and friends as they wait to learn the reason for the stop. Other helpful features are the indication of the lap that each rider is on, and the light over the rider's name that comes on when he reaches Cronk ny Mona, thus serving as an early warning signal of his impending arrival at the Finish.

Thoughts have been expressed down the years that the scoreboard should be *'updated'* and there has been talk of *'moving with the times'* but nobody has yet devised a viable alternative. Perhaps the first area of change may come in the Pits, where crews with their own computers might be linked to the organisers time-keeping system that gets more and more of its information from transponders fitted to all race machines. Electronically operated scoreboards may well follow, but will they be as clear and comprehensive as the present manual ones?

SCRUTINEERING

The official scrutineering of bikes before they go onto the TT Course is not the most popular of activities with riders, but it is an essential one. The main purposes of the detailed inspections that constitute the scrutineering process are to ensure that machines comply with the regulations for the event and are in a safe condition to race. In addition, since the requirement to wear crash-helmets was introduced in 1914, head-gear and general riding-gear have also been inspected. At one such early inspection of crash-helmets, several were confiscated for being in such poor condition that *'they wouldn't even keep the rain out'*. In a late 1940s helmet inspection episode, Vic Willoughby, later to join 'The Motor Cycle', told how a Scrutineer: *'put my "pudding basin" under his arm and, with an almighty tug, ripped out the inner harness. I protested that no prang could produce such a result but he insisted I should get another helmet. On a phoney pretext I persuaded him to release the damaged lid and took it to a cobbler who restitched the harness right through the shell. To camouflage the large stitches showing on the outside, I painted the whole thing black'*. Vic's helmet was accepted when next presented for inspection.

It is unlikely that the helmet of five times MGP winner Denis Parkinson would have stood up to test when he retired from racing in 1954. An obituary of Denis, who died in 2004, told how he acquired his helmet from Stanley Woods in 1936 for the sum of £2.50 and used it for the rest of his extensive racing career - one that included wins in Lightweight, Junior and Senior MGP races.

Today's thorough pre-race inspections aim to ensure that a rider will not go out in faulty riding-gear or on an inadequately prepared machine. But motorcycle racers are, by nature, risk takers and although aware of the demands that the TT Course puts upon their machines, most Scrutineers still have horror stories to tell about riders presenting bikes with major faults and poor preparation. One former Chief Scrutineer spoke of having *'scrutineered bikes which I wouldn't pass fit for a trip to the shops, let alone the TT Course'*.

Busy scenes like this are common as bikes queue to be scrutineered before every practice and race.

It was not so many years ago that sidecars presented considerable problems to scrutineers, for the demands of the Mountain Course required the strengthening of certain components. That was a fact not always well received by riders who, after presenting the outfits that they had been using at UK short-circuits for scrutineering, were told that they were not acceptable for the TT. The supplementary regulations now require that all UK based sidecars must be inspected and approved prior to travelling to the Isle of Man. In a move to ensure that the current high standards of preparation and appearance are maintained, the regulations also provide that *'Machines will not be approved if their appearance is not appropriate to the status of the event'.*

Despite the close attention of scrutineers, solo and sidecar machines can still get through with faults. (The busiest of MGP practice sessions can see almost 400 machines scrutineered). Whatever the reasons for that, there are recorded instances that have proved a shock to riders, mechanics and scrutineers. Things like the rider of a modern 600 who, part-way round his second lap, was forced to pull in and retire with his front brake caliper completely detached from the fork-leg and waving in the wind on the end of the hydraulic hose. The bolts that should have held it to the fork-leg were gone, and the rider was noticeably pale from thinking of the consequences of the caliper going into his front wheel at 150 mph.

It is now an accepted fact that the scrutineering process is designed to prevent accidents and save riders from injury. Well, a few years before his victory in the 1973 Lightweight MGP, Dave Arnold was down to race a Lightweight Ducati. It was in the days before the current brick-built scrutineering garages and the job was either done in a tent or, if the weather was fair, out in the open.

Bikes were wheeled up a wooden ramp onto a narrow platform, and with rider and scrutineer standing each side of the bike, the inspection - that involved pulling, pushing and squeezing various components - took place. At one critical moment in this particular inspection the Scrutineer thought that Dave was holding the bike and he thought that the Scrutineer was. Poised without means of support for a split second, the Ducati heeled towards Dave on its plunge to the ground. Months of preparation had gone into that bike and the rider instantly reached out to catch it. Lightweight it might have been by name but its impact was enough to break his arm. As a result, he acquired the unwanted status of being the only rider to be put out of a race through injuries sustained during scrutineering.

In another incident a Scrutineer was holding George Barker's Kawasaki by the left handlebar grip during pre-race inspection at the 1972 TT. The weight of the bike tipped slightly to the right and, suddenly, the Scrutineer was left holding only the rubber handlebar grip as the bike crashed to the ground. Maybe it was of some consolation to the rider that the grip came off in Scrutineering, rather than when he was fighting the bike at the bottom of Bray Hill. It is customary for grips to be wired on to the 'bars nowadays.

Scrutineers have the sometimes unenviable task of enforcing the FIM's detailed rules about machine construction and specification, and this can be a particular cause of aggravation where the rule is a fairly recent introduction and is one that riders have not made themselves fully aware of, (usually because they do not agree with it).

Scrutineering in progress during the 1970s. Nowadays the job is carried out in a brick building close to the Pits.

Although, in such circumstances, Scrutineers are only doing their job in enforcing the rules, that is not necessarily how riders see things, and they sometimes use their lack of agreement with, or ignorance of the rules as an excuse to make claims of officiousness that reflect unfairly on those who volunteer their services for the job of scrutineering. In an incident back in the early 1960s when former rider and Travelling Marshal Angus Herbert was Chief Scrutineer, he was faced with making a decision in accordance with the FIM rule-book in respect of new provisions regarding rear mudguards that would have seen the exclusion of all the 'works' teams and many of the private entries. In the ensuing uproar the Race Stewards found it expedient to by-pass the new rule, and the races went ahead.

Winner of the 1970 Senior MGP on a Cowles Matchless was Roger Sutcliffe and, as tradition dictates, that meant that he was not eligible to compete in the Manx the following year (he went on to the TT). However, at the 1971 Manx, Roger responded to a request to help out with scrutineering, and at the weigh-in before Thursday's Senior race he found himself in the unique position of scrutineering the same Ray Cowles Matchless that he had ridden to MGP victory the year before. The rider in 1971 was Neil Kelly, and he brought it home in an honourable 4th position.

Nowadays, it is part of the Scrutineers duties to be in attendance at pit-stops, where they do a quick visual inspection of machines as they are being refuelled or repaired. This they must do in an adrenalin-charged situation without tripping over bike, rider, pit-attendants, camera men, a roving commentator, and the on-going activity in the adjoining Pits.

The post-race measurement of engines can be seen as part of the scrutineering process (several Scrutineers are licensed Engine Measurers) and is always a time of tension for those involved in stripping the engines for measurement. Usually restricted to the first three finishers plus the bike that sets the fastest lap, it is a fairly private process, for not every racer wants his bike's inner secrets revealed to the world at large and the stripping is usually done by a mechanic. There was a slight raising of eyebrows when the call came for the engines of the first three finishers in the 1950 Clubman's (1,000cc) race to be stripped, for the man who stepped forward to pull-down the engine of the winning bike was the actual rider of that race winner, Alex Phillip. After the strip-down, Alex then had to reassemble it, for it was his only transport for the 300 mile trip home to Scotland for he and his wife.

Today the measuring process will go beyond engines, particularly in the difficult to police Production classes. Exhausts, petrol tanks and carburettors are all measured in an attempt to see that the bikes meet the regulations and fuel is analysed. Just how some of todays engine management systems are configured sometimes remains a mystery but, although they have the authority to do so, the organisers have yet to call for Production bikes to submit to power output measurements on a dynomometer as prescribed in the regulations. Understandable really, because who wants to be the unlucky man holding a rider's expensively prepared Fireblade at maximum throttle for output measuring, only for its engine to blow? Should the regulation ever be enforced, the job will probably fall onto the broad-shoulders of a Scrutineer.

SEEING THE WAY

It would seem to be a pre-requisite for racing over the demanding Mountain Course that riders can see where they are going. However, Mother Nature in her varied forms has often conspired to prevent this. One of her biggest influences is on the weather, which can be extremely varied over both practice and race periods at TT and MGP. On occasions 80-90% of the Course can be fit for racing but the remainder be unsuitable. This can be very frustrating, and there have even been instances where sea-mist has drifted in to reduce visibility on the Cronk y Voddy section, leaving well over 95% of the Course clear for racing and a tantalising few percent unsafe. Even when not combined with mist (as it often is), rain is another deterrent to riders seeing the way. In the days when goggles were used they were often discarded when they got misted-up and waterlogged.

Freddie Dixon was a TT winner who did not believe in using goggles. Getting minimal protection from a basic gauze fly-screen he took victory in the 1923 Sidecar and 1927 Junior TTs without any form of eye-protection. The tale is told that when regulations were introduced requiring riders to wear goggles while racing, Freddie wore a pair without lenses.

Freddie Dixon rounds Ramsey Hairpin on the way to third place in the 1924 Senior TT on a Douglas. He spurned the use of goggles even though he averaged over 60mph and was racing for nearly 4 hours.

Manxman Graham Oates was a former despatch rider in the First World War who lost the sight of one eye and suffered damage to the other after a gas attack. He was a man who went on to a remarkable career (described in 'Aurora To Ariel' by Bill Snelling) that included a ride in the 1924 Ultra-Lightweight TT on a two-stroke Powell. Given his limited vision, it was bad news for Graham when his one-and-only pair of spectacles were smashed by a stone thrown up by a fellow competitor during practice. Despite promises of speedy replacement after leaving them at the shop of a local optician, in Graham's words: *'Race morning on the way to the start, and panic - shop closed! Left one of the Powell chaps to find specs mender, grab the glasses and taxi in haste to the start'.* As the specs failed to arrive before his appointed start-time, he started without them *'. . . like a blind man, worried as much for others as myself'.* Somehow he reached half-distance and at his pit-stop his attendant thrust the glasses into his hands. Putting them on and setting off again he found *'Ye gods, I can actually see my way down Bray Hill without guessing where the road should be!'* Pressing on with an under-powered two-stroke that began to ail and with a front-brake that failed at Ramsey, he came home in eighth place.

The restricting effects of fog and rain on visibility and thus on riders and racing is understandable, but another Island hazard for competitors is bright sun. With morning and evening practice formerly taking place at sunrise and sunset, riders could be almost blinded by low sun on parts of the Course, and accidents have resulted from them suddenly coming upon such conditions. The organisers are aware of the points where the riders are first affected by the sun (Kirk Michael in the mornings heading east and Crosby in the evenings heading west) and a combination of permanent warning boards and marshals' flags are used to warn them. The abolition of morning practice has solved part of the problem.

It is not just the weather that affects a rider's capacity to see his way around the Island, for as Mother Nature distributes physical talents that vary from person to person, so it is with riders eyesight, some being blessed with better vision than others. The man who best illustrates this is Harold Daniell. Forced to wear what were almost pebble-lenses, turned down for war service due to poor eyesight, one feels that Harold should not really have been racing. But that was not how he saw it. Riding through his eyesight problems, he took second place in the Senior MGP and followed it with three Senior TT victories (1938, 1947, 1949) and numerous leaderboard placings.

One man well-versed in the problems of seeing the way was several times MGP winner Ken Bills, for he was an Optician and spectacles wearer. Ken turned his skills to producing prescription lenses for riders goggles, thus allowing them to dispense with their spectacles whilst racing.

An unusual way of carrying a spare pair of goggles is shown by this sidecar crew.

The old remedies for eyesight problems of spectacles, special goggles, etc, have all been overtaken nowadays by the use of modern contact lenses, but it was the use of such 'high-tech' visual aids that cost Michael Rutter victory in the Formula 1 race in 1998. Michael and Ian Simpson, both sons of former TT winners and both mounted on Honda RC45s, were race favourites and Michael led Ian for the first three laps. It was then that he lost a contact lens, which forced him to reduce speed. That resulted in his lead being whittled away, and him losing the race by 17 seconds. It was a bitter blow and one that was not eased by the fact that he also lost the Senior to Ian after leading for two laps, before being forced to retire with a puncture.

Riders now wear full-face helmets and built-in visors that yield improved safety and vision, but Mother Nature continues to create obstacles to vision, in this case millions of them in the form of insects that splatter themselves against riders windscreens and visors. It is customary for riders to fit transparent 'tear-offs' over the visor that can be removed as they get coated with flies, oil, dust etc, thus leaving a clean surface beneath. In addition, most riders will change their visor at their pit-stop - some even change helmets. Before the move to visors, riders wearing goggles sometimes kept a cleaning device behind the fairing. One favourite was a tennis ball with a slice cut out. Mounted somewhere in the handlebar region, it contained a piece of damp sponge which the rider would reach for, wipe his goggles and then return it to its holder. An even more basic method of fly removal was recommended by Graham Walker when he wrote some notes for beginners to the races in the late 1940s. In them he said: *'a sucked glove finger quickly applied to the goggles will remove squashed flies before they congeal'*. The snag with that system came on the second occasion that the rider wanted to suck a glove finger - which one had he used before?

SIDECARS

Described by more than one writer as 'A Breed Apart', to many sidecar racers the TT is the highlight of their racing year. Not usually blessed with the financial support that often flows in the direction of solo riders, in the words of Nick Harris, sidecar racing *'has produced a breed of racers that still seek difficult mountains to climb while not always taking the easiest way out of situations'*.

The first Sidecar TT was held in 1923 when the three-wheelers were literally faced with a mountain to climb. Still a narrow track, the Snaefell Mountain Road presented extreme difficulty to anyone wanting to pass with a 'chair, and taking to the grass verge was the usual procedure. There were only 9 starters in that first race and sidecars lasted for just 3 years. Although the races were accepted by the motorcycle manufacturers, they did not find favour with the sidecar makers due, so it was claimed, to the bad publicity that could ensue from the antics of the passengers and the alarming flexing of the bikes' girder forks while cornering. This flexing was visible to everyone, and it led to the addition of crude bracing in an attempt to reduce the problem.

Leaping Ballig Bridge in the 1920s. This was not the sort of image that sidecar manufacturers sought for their family-orientated products.

Unlike today, where solos and sidecars have their own practice sessions, no attempt was made to separate two and three-wheel classes during the 1920s and they all went out and practised together.

An attempt to restore the three-wheelers to the TT in 1933 failed due to lack of entries, but when sidecars gained their own World Championship they returned to the Island in 1954 and initially raced on the Clypse Course. The Clypse was generally very narrow making passing rather difficult. In addition, British sidecar outfits had the 'chair' on the left, whilst Continentals invariably had theirs on the right, which could create more problems. Towards the end of the 1958 race, British crew

Ernie Walker and passenger Don Roberts were lapped by race winners Walter Schneider and Hans Stauss. To draw attention to the fact that they wanted to pass, German passenger Stauss grabbed English passenger Roberts leg and shook it! In 1960 Sidecars moved back to the Mountain Course, where they have delivered exciting racing ever since.

Although Eric Oliver won the returning Sidecar TT in 1954 on a Norton, his victory was down to his superior riding skills, for BMW outfits - with an advantage of some 10 bhp - dominated sidecar racing through the remainder of the 1950s, the 1960s (apart from Chris Vincent's victory on a BSA in 1962) and into the 1970s. BSA achieved more success when a sidecar race for 750 machines was introduced in 1968, but the Japanese took over in the 1970s, firstly with two-stroke machines from Yamaha and then with four-stroke fours from several of the Japanese manufacturers.

During the 1950s specialist sidecar manufacturers supplied their 'chairs' to be bolted on to a solo. Keen to obtain publicity for their wares, the sidecar race made provision for a 'Manufacturers Award' that went to the sidecar maker with the best team of three drivers who used his product. Strange as it may seem, it did not matter that they might be driving three different makes of motorcycle.

Eric Oliver as seen by 'Sallon'.

The sidecars have never fitted 'seamlessly' into the TT meeting. For their part they feel that they are treated as second-best to the solos, whilst solo runners sometimes question why sidecars are there at all. This occasionally creates the perception that sidecar folk are given to moaning but, sometimes, they are justified in doing so. They certainly wondered why they had been singled out when the organisers introduced a 'No Overtaking' zone for the three-wheelers at the 1965 event. On the twisty approach to Ballaugh, road-signs were erected to prevent the chairs from passing each other. Penalty for breaking the new rule was exclusion.

Chris Vincent and Eric Bliss riding to victory with their BSA outfit in 1962.

George O'Dell's 'Seymaz' was the best sidecar outfit that money could buy in the late 1970s. Power was provided by Yamaha two-stroke engines of 500 or 750 capacity.

One man who drove his first Sidecar TT in 1966 is Roy Hanks and he is still racing at the top level. An essential element in sidecar racing is the passenger and Roy said of the breed: *'There are people who can ride as a passenger without thinking. Then there are passengers who have to work hard at being good and there's those that just hang on'.* Acting as a passenger on a sidecar outfit at the TT has always been the preserve of those with a different mindset to the majority of the population. The racing of three-wheelers can be more physical than riding a solo, and this is particularly so during the long TT races - for both driver and passenger. A driver usually builds-up speed during practice, finding more and more bumps and making the passenger's job of holding on to a flat platform an ever more difficult business. After the Thursday afternoon practice session in 1983, former winner Trevor Ireson was informed by his passenger that he had reached his personal limit and could not go on. By the end of practice week a couple more passengers had given up. Indeed, one of them just disappeared without trace, leaving his driver to assume that he had departed the Island and returned home.

It was not only passengers who were concerned at the speed of the outfits during the 1980s, for they also became a worry to the organisers. A Formula 2 sidecar class was introduced to run with the main sidecar races in 1984 and it was for up to 350cc two-strokes and up to 600cc four-strokes. In 1990, in a move aimed at cutting speeds, the Formula 2 class became the only one available to the three-wheelers and the previous main sidecar class of up to 1,000cc machines was dropped. Although the two-strokes had dominated the Formula 2 class when it was introduced, soon after 1990 the four-cylinder 600cc four-strokes became the winning motors. Indeed, within a few years they were lapping faster than the previous 'big' class had done and are now lapping in under 20 minutes, giving a lap speed of 115 mph.

SPEEDS

Speed - always the big attraction, to both riders and spectators. The organisers of the first TT wanted speed from their competing machines, but they wanted it to be allied to reliability, respectable fuel consumption, and to be achieved from motorcycles of a touring nature. However, the competitive spirit in which the event was held meant that their high ideals were soon eroded, as manufacturers concentrated on getting ever more speed in order to overcome the competition. First to go were the fuel consumption limits, followed by the requirement for effective silencers, then riders were no longer obliged to carry tools. The competing machines - initially lightly converted road-going models - soon became competition specials built with racing in mind, and the most successful reflected the words of Norton's famous competition manager, Joe Craig, who said: *'the ideal racing engine has power designed into it'.* Some manufacturers could not afford to go down that route and had to tune their roadster engines for TT racing, but they stood little chance of winning against the purpose designed racers of a firm like Norton, who not only set up special competition departments to ensure continuous development but, to make doubly certain of success, they also employed the most talented riders of the day.

Joe Craig (left) oversees preparations for a test on a Norton race engine.

For over 50 years from the mid-1920s well into the 1970s, out-and-out racing bikes ruled the roost at the TT. The position was summarised by the words of TT journalist and author Laurie Cade in the mid-1950s with: *'they have entirely departed from the original terms of reference, and are no more like tourist machines than a racehorse is like a farmhorse'.*

The introduction of 'Formula' events (first tried in 1959 but quickly dropped) was supposed to create classes for machines that were the same as you could buy, thus excluding the no-expense-spared factory specials. Reintroduced in the 1970s, they achieved some degree of success, but the Formula bikes raced by the Honda factory riders were hardly thick on the showroom floors and the 'Formula' regulations seemed to allow ever more specialised and expensive racing machinery.

So, just what speeds have been achieved down the years? Rem Fowler set the fastest lap at the first TT in 1907 at an average speed of 42.91 mph, and estimated that his maximum speed was about 60 mph. By 1920, Norton estimated that their bikes were capable of 70 mph on the flat and 76 mph downhill. The roads of the Course improved considerably during the mid-1920s, as did race engines, and in 1927 the 500cc Nortons of Stanley Woods and Joe Craig both averaged 93.7 mph over a one-mile stretch of the Sulby Straight. That location became a favourite timing point for many years, but the published information on the speeds achieved there sometimes omitted to mention such factors as road and weather conditions which could materially affect the speeds achieved. It was no coincidence that the best riders invariably set the fastest times on the Sulby Straight, because the speeds reached depended on the exit speed from the preceding Quarry Bends, and how late a rider left his braking for Sulby Bridge. Figures from the 1930s reveal the continuing increases in speeds:

1934 TT, Jimmy Simpson (Norton) 106.5 mph.
1935 TT, Stanley Woods (Moto Guzzi) 112.5 mph.
1937 TT, Stanley Woods (Velocette) 122.49 mph
1938 TT, Jock West (BMW) 130.4 mph

The sort of postcard that TT fans send to their friends from the Island has always been the type that extols the speed aspect of the races rather than scenic views of Douglas.

It was inevitable that riders got to know where and when timing operations were in progress and some resorted to 'foxing' by easing the throttle and so concealing their true speeds. They were probably the same riders who rarely recorded fast laps in practice when timed just from the Grandstand. However, when timed from Ballaugh to Ballaugh or Ramsey to Ramsey they were usually much quicker.

Racers rely on the information provided by revolution counters (that measure engine speed rather than road speed). If road speed needs to be known it has to be calculated from rev counter readings, taking account of factors like the gearing used.

The need to run the racers on 72 octane petrol in the immediate post-war period served to restrict speeds for several years. By 1951 (when running on 80 octane) factory rider Bill Doran (AJS) hit 124.14 mph at Sulby, but was reported as reaching an incredible 133 mph on the Mountain Mile with a strong following wind. The speeds of non-works runners at the TT always tends to be lower than the 'works' men, as do the speeds recorded at the MGP.

Speeds continued to rise, with Les Graham (MV Agusta) reaching 128.57 mph at Sulby in 1952. As streamlining came into use in the 1950s it seemed to add a few more mph and by the end of the decade the big MV Agustas were hitting 138 mph at Sulby, whilst the best private runners on British singles were just breaking 125 mph. On such a fast Course no amount of spirited riding could make up for such a deficiency in speed between singles and multis. In the early 1960s 'The TT Special' put its watches on other classes at Sulby, with sidecars clocked at 118.45 mph and the best 50cc at 86.97 mph. The Sulby Straight was by no means the fastest part of the Course but it did allow for timing over a one-mile stretch. By the mid-1960s not only were the British singles running at a huge speed disadvantage to the big Italian multis, they were also losing out in straight-line speed to the Japanese Lightweights. This is shown by the speeds recorded by Mike Duff as he passed The Highlander in 1965. Mike was a top-flight rider with quality machinery, and his bikes were amongst the fastest in each class. The figures recorded for the four classes in which he rode were:

125cc Yamaha	125 mph
250cc Yamaha	143.4 mph
350cc AJS 7R	122.9 mph
500cc Matchless	137.1 mph

New records were set for the sidecars in 1973, with the Konig powered outfit of Jeff Gawley hitting 136 mph. 'The TT Special' gradually dropped the measuring of speeds, but those of the Japanese race machines continued to grow. 'Motorcycle News' dabbled with a speed gun occasionally and in 1980 they took times on the drop from Creg ny Baa to Brandish, a stretch considered by many to be the fastest on the Course. Top figures from the damp Formula 1 race were set by Graeme Crosby (Suzuki) 163 mph and Mick Grant (Honda) 159 mph, with the fastest sidecars managing 141 mph.

The accurate recording and publication of maximum speeds now seems to be a thing of the past. Maybe it is a good thing because, for the average spectator they can be truly frightening. The fastest publicised speed at the TT was that of Steve Hislop in the early 1990s, when he was timed by radar at 192 mph on the Sulby Straight and about which he said: *'That's scary - it's frightenly fast - at the speeds we're doing you just head for the gaps between the green bits'.* But competitors in the Grandstand are now aware of the speeds of riders who flash by on the narrow ribbon of road in the Start and Finish area, because they are shown by a large digital display. The fastest Formula 1 and Senior runners are hitting an incredible 168 mph in 5th gear, with 600s some 10 mph slower. Throughout the TT's history it has taken a special sort of rider to get the maximum out of the race machines of each era, and it is little wonder that the top riders of each generation have been regarded in awe by knowledgeable spectators and the man in the street.

STARTERS/FINISHERS

The number of starters and finishers in TT races has varied considerably down the years. At the first, held on 28th May 1907, there were 25 machines and riders lined up opposite Tynwald Hill at St Johns, ready to tackle 10 laps of the 15 mile and 1,430 yard course. Private owners had each paid a 3 guinea entry, whilst entries made by 'manufacturers or agents engaged in the motorcycle trade' paid 5 guineas. Soon after 10.00 am the first two riders were despatched, followed one minute later by the next pair.

Riders in the first TT were required to make a 10 minute stop at half-distance, after which the 16 remaining competitors set off on another 5 laps. A little over four hours after he had started, Charlie Collier (Matchless) crossed the finishing line at the end of his 10th lap to take first place in the single-cylinder class. Rem Fowler (Norton) was the first man home in the multi-cylinder class. Last man to finish was 'Pa' Applebee who scraped in at one minute before 4 o'clock, the time when the roads of the Course were due to be reopened to the public. In total, there were 11 finishers.

Riders who were known to be 'works' entries at the TT tended to be held in slight awe by spectators, but a look at the entry list for the 1928 Lightweight TT shows that out of 27 entries a total of 22 were 'works' entries. Of the 5 remaining, 4 were entered by companies in the motorcycle trade and only one entry, that of Harry Meageen on a 2.46 HP Rex Acme (JAP), had the appearance of a genuine private entry made by the rider himself. Manufacturers with entries in the race were The Cotton Motor Co., Dot Motors (1926) Ltd., The Excelsior Motor Co. Ltd., New Gerrard Motors (Edinburgh), New Imperial Motors (1927) Ltd., O.K. Supreme Motors Ltd., The Rex Motor Manufacturing Co. Ltd., The Enfield Cycle Co. Ltd.

Entries were down in all classes during the late 1930s, although public enthusiasm for the races remained high. There are invariably a few non-starters for practice from those whose entries are accepted, and by race-day a few more are usually missing. However there were 42 entries for the 1937 Junior and 39 turned up to practice. Unusually, all 39 also started the race. Numbers were also low in the Lightweight TT of 1962, although the lack of quantity was made up with much quality. The race received only 38 entries, but 18 different makes were represented, including the very best works machines and riders in what was a golden era for the TT.

When the MGP restarted after the Second World War the Lightweight class was run concurrently with the Junior. In 1947, out of 157 entries in those two classes, 140 riders started the race and they were despatched at 10 second intervals. The first rider was reckoned to be past Creg ny Baa before the last one was sent on his way, and it was probably the most crowded field in an Island race. Eric Briggs took victory in the Junior on a Norton at an average speed of 74.64 mph and Austin Munks brought his Moto Guzzi home at the head of the Lightweight field at 70.63 mph.

140 riders queue to start the combined Junior and Lightweight MGP of 1947.

Most TT races have been of the interval start type, with riders departing singly or in pairs, at intervals that have ranged from ten seconds to one minute. It is a system that does not make a race easy to follow for the uninitiated, but it gives a unique character to the TT where riders race against the clock with some opponents, as well as racing wheel to wheel with others. It is exciting enough but, perhaps in an attempt to add to the drama, the ACU proposed to start riders in groups of nine at 90 second intervals at the 1970 TT. The new system was tried in the Thursday afternoon and, whatever the views of spectators, it received a firm thumbs down from riders and was not used for the races. The 1970 event received a record 667 entries across all classes and by 1989 that had risen to 759. In 2003 a total of 660 entries were accepted, although the event was over-subscribed and some entries had to be refused.

A typical TT will see competitors riding a total of some 4,000 laps over the practice and race periods and that equates to about 150,000 miles. The event is known to be hard on machinery and an analysis of race retirements over the 20 year period of 1952-71 showed that the percentage of retirements across all classes varied between a high of 69% and a low of 43%. With the trend towards racing of production-based machines, reliability levels at today's TT are higher than they have ever been and finishing rates of over 75% are quite common, indeed, in the Junior MGP of 1996 an incredible 90% of starters finished the race.

The 2000 Lightweight 400 TT saw every rider who finished claiming either a silver or bronze replica. New Zealand's Brett Richmond (Honda) pictured at Stella Maris was the victor.
Inset: Bill Smith (Yamaha) was the last finisher. Bill was riding his last TT in a career that spanned 43 years, countless replicas and 4 TT wins.

CHAPTER 9

TALES OF . . .

STRANGE BUT TRUE

The excitement generated at Ballacraine by the early TT races was too much for one Manxman. The 'Peel City Guardian' reported of a race before 1910 that *'Most probably as an outcome of the motorcycle race practising, the death occurred on Friday evening of Mr. John Crellin, dyer of Ballacraine, aged 73. He was lying against a hedge, where he had full view of the riders in their difficult task of rounding Ballacraine corner. Suddenly he collapsed and fell. Quickly lifted up, in a few seconds he was found to be dead'.*

*

One of the biggest problems in the early TT races was the amount of dust thrown up by the riders. Jack Marshall who won the single-cylinder class on his Triumph in 1908 recalled that there were several proprietary solutions that were supposed to minimise dust and *'In an attempt to damp down the dust, the officials sprayed the course with an acid solution which was supposed to keep things moist. The acid got on to our clothes and in a couple of days they looked as if the rats had been at them!'*

*

In today's world, where everyone expects instant information about all aspects of a sporting event, it is difficult to realise that the early TT races had no public address system and certainly no Manx Radio. The only means of dispensing information was via a man with a megaphone who would tour the front of the Grandstand area advising spectators on race positions, retirements, etc. Those watching elsewhere would have to maintain their race cards and indulge in a little amateur time-keeping to follow the progress of the race, but even then they were never completely sure of the results until they got back into Douglas. Sometimes the Roads Open car carried a board with the first three finishers numbers displayed, and the Grandstand area eventually gained a public address system, but it was not until 1955 that this was extended to about five locations around the Course.

Frank Sheene waits to go out for practice on his BSA Gold Star at the 1953 TT.

*

It is well known that after sampling the TT, Barry Sheene decided that the event was not for him and he never missed an opportunity to say so. But his father, Frank, had earlier found Island racing much more to his liking and competed in five Clubman's TTs and four MGP.

*

Manxman Neil Kelly is the only TT winner to have been born on the TT Course. Living on Bray Hill, Neil became accustomed to motorcycles passing his front door at high speed and after army service that involved a spell in one of their motorcycle display teams, he came back to the Island and started racing. He has gone down in history as winning the 500cc class of the 1967 Production TT, and by doing it on a Velocette he also has the distinction of being the last man to take an Island victory on that marque.

Neil Kelly served as a Travelling Marshal after he stopped racing. Here he launches a BSA Rocket Three over Ballaugh. The inclined engine distinguishes it from the Triumph Trident, although somewhere along the way this BSA has collected Triumph tank-badges.

*

Mick Grant was threatening to win a TT in the early 1970s and was capable of very quick laps. However, in an attempt to improve both his Course knowledge and riding he did several laps in a van with veteran Billy McCosh. Now both recognised that Mick already lapped appreciably faster than Billy, but Mick also realised that he could still learn from Billy's extra experience. This proved to be the case and, after some persuading, Mick accepted that Billy had a better line at Sarah's Cottage and Rhencullen, whilst Billy found it difficult to believe just how quick Mick was taking some parts, including his flat-out passage through the bottom of Barregarrow.

Riding a Bantam, jumping Ballaugh Bridge and smoking a cigarette - how did he do it?

*

The organisers experimented with computerisation of the TT race results during Mike Hailwood's come-back year of 1978. The experiment was abandoned when, after the Formula 1 race, test material got mixed up with the real results and showed the winner to be Mike Hailwood on a 50cc Vespa at a race average speed of 240 mph.

*

There was a strange incident in the Senior race of 1982 when Dave Dean saw a spectator waving a red jacket at the scene of a two-man accident at the sweeping Doran's Bend. Dave took it as a signal that the race had been stopped and toured to Kirk Michael before waking-up to the fact that the race was still very much on. Although the Clerk of the Course was willing to credit him with the three minutes that he was estimated to have lost, the International Jury (who are the top appeal body on race matters) would not do so. Dave therefore finished 15th instead of 10th.

*

Everyone knows that the humble BSA Bantam started out at 125cc, so a glance at the results of the 1989 Production TT indicating that the Bantam Racing Club won the Team Award in the 1300cc class requires a second read. It turned out to be true and, for good measure, they repeated it in the Formula 1 race. Seems that you do not actually need a Bantam to be a member of the Bantam Racing Club - a big Yamaha, Honda or Suzuki will do nicely.

*

Jim Moodie finished 8th in the Supersport 400 TT in 1990 and immediately submitted a protest on the grounds that the bikes of the first seven finishers did not comply with the race regulations. Strangely, the organisers seemed more concerned as to whether Jim had complied with the correct procedures for submitting a protest than they did about the legality of the first seven finishers, several of whom admitted breaking the rules in the manner that Jim was protesting about. Refusing to enforce their own regulations against the infringers, the organisers dismissed the protest!

*

It may seem strange, but races have been won and lost through incidents involving filler-caps, so a good reliable filler-cap is much prized. Joey Dunlop was a man who had experienced his share of problems with ill-fitting caps, so was careful of the ones he used. In 1995 he retired in the morning's Ultra-Lightweight race at The Hawthorn and hitched a lift back to the Start in the Course Inspection car. It was only later, when his Castrol Honda was being fuelled-up for the afternoon's Lightweight race, he remembered that, incredible as it may seem, he used the same filler-cap on the 250 as he did on the 125. It was too late to recover the one from his stranded 125 at The Hawthorn, so another cap was chosen for the 250 and, being very careful at his pit-stop, Joey went on to win the race.

*

The opening Formula 1 race at the 1998 TT was postponed from Saturday to Sunday due to bad weather. For most riders that was an inconvenience, but for potential winner Bob Jackson it was a disaster because his sponsor, Winston McAdoo, would not allow his bikes to be raced on a Sunday on religious grounds. Another strange incident deserving the title of disaster befell top rider Iain Duffus the same year. He slipped in the Paddock, broke his leg and put himself well and truly out of the TT.

*

The 1999 MGP meeting saw a bizarre incident occur on the Mountain Road above Ramsey. It was just before the roads closed for Wednesday evening's practice that a van coming down the Mountain had a brake disc shatter. Hot fragments of disc finished in the roadside heather, setting it on fire. Despite the best efforts of the Fire Brigade (handicapped by lack of water), the fire continued to blaze and, although affecting only a relatively short stretch of the Course, smoke and flames were so thick that the practice session was abandoned.

*

In the early years of the new millenium the local Health & Safety set-up turned their attention to the TT races. First thoughts suggest that was bound to be a meeting of opposites, but, fortunately, they confined their initial activities to the Pits and Paddock areas, looking at things like refuelling, unprotected trailing cables from tyre-warmers, etc. However, there is on-going Health & Safety interest in the TT and MGP meetings, with other areas being subject to Risk Assessment. Let us hope that does not impinge on the racing, for the Inspectors would certainly be most unwelcome if they tried to dictate how fast riders could take Quarter Bridge, Ballacraine, and such.

Carlo Ubbiali peels into Parkfield Corner riding his fully streamlined 125cc MV on the Clypse Course in 1957.

STREAMLINING

Today streamlining is accepted as the norm. Indeed, with the growth in racing of production-based bikes, many of the machines out on the TT Course are difficult to distinguish from showroom models, although most will have had their standard plastics replaced with identical, but lighter, race versions.

A little over fifty years ago streamlining was in its infancy on race bikes, even though basic forms of enclosure had been used on some pre-war record breakers. The streamlining that we now take for granted was the subject of much experimentation and in the early 1950s became almost all-enveloping.

Initially there were few regulations covering the use of streamlining, although the FIM ruled against the use of total enclosure of man and machine by specifying that a rider must be able to separate from his bike in the case of an accident. It was a wise move because, even without the rider completely enclosed, there were several mystery crashes that were put down to the build up of fumes within the fairing affecting riders responses as they crouched behind their screens. In 1958 the FIM ruled that streamlining had to be of the 'dolphin' variety that we are familiar with today, so leaving the front wheel mostly exposed.

Whilst factories welcomed the speed advantage to be gained from streamlining, riders were also glad of the increased protection from wind buffeting, rain, insects, etc. Machine enclosure is taken for granted nowadays, but fairings and belly-pans still need careful attention to design to withstand the rigours of the TT Course. If a mounting breaks loose it can lead to a very dangerous situation and, although riders will seek the lightest possible plastics, they must not be too flimsy. In the 1989 F1 event, the fairing on Steve Hislop's factory Honda was so light that the nose caved in during the race.

Steve Hislop en-route to a 120 mph lap in 1989. Such was his speed that it caused the nose of his fairing to collapse.

The streamlining of sidecars has progressed through the fitting of separate fairings on bike and chair, to the quickly-detachable, one-piece type that covers the whole outfit.

TESTING THE WINNERS

For many years through the 1930s to the 1960s it was the custom for the manufacturers of British-built TT winners to make their actual race-winning machines available to 'The Motor Cycle' and 'Motor Cycling' for test after the race. Amazing as it may seem, most of those tests were carried out up on the Mountain Mile on open roads, usually very early in the morning following the race.

Vic Willoughby prepares to test Ray Amm's 1953 TT winning Norton on the Mountain. Amongst his audience are Ray Amm (leaning on bonnet) and his wife, with Graham Walker (far right) and Norton race supremo Joe Craig (second right).

The factories must sometimes have felt some concern at handing over their precious models for test, although they were probably reasonably happy when the testing was done by someone like former TT runner Vic Willoughby when he was on the staff of 'The Motor Cycle'.

Just as difficult to believe nowadays is an article that appeared in 'The Motor Cycle' of January 1934 in which they reported doing a genuine road-test of Stanley Woods Senior TT winning Norton. It was fitted with a speedometer, silencer and bulb-horn as a gesture to road legality, although they also speed-tested it on an open pipe and revised jetting. Their assessment was that: *'In sheer speed*

Bruce Anstey on the 600cc Triumph that he rode to victory in the 2003 Junior TT.

and acceleration the machine is . . . in no way specially outstanding. The honest-to-goodness maximum speed is probably very little over 105 mph, and there are quite a number of TT mounts capable of much the same'. The tester, 'Torrens' (pen-name for the magazine's Editor, Arthur Bourne), went on to attribute the bike's TT success to its steering, road-holding and cornering - plus a little input from Stanley and the Norton race organisation.

It seemed to be mainly the British factories that loaned their machines for testing and when they stopped winning in the mid-1950s, the testing stopped soon after, (although Vic Willoughby did manage a few rides on foreign machines). But, in 2003 Bruce Anstey rode a Triumph Daytona 600 to victory in the Junior TT and, perhaps coincidentally, the bike was later made available for Frank Melling to test on behalf of Britain's longest-running magazine 'Motor Cycle Sport and Leisure'.

The days of testing racing bikes on the Mountain were over and Frank Melling used a short circuit. Also, on his own admission, most of his racing was done on classic machinery so he was not the man to push the Triumph to its limits. But his familiarity with the old British singles did allow him to make pertinent comparison between the nature of the bikes used to win TT races in the 1950s and those used today. In his words: *'ride a current race bike and it will not let you have a peaceful time. It accelerates constantly; brakes ruthlessly; corners without the need to be coaxed or persuaded. There are no mental respites for the rider on straights and hills do not exist. The acceleration and braking is simply unbroken, relentless and all consuming'.* By comparison: *'Braking, acceleration and cornering all demand negotiation with a classic . . . the physical workload is much lower on a classic but the distractions from the act of racing are much, much higher'.*

THE CHEQUERED FLAG

Whilst it is a less common occurrence in Isle of Man racing now that riders are seeded for start numbers, it can still happen that the first rider to receive the chequered flag for finishing a race is not the actual race winner. This may seem a strange business to those accustomed to watching races that employ a massed-start, but it is due to the TT and MGP use of the interval starting system. In such a case the winner may have started, say, 50 seconds after the rider who started first. If the winner completes his race in 30 seconds less than the rider who both started and finished first on the road, he will still take the chequered flag 20 seconds after his rival. It is not an easy scenario for fans of massed-start races to understand, but it is all part of Island racing.

When the chequered flag was introduced it was a big device, sometimes up to five feet square. Now that was no problem for the flag-waver in the adrenalin-filled moments of greeting the first few finishers, but after that it began to get a bit heavy and, whilst not obliged to wave it at the later runners, even holding it out became a bit of a chore. Should it be a wet finish to the race, then the ever-increasing weight of the flag could make it difficult even to hold out.

In conventional massed-start races, once the chequered flag goes out it signals the end of the race for each rider that passes it. But that is not always the way in the interval start Island races, for the rider who crosses the line seconds, even minutes, after the winner could be starting another lap, and the regulations allow him to do so. The rule of thumb operated by the organisers is that riders will be allowed through to start another lap for as long as there is a reasonable expectation that they may be able to finish within the time needed to win a Replica (or other award).

The business of some riders having to be flagged off and others being allowed to go through for another lap has been known to cause confusion. There was no real problem in the 1920s and 1930s when fields were relatively small and competitors were despatched at 1 minute intervals. Indeed, there was frequently enough time for the organisers to produce a card with the rider's number on that was displayed with the chequered flag.

Winner of the Senior MGP in 1955 was Geoff Tanner (Norton). Here he takes the chequered flag while a marshal also holds out a board with his riding number on (no.1) to avoid any confusion. Geoff also won the Junior the same year, but in that race his riding number was 104 which meant that he had a lot more traffic to negotiate. Note that the MGP organisers waved their chequered flag from the opposite side of the road to those running the TT.

Nowadays the waver of the chequered flag has a small team feeding him with information and he will try, by a combination of waving and finger-pointing, to convey to riders travelling at 150 mph, exactly who is to do what. It is hardly surprising that there have been occasional misunderstandings and some riders have gone through to start unnecessary extra laps. Although they soon get stopped, the occasional one has made it as far as

It is a two-handed job for the flagman to signal the end of the race for Freddie Frith as he crosses the line to take third place in the 1938 Senior TT.

Ballacraine. Whilst no real harm is done if the confusion results in a rider starting an extra lap, there have been instances wherea competitor has come in a lap early as a result of seeing the chequered flag waved for someone else. When that happened the organisers, if convinced of the genuiness of the mistake, ask the timekeepers to calculate an average lap time, add it to the rider's recorded time and accord him a finish.

Finishing line officials checking and double-checking that they will put the chequered flag out at the right moment.

THE PITS

A Pit is the name given to the Course-side space allocated to a rider to carry out refuelling and repairs, and at the TT the provision has always been very basic. When the event first moved to the Mountain Course in 1911 the Start and Finish was located between the bottom of Bray Hill and the Quarter Bridge. There was no room for Pits at that spot and riders could choose to refuel at Braddan Bridge or Ramsey. By 1914 the Start had moved to the top of Bray Hill where small timber-framed cubicles at the side of the Course were provided for each rider and that became the only point at which they were allowed to refuel.

Matchless rider Bert Colver refuels and makes adjustments in 1914.

Similar provision was made when the Start was moved to the Glencrutchery Road in 1920 and the principle of allocating each rider a cramped space of barely a machine's length endures to this day.

A well-worn cliché that has, nevertheless, been proved to be true, is that a TT race can be won or lost in the Pits. At early TT races riders were required by the rules to carry tools and they often needed them for repairs out on the Course. That requirement was eventually dropped and in the search for weight-saving and increased speed, most riders left tools in the Pits and put thoughts of Course-side repairs out of their minds. Riders have always been prohibited from receiving any assistance with repairs or refuelling outside their Pits and the penalty for infringing that provision was exclusion. Indeed, it was not until 1935 that a rider's Pit-Attendant was allowed to assist with machine repairs at the Pit, prior to that he could only help with refuelling.

If a rider struck trouble on the Course in days gone by and could get his stricken machine to the Pits, he could, with the assistance of a good Attendant, carry out fairly major repairs and still get back in the race. Replacement of footrests, wiring-up of exhausts and broken bracketry, even replacement of a clutch were possible, if he had the right tools and spares. Nowadays riders do not really expect to carry out repairs mid-race and a fault usually means retirement. Pit-stops are now made with the primary aims of refuelling, changing a visor (or helmet), taking a drink and, in some cases, replacing the rear-wheel to obtain the benefits of a new tyre. But, in today's close-fought races, those tasks must be carried out with the maximum efficiency and in the minimum of time, because the old

" Now, all you've gotta' do is to keep cool and the race is in your pocket ! "

This cartoon first appeared in 'The Story of the TT' by Geoff Davison. Whilst there has always been scope for confusion at a Pit-stop, today a rider is permitted two Pit Attendants and a Timekeeper (who may clean his screen and change his visor). The rider may also attract the attention of a scrutineer, camera-man, commentator and, frequently, the close proximity of riders and crews in the adjoining pits.

cliché still holds good and the loss of a few seconds to an opponent whilst stationary really can cost a rider the race. One man who knows the truth of this is Bob Jackson, a privateer who had threatened to achieve a TT win for several years in the 1990s. Riding a Kawasaki that was fractionally off the pace of the works Honda RC45s of Michael Rutter and Ian Simpson at the 1998 TT, Bob fitted an enlarged petrol tank for the 6 lap Senior race, meaning he needed to stop once to refuel while his opponents stopped twice. Come the race and Rutter held the lead initially before getting a puncture and retiring. Simpson moved into the lead but lost it when he stopped his Honda for petrol at the end of the second lap and Jackson went straight through and into the lead. He then came in for his single stop at the end of the third lap and was on schedule for victory until delayed by a filler-cap that was reluctant to screw back in place. The extra 40 seconds that were spent fumbling with the filler cap in the Pits cost Bob the race - by a margin of just 3.7 seconds.

THE TRADE

The Trade is the name given to the suppliers of components such as sparking-plugs, brake-linings, carburettors, tyres, petrol and oil, who have always provided essential support to manufacturers, riders and tuners throughout the practice and race periods. Eric Williams, who won the 1914 Junior TT on an AJS, told how *'The Trade Barons waited on competitors with their respective green, red, brown and gilded tins, to fill or top you up before you could as much as bat an eyelid - and paid you a bonus to allow them to do it!'.*

Each Trade 'Baron' would normally base himself at a hotel or garage that would serve as his headquarters. Depending on the service offered, riders and manufacturers would either visit the Trade garages or the representative would visit them at their garages. They would be present in the Paddock area at all practice or race sessions and would often dispense hospitality to riders, journalists and factory executives at their hotels of an evening, hoping to mix business with pleasure. Race entrants often tried new developments at the TT and would look for expert advice and cooperation from the Trade in solving problems relating to carburation, ignition, lubrication, etc, often in conditions of secrecy. In return, the Trade representatives would go back to their factories with information on how their products performed in the most testing of conditions.

Dunlop have been involved with the TT since 1907 and always had a large presence at early events. In the mid 1920s they would bring 400-500 tyres, plus rims, saddles and accessories. To deal with demand they would have three tyre fitters, one wheel builder and a saddle fitter on duty. By the late 1940s their Competitions Manager, Dickie Davies, would bring an eight-man team with their own benches, wheel-building equipment, cylinders of compressed air, publicity banners and sufficient tyres to cope with hundreds of motorcycles across different capacity classes. However, there were no special wet weather tyres, variations in compound, or changing of tyres mid-race in those days. In Dickie's words: *'A rider uses one pair of tyres for practising and another pair for the race'.* It was a very different situation to the one imposed by today's tyre-hungry machines and riders.

A Dunlop tyre fitter.

Each rider would be contracted to particular suppliers and would be rewarded by the payment of bonuses from those Trade suppliers for successful performances. The amount of bonus paid has varied down the years, with perhaps the 1920s being the most financially rewarding period for riders. Indeed, it got so rewarding for riders and so expensive for the companies involved that members of the Trade got together and set maximum bonus figures.

The Trade (in particular the petrol and oil companies) has always had a huge influence on motorcycle racing and on riders' careers, for the members could dictate who their contracted riders rode for. Over many years the money paid out in Trade bonuses literally kept the wheels of racing turning, and it continues to make an important contribution to financing the sport.

Supporting the TAS Suzuki team, Putoline oils were able to publicise TT wins by riders like David Jefferies and Adrian Archibald.

THE UNEXPECTED

It used to be the custom for the start and finish of each TT and MGP race to be signalled by the firing of a maroon (a rocket that was fired into the sky and exploded several hundred feet above ground with a resounding bang!). It wasn't only spectators in the Grandstand who could hear the maroon, for the sound carried for several miles and could usefully be heard at places like Hillberry and Cronk ny Mona. In an incredible bit of bad luck for a passing seagull, the maroon launched to signal the finish of the 1935 Junior scored a direct hit and brought it crashing to the ground.

*

In the 1953 Clubman's races, late-number rider Joe Finch had his worst dreams come true when he stopped to refuel and found the petrol replenishment container supplied by the organisers to be empty. He had to make-do with what was left in the filler at the adjoining Pit. Unfortunately this was insufficient and he ran out of petrol at Creg ny Baa on the last lap and pushed in for a belated finish.

*

Mac McDiarmid had a successful 1984 TT on a 250cc Suzuki Super Six when he won his class in the one and only Historic TT (for 'Classic' bikes). Come the 1985 races and the 'Isle of Man Gazette' considered that 'one of the most comical stories' of that TT concerned Mac, after he had pulled in at Ballacraine on his Production 998 BMW to make adjustments during the final practice session. Taking off helmet and gloves and resting them on the seat, it did not take long to sort the bike problem. A bigger one then loomed for he could not find his gloves. Looking all around the bike they were nowhere to be seen, but glancing over the hedge against which the bike was leaning, he saw a horse in the act of swallowing the last few protruding fingers of his precious riding gloves. Fortunately, swift action by marshals recovered the gloves before they disappeared.

*

In his TT debut year, New Zealand rider Robert Holden had an unexpected moment during practice week, but it was not on the TT Course. Like many other riders at TT time he went to Jurby airfield between official TT practice sessions to test some modifications made to his machine. Steaming up Jurby's main runway at 140 mph on his GSX-R750 Suzuki, Robert lifted his head from under the screen to see a light aircraft coming in to land! Swerving to the edge of the runway and slowing, he watched over his shoulder as the plane passed and touched-down. Seems that it had permission to make an emergency landing, but there had not been enough warning to clear the runway.

TOO FAST

After the first TT of 1907 'The Motor Cycle' wrote: *'It is useless to say fast speeds are not to be encouraged, human nature being what it is'*, but a cry that has been repeated at regular intervals down the years is that racing motorcycles have got too fast for the TT Course. As early as 1920 there was agitation to limit future races to 350s because

The aircraft was not Robert Holden's only close encounter! Holden (4, Ducati) nearly gets T-boned by Jim Moodie (5, Harris Yamaha) at Governor's Bridge. Moodie appears to acknowledge he may have been in the wrong in the second shot.

the 500s were considered too fast. With the 500's fastest lap in 1920 being 55 mph that may seem to have been a ludicrous claim when weighed against the almost 130 mph laps achieved by today's 1000cc projectiles. But there was merit in the claim because, as several riders of the day pointed out in later years, the engines of 1920, although side-valves of modest output, were still too fast for the steering, brakes and road conditions of the time. Weighing some 230 lbs and capable of about 70 mph on the flat and 75 mph down the Mountain, it was not compulsory to fit a front-brake until 1923. Even the 'works' Norton bikes of 1920 were only fitted with stirrup-type front brakes (as on a kiddies push-bike) and the heavier Indian of Freddie Dixon had no front brake.

Freddie Dixon with the Indian on which he finished second in the 1921 Senior TT at an average speed of 54.02 mph, without the use of a front-brake.

The ACU again considered the abolition of the 500 cc class at the end of 1923, and actually made a formal decision to do so. It was a decision that was not enforced. In those early years a bike's lack of suspension, the heavy engine vibration, hand gear-change, hand-operated oil-pump, levers for throttle and air control, absence of steering damping and the atrocious condition of the roads, all combined to make a six-lap, 226 mile, Senior TT an exhausting ride. Well known competitor, 'Pa' Applebee, was quoted as saying of pre-1914 days: *'a rider was considered amazingly fresh if he could stand at the end of a race'.*

As lap speeds climbed rapidly through the 60, 70 and 80 mph marks during the 1920s and 1930s, the motorcycle press regularly asked how much faster could motorcycles lap the Mountain Course, and there was excitement and an air of disbelief as Freddie Frith set the first 90 mph lap in 1937 when winning the Senior event on a Norton.

In 1954 came serious proposals from the FIM (the world ruling body for motorcycle sport), for the elimination of the 500cc class from international racing by 1956, to be followed by the 350s soon after. Fortunately, their proposals were not implemented, and Bob McIntyre set the first 100 mph lap when winning the Senior TT of 1957.

It was not just the solos that were getting faster, for the sidecars were also piling on the speed. This could hardly have been a surprise considering that the organisers introduced a 750cc class in the 1960s and later upped the maximum capacity to 1000cc. But with rising concern over the speeds being achieved, the engine capacity limit for sidecars was reduced from 1,000 cc to 600cc four-strokes and 350cc two-strokes in 1990. Many riders were against the move, but perhaps they did not realise how quickly the development of four-cylinder 600cc motors would progress, for speeds continued to grow and by 1996 the smaller-engined bikes had broken the lap record for 1,000cc machines set 7 years earlier. The organisers again tried to curb rising speeds amongst sidecar racers when, for 1994, they introduced a rule reducing carburettor choke size to a maximum of 32 mm. On paper it should have slowed the outfits, but the fast men were ahead of the game, for they had already reduced to that size, having found that it actually made their outfits go faster.

After reflecting on their record breaking performances in the 1992 Senior TT, Steve Hislop and Carl Fogarty called for a reduction of upper engine capacity for the main solo races and asked for a top capacity of 600cc to be introduced. Both felt the bigger bikes were too fast for the Mountain Course, with Steve saying: *'it would limit the mind-numbing spots like Sulby Straight and Glen Duff, where the 750s are going so quick on the bumps you can't focus properly'.* Not everyone agreed, but Steve knew that ever faster bikes were on their way, and that was clearly something that he did not relish. Indeed, he left the TT in 1992 indicating that he would not be back (although he did return). No reduction in engine capacity was

A world-class trio of riders, all of whom have TT or World Championship victories to their credit, peel their Yamahas into Ballacraine. Takazumi Katayama (Yamaha) leads Joey Dunlop (Yamaha) and Mike Hailwood, 1978 Junior TT.

made and 600cc machines are now lapping within 1 mph of the lap record set by Carl Fogarty in that tremendous 1992 race (when the gap between 600 and 750cc race records was about 6½ mph).

TRAVELLING MARSHALS

The Travelling Marshal service was introduced at the TT in 1935 and was soon extended to cover the MGP. Initially comprising two former TT riders (Vic Brittain and Arthur Simcock) mounted on race bikes operating only during the races, the service has grown to eight riders on high-powered Honda road bikes who are out in all practice sessions and races. The men chosen to serve as Travelling Marshals are former competitors and the job frequently finds them in the thick of the action.

Practice and racing over the Mountain Course is supervised by the Clerk of the Course and his Controllers (plus Race Jury/Stewards on race-days), who are located high in the Control Tower above the Grandstand in Douglas. Communication by radio and telephone with the many marshal posts around the famous 37¾ miles helps the Clerk of the Course to keep a check on the racing, but that does not give him a wide enough picture. To achieve that he needs the services of mobile 'eyes and ears' with race experience who can get to any point on the Course, make on-the-spot assessments to an agreed set of standards and report back with the minimum of delay. This is the job of Travelling Marshals (known within the race organisation as 'TMs'). Doing pre-race Course inspections to ensure that everything is fit for racing, they then position themselves at recognised 'stations' (Ballacraine, Sulby Bridge, etc), where they are in position to give an instant response to a request to attend a practice or race incident. Upon arrival at an incident they take control and see that all tasks are carried out by marshals at the scene.

As coming off a motorcycle on the TT Course frequently results in injury to the rider, there have been investigations down the years into the feasibility of having motorcycle-mounted Travelling Doctors, or having doctors ride pillion to

Travelling Marshals. The usual bogey of insurance problems has prevented the introduction of any such schemes, although before the introduction of the rescue-helicopter, a doctor occasionally hitched a lift with a Travelling Marshal to an incident on a remote part of the Course. Today a rapid and effective response is guaranteed, for the current force of Travelling Marshals are trained in first-aid and a rescue helicopter is always quickly at the scene. In addition, many locations on the Course have a doctor, paramedic or member of the Red Cross or St Johns in attendance.

The tales told by and about Travelling Marshals are legion, and almost all are favourable, even when, on occasions, they themselves fall off. In the early days of the service they spent much time circulating the Course, something which suited those experienced racers admirably. But the proximity of former adversaries sometimes overcame the need for disciplined riding, with the result that it was not uncommon for a Travelling Marshal to be called in by the Clerk of the Course and given a ticking-off for racing on duty. Today that distraction is much reduced, because with much higher speeds involved, more competitors on track and a greater number of Travelling Marshals on duty, they spend more time on 'station' and far less time circulating the Course.

The 1950s saw world champions Freddie Frith, Les Graham, Bob Foster, Geoff Duke and Cecil Sandford doing turns of duty as Travelling Marshals, and it was not only newcomers who could have learnt from those men, for even the experienced would surely have gained something from a lap in their wheeltracks. In 1956 police-type radios were fitted to the Triumphs used by Travelling Marshals as an experiment. The radios were not a total success but could have been developed to be so. Strangely, although everyone recognised the advantages offered by such a form of instant communication, it was not until 1980 that radios came into regular use.

Being a Travelling Marshal does have plenty of lighter moments. Jack Harding did the job for many years and recalls an incident from 1963. A rider passed Jack on the approach to Braddan Bridge but arrived there going far too quickly, so he took to the slip-road and slid off gently under final braking. A nearby policeman went to assist the fallen rider and looked in surprise as Jack drew up alongside. Giving him a moment to stop his engine he said in a tone of admiration: *'You chaps*

There is some 50 years between these two photographs, but in each case a Travelling Marshal was on hand to assist after a rider stopped with machine trouble in front of the Central Hotel in Parliament Square, Ramsey.

usually arrive pretty quickly, but I've never seen service like this before'.

A stylish Colin Broughton takes his radio-equpped Triumph through Whitegates at the 1956 TT.

The photograph above shows the best part of a Travelling Marshals job, but the worst side is dealing with rider accidents. Those vary from a simple fall to a fatality and the men appointed as Travelling Marshals must be able to cope with the effects of such events and get back on the bike and go off to the next job. Ewan Haldane did the job in the late 1950s and recalls a particularly sad incident when he attended a fatality on the Mountain to a rider who was on the Island with his wife and young child. Returning to the Grandstand, Ewan was aware as he walked to the organisers office to give his report on the incident that the wife and child were making their way to the office a little way behind him. After giving a quick report to the Clerk of the Course, he was glad to be able to slip away from the unenviable job of breaking the tragic news.

Allan Killip prepares for a lap of filming with this helmet camera

Allan 'Kipper' Killip did Travelling Marshal duty every year from 1962 to 1998 at both the TT and MGP. Riding everything from 40 bhp AJS twins to 140 bhp Honda multis, he only had one minor spill (at Quarter Bridge) - others clocked up a much higher number of 'offs' in far shorter careers! Kipper enjoyed his rides alongside the greats in TT history without being overawed by them. Taking everything in his stride, he eventually retired from riding duties in 1998 to be succeeded by another long-server, Des Evans.

An unusual incident during the Newcomers race at the 1982 MGP, saw Travelling Marshal Mike Kneen receive a message from Race Control to black-flag and stop his brother Richard, who was riding a Yamaha in the Senior Newcomers class. Receiving a far from brotherly look and a few blunt words for his pains, Mike was able to give the bike the all-clear and a relieved Richard rode off to take a fine second place.

After some forty years of using British bikes, the Travelling Marshal service switched to Hondas in 1977 and have used them ever since. Some of the Hondas have been better suited to the job than others, with the CBX1000s of 1978 being a bit of a handful and the Pan European's of 1990 suffering from an excess of bulk and a shortage of speed.

Past MGP winner Robin Sherry was a regular Travelling Marshal during the 1980s and lived at Union Mills. Whereas nowadays at the completion of a practice or race the Roads Open car receives a radio message telling it to depart from the top of Bray Hill and re-open the roads to the public, in Robin's time a Travelling Marshal would take a note of authority from the Clerk of the Course and deliver it to the driver of the car. On a nice morning this would offer an ideal opportunity to the Travelling Marshal to slip in front of the car and put in a high-speed lap on virtually empty roads - nice work if you can get it! One such morning Robin was the bearer of the note but he turned down the opportunity of a lap and tagged on close behind the car as it plunged down Bray Hill and out to Union Mills where he pulled off for his breakfast. The next practice session brought a shock when he was told that a policeman had reported him for speeding down Bray Hill, missing out the roundabout at Quarter Bridge, plus one or two other traffic offences on roads that were technically open and subject to normal traffic laws once the Roads Open car had passed. The incident blew over, but what particularly annoyed Robin was that a couple of days earlier he had been riding to his appointed 'station' on closed roads before practice and had met a police van travelling in the 'wrong' direction on the Course. Now, that was a serious offence. Robin's last spell of duty was at the 1992 MGP when, in a busy fortnight for Travelling Marshals, competitors covered the huge total of 213,305 miles in practice and racing.

Express delivery from Travelling Marshal Roger Sutcliffe.

All Travelling Marshals are Manx residents and they all hold-down full-time jobs, so getting time off for their duties often interferes with their work. Former MGP winner Roger Sutcliffe did a Travelling Marshal's job for several years during the 1980s whilst also running his plumbing business. Just about to leave work for duty at a long Thursday afternoon practice period, Roger received a call from one of his men who had urgent need for a new ball-valve to complete a job in a house at the side of the Course in Kirk Michael. Roger collected one from his Stores, took it with him to the Grandstand, had a brief word with the Clerk of the Course and set off on closed roads. Less than 10 minutes later he handed the ball-valve to his waiting plumber 14 miles away in Kirk Michael, then carried on to his appointed 'station' at Sulby Bridge.

The last words on Travelling Marshals goes to the man who did the job for 36 years, Allan 'Kipper' Killip. Explaining how he picked men for the job he stressed that it was not the fastest riders that he looked for because, in his words: *'it's their personal qualities that count most'.*

TRIUMPH AND TRAGEDY

Supporters of the TT recognise the challenge that riders undertake in racing over the ultra-demanding Mountain Course, and they admire the courage and skill that is required to do so. Opponents of the races concentrate on the price that sometimes has to be paid by those brave enough to take on the challenge, one that can result in death or serious injury. In todays language, supporters and opponents are approaching the event from different directions - and there is little chance that they will ever meet.

It is self-evident that the Mountain Course with its kerbs, walls and lack of run-off space can be more dangerous than the billiard-smooth, purpose-built circuits with gravel traps and huge run-off spaces that are used for World Championship events. But the former requires to be ridden with an element of restraint (not easy), whilst the latter always requires to be ridden on the limit, and often beyond. It is a sad fact that recent 500cc World Champions Wayne Rainey, Wayne Gardner, Kevin

You shouldn't have done it

"Dangerous? — of course it's dangerous — bloody dangerous!"

Schwantz and Mick Doohan, were all forced into early retirement because they could not continue with the constant injuries that they sustained as a result of riding on, and over, the limit in circuit racing.

A TT win is still regarded as a major triumph in a rider's racing career. Today, with the polarisation of the sport into road and circuit racing, it is mostly exponents of the former who strive for victory over the Mountain. But, although the sport began its divergence into road and circuit events some 35 years ago, there are many circuit riders who are aware of the value of a TT win, with some successfully mixing both disciplines and others harbouring a secret wish to contest a race on the Mountain Course. They know that a TT triumph still serves to broadcast a rider's name far and wide in the world of motorcycle racing and also allows him to be compared with some of the greatest riders of the past.

The TT is used to annual attacks from journalists with little knowledge of the event who trot out a string of familiar cliches, without regard for factors like the huge number of racing miles covered compared to races on short circuits. But sometimes appearing in the same newspaper as an anti-article, are the reasoned words of reporters with years of TT experience who seek to convey the excitement (and danger) of the event to their readers. It was the late George Turnbull writing in 'The Daily Telegraph' who captured the impact of the races on all concerned when he wrote: *'The TT Mountain Course plays more havoc with the human emotions in one week of racing than any other circuit in the world. Joy, sorrow, exhilaration and fear - all are imposed on competitors and spectators by the unforgiving 37¾ miles of everyday road which for a short time each year become the most fearsome race arena devised for high speed sport'.*

There are many examples of where the initials TT can be shown to stand for Triumph and Tragedy, as well as for Tourist Trophy. The Japanese manufacturers had created intense interest in the early 1960s, but the excitement, spectacle, joy and glory of the 1962 series, was overshadowed by the death of a fine rider. Australian Tom Phillis was killed in the 350cc race at Laurel Bank when lying third on his 'works' Honda and trying hard to catch Gary Hocking and Mike Hailwood on their MVs.

In the early 1960s not only was there intense

Tom Phillis takes Quarter Bridge on his last lap, 1962 Junior TT.

competition between opposing teams but there was also fierce rivalry between riders in the same teams, for the number of coveted 'works' rides were few while the number of riders who aspired to them were many. Tom Phillis's death had a major effect on his close friends in motorcycle racing. Fellow Honda teamster Jim Redman had serious thoughts of quitting but was persuaded by Bob McIntyre to keep riding. Gary Hocking felt that all the riders were being forced to press each other too hard and he persuaded Count Agusta to release him from his MV contract. The dreadful irony that ensued was that whilst Redman did continue racing, McIntyre was killed a few months later at Oulton Park and Hocking died in a car race in his native Rhodesia before the year ended.

Looking at more recent incidents, Dave Saville experienced multiple TT triumphs with 9 wins in the Formula 2 sidecar class between 1985 and 1990. Popular with spectators and fellow competitors, Dave looked to vary his experience over the Mountain Course by entering the Classic MGP in the early 1990s, but a heavy fall at Creg ny Baa turned into a tragedy that ended his racing career and left him in a wheelchair. Riders slide off at Creg ny Baa at almost every TT and MGP, and most of them get up and walk away - why was he so unlucky?

This is Simon Beck Kawasaki-mounted at the 1998 TT where he was fastest in practice for both the Formula 1 and Senior races.

Gilberto Parlotti (Morbidelli) lost his life at the Verandah in the 1972 Lightweight 125 race. Leading the 125cc World Championship at the time, his death triggered massive protests from the other star riders of the day and can be seen as the catalyst for the TT's eventual loss of World Championship status in the conventional race classes.

Simon Beck was a former Senior MGP winner who moved to the TT and during the 1990s worked his way up through the ranks, improving year on year. In 1999 he was rewarded for his sterling privateer efforts with support from Honda on an RC45. But tragedy struck during Tuesday evening's practice when he crashed at the 33rd Milestone and was killed. Simon had just set the fastest practice lap before his accident.

The Jefferies family experienced many triumphs in Island racing. Alan was second in the 500cc Clubman's race in 1947, son Tony took victory in the Junior and Formula 750 TTs of 1971, and second son Nick was a MGP winner in 1983 and victor in the Formula 1 race of 1993. Their efforts were surpassed by the efforts of Tony's son David. Coming to the 2003 TT with 9 wins under his belt, family triumph turned to tragedy when David was killed during practice.

Some critics of the TT quote the number of fatalities that have occurred in Island racing, but all that does is prove that the event is dangerous, something that riders, organisers and supporters readily admit. The Sports Editor of Isle of Man Newspapers, John Watterson, wrote in 2003, *'We all know it's a dangerous circuit and pastime. If we stand back and assess the TT it is at times difficult to defend . . . it is an addiction and one, like it or loathe it, we are all proud of'*. Those who concentrate on fatality figures are probably unaware of the sad fact that many TT and MGP competitors have been killed in motorcycle racing off the Island, in car racing and in other forms of accidental death. Whether those men had raced motorcycles or not, they would certainly have lived life in the fast-lane, shrugging off its attendant risks in a manner difficult to understand by the non-risk taking populace at large. The non-racing public of the time would have had similar difficulty in understanding a report in 'The Motor Cycle' that described a fatality at Brooklands in the very early days of motorcycle competition with: *'The cause of the accident was the splendid self-confidence without which daring deeds can never be done'*.

A wheelie and a half for Simon 'Ronnie' Smith at Ballaugh in the Junior TT of 1999. Within a few weeks of putting in his best ever performances at TT 2002, 'Ronnie' was killed in a road traffic accident.

CHAPTER 10

TALES OF . . .

TRUE GRIT

A rider's planning and anticipation of a TT meeting can be the result of months of preparation, with some basing the whole of their racing year around an Island race. Top runners only consider such a race to have been a success if they get to stand on the winner's rostrum, but for most just getting to the finish is sufficient reward. Such intensity of feeling about Island racing has created many tales of riders striving to overcome adversity to achieve a coveted race finish.

Graham Walker is remembered by some as the father of commentator Murray Walker, but he was also an accomplished TT rider over many years and one-time winner (the 1931 Lightweight race on a Rudge). Graham was a big man and he had the requisite strength to fight his machines over the poor roads of the early 1920s. In the six-lap 1920 Senior he was entered on a Norton and the records show that he finished in a not-so-special 13th place. However, what they do not show is that he came off on the first lap *'due to the front brake blocks getting mixed up with the spokes'*, gashed his knee, damaged the saddle and bent his handlebars. He got back into the race, but subsequently changed 5 sparking plugs, one rear tube and, in his words: *'the shape of my stern'*. The latter problem can be explained by the fact that soon after the crash he lost the top of his saddle and spent the remaining 5½ laps (200 miles) sitting on the mudguard. It was even before the days when a pad was fitted on the rear mudguard to enable riders to *'get down to it'*, so it must have been an incredibly uncomfortable way to ride and sitting so far back would have done nothing for his machine control.

In the 1914 Junior TT, Douggie Alexander lost the top of the saddle from his Royal Enfield on the second lap but still rode to the finish of the six-lap race. Graham Walker performed a similar feat on his Norton for five laps of the 1920 Senior race.

There have been many wet Island races, with some run in conditions that would not be tolerated in the 21st century. The 1946 MGP was the first post-Second World War event to be held over the Mountain Course and victory went to Ernie Lyons in some of the wettest conditions ever experienced. Showing incredible courage and fortitude over 6 laps, Ernie was not helped by the fact that his Triumph GP twin broke its frame during the race. Asked if he knew when the frame broke, he jokingly replied: *'I think it must have been when the bicycle began to steer much better'*.

A good privateer of the late 1940s and early 1950s was Phil Heath. He had an entry in the Junior and Senior classes of the 1951 TT but, come Junior race-day he suffered one of his recurring attacks of malaria (contracted on war-time service in the Far East). Normally these were not too severe: *'a slight giddiness which lasted 24 hours and as long as I stayed in bed or sat quietly and didn't move my head from side to side I was okay'*. It was a hardly a condition suitable for a rider to complete seven racing laps of the TT Course, but Phil was reluctant to lose his ride in the Junior event. Acknowledging that he should not have raced, he recalls: *'I started okay and as long as I kept my head steady looking straight ahead I could cope. Once I thought I heard a funny noise in the transmission and looked down, whereupon everything went topsy turvy but quickly I managed to get back to normal'.* He felt very shaky at his pit-stop, had difficulty restarting, but once under way, he pressed on to the finish. Understandably riding slower than usual, he completed the race in 17th place.

Phil Heath was back to full fitness for the 1952 TT. Here he tackles Bray Hill at speed in the Senior.

The 1959 Senior TT was another very wet race. Postponed from Friday to Saturday, it started in the dry, but ensuing torrential rain and hail saw winner John Surtees having to be lifted from his machine at the Finish due to cold and exhaustion. John observed that, so strong was the hail, it *'was capable of stripping the paint from the fairing of the MV'.* Although the atrocious conditions resulted in a slow average race speed, fellow competitors still told of John howling past them in clouds of spray on the way to his win.

In days gone by motorcycle footrests were not of the folding type fitted to the majority of today's machines, and this meant that in a spill a footrest was vulnerable to be bent or snapped off. It was simple enough job to straighten a bent one, but it was a process that could weaken it to the extent that it could later snap under a rider's weight. Graham Downes managed to snap one on his AJS 7R whilst descending Bray Hill in the 1957 Junior MGP. After a few shaky moments controlling the 7R, Graham's attitude is revealed by his post-race comment: *'There was no question of retiring, but it was a most uncomfortable ride, the large tank I had borrowed meant that I could not rest my foot on the chaincase, so it had to dangle for the next four laps'.* Norton 'works' rider from 1929-1933, Tim Hunt went one better in the 1929 Senior TT when he fell twice in the race (once on each side) and broke-off both footrests. Trying to support as much weight as possible by sitting on the back mudguard, he still finished in fourth place.

Tim Hunt in 1931 when - with footrests in place - he took his Nortons to victory in the Junior and Senior TTs.

Mention is made elsewhere of Mike Hailwood's brave ride to victory on his battered MV Agusta after he dropped and bent it badly in the 1965 Senior race, also Joey Dunlop's courageous ride to win the 1980 Classic TT while holding the 8 gallon petrol tank of his Yamaha on with his knees after the retaining strap broke in the early laps. Both showed the determination to finish the race which is a characteristic of most TT riders.

In what was a major surprise to rider Allan 'Grandad' Warner (and probably to Honda), the rear-shock of his Honda VTR1000 snapped as he went through the bottom of Barregarrow during the last lap of a race at the 1997 TT. It is a spot that puts abnormal loading on cycle parts and suspension and has resulted in broken frames, holed exhausts, etc, for several riders over the years. It made Allan's bike extremely low at the rear, but with the prospect of a finish still a possibility he continued at much reduced pace, did his best to keep out of the way of passing riders, and eventually took the chequered flag to gain his hard-earned Finishers award - something that he immediately presented to his mechanic for a fortnight of application to his bikes that went well beyond the call of duty. Allan's experience showed that even after so many years of racing and development the ultra-demanding Mountain Course can still find weaknesses in the best of modern machinery, whilst his action was typical of that of many riders down the years who have been determined to get to the finish of a race.

TT REPLICAS

The winner of each race at the TT and MGP receives a substantial award modelled on the original Tourist Trophy presented to the winner of the first race in 1907 by the Marquis de Mouzilly St Mars. It is the winner of the Senior race who receives the original Tourist Trophy, and in the early days of the races those who finished within half an hour of the winner were awarded gold medals. From 1922, miniature silver and (later) bronze replicas of the original Tourist Trophy have been awarded to riders who finish within a specified fraction (or percentage) of the winner's time - although initially silver replicas only went to those finishing in the first six.

This was Norton Motors impressive collection of TT Replicas that they sometimes allowed to be displayed in the showrooms of their dealers. In this photograph from the 1960s Norton's Bert Hopwood is on the far left and MGP and TT rider Albert Moule, an executive of the Colmore Depot, is on the far right.

For those who know that a TT win is beyond them, the target is always to win a 'Rep', as riders call the lesser but still much coveted awards. Because the number of replicas allocated relates directly to the time taken by the winner to complete a race, those elite men good enough to win yet modest enough to want to be considered sportsmen, sometimes sought to ride with half a mind to the matter of the post-race allocation of Replicas. In essence, the slower the speed at which they won a race, the greater the number of TT Replicas awarded, allowing more riders to go home satisfied. Such tactics are rarely used nowadays, particularly because the competitor with the 'fastest' aggregate time in the Formula 1 and Senior TT stands to win the Joey Dunlop Trophy and, more importantly to a professional rider, accompanying prize-money of £10,000.

A spin-off from the award to successful riders of TT Replicas was that the title was adopted as the name for several ultra-sporting road-going models that claimed to be derived from their successful TT racing brethren. One company to do so was AJS with their all-conquering ohv models of the early 1920s, and many others followed suit into the late-1930s, some companies being more justified in using the title for their products than others.

Sidecar racers often complain that they are the poor relations at the TT. Whilst some of their claims may be justified, spare a thought for sidecar passengers who, surely, are the poorest of the poor! Seen as little more than compulsory ballast by some riders - and treated as such - it was not until 1957 that sidecar passengers received replicas on same basis as their drivers.

The first man to win four replicas in a week was Bill Lomas in 1955 (there were only four solo classes at the time) and he was followed by Mike Hailwood in 1958 when he won four replicas on what was his TT debut year.

Every Replica has a story to tell, for each represents a moment of TT and MGP history. Whilst it is riders who make most of that history, in exceptional cases an occasional replica has been presented to a long-serving official of the races - suitably inscribed so that they could not be confused with those awarded to competitors.

Winner of the 1921 Senior, Howard Davies, is shown here before the start of the 1922 Senior wearing the number 1 plate. His bike is positioned in what was known as the 'Island Square', a white painted box from which he would start the race.

TT TERMS

There are a few terms that have developed with regard to Island racing down the years. 'Early morning practice' was peculiar to the TT and MGP for almost 100 years, but with its abolition in 2004 it will now fade away. Associated with early morning practice was the expression 'bird scarer', which used to be applied to the first man away. He was bound to find pigeons, rooks, jackdaws and similar strutting around in the road - despite the efforts of marshals - and he would also serve as a rabbit and sheep scarer.

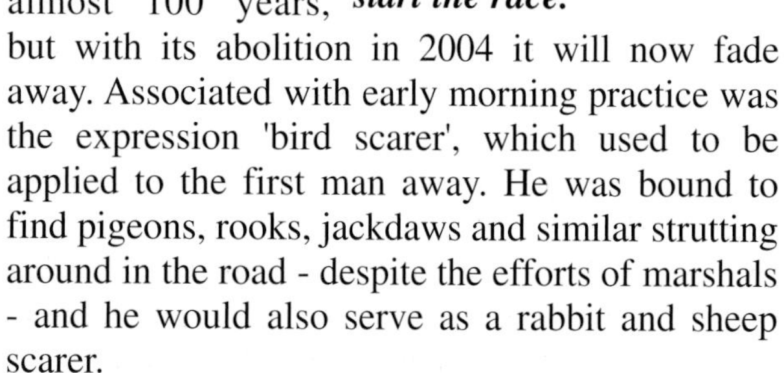

Another expression that has gone out of use is reference to the 'Island Square'. Before riders were seeded for starting numbers, the honour of starting at number 1 was usually offered to the winner of the previous year's race, and he would start from the 'Island Square'.

In principle, only a rider or his pit-attendant is allowed to touch his machine during a race, but a Travelling Marshal may do so for the purposes of inspection if a rider is stopped on the Course under Black Flag procedures, a Scrutineer may do so for safety reasons during a pit-stop, and a marshal may hold a bike for a rider while he works on it and may also help him to push-start it, (the latter was not allowed in the past). Any other form of third-party involvement during a race can be construed as 'outside assistance' and renders a rider liable to disqualification. Given the length of the Course and the nature of Island racing, 'outside assistance' can, and has, taken the form of loan of a spanner or taking on petrol other than in the pits. Such assistance may have been provided, often unwittingly, by a helpful marshal or spectator, but it can also result in the rider losing a hard-earned Finishers Award.

Another TT term is 'Paddock Hotel'. It does not refer to a multi-storey establishment for wealthy visitors, but to the areas at the back of the Grandstand that house the colourful multitude of tents and motorhomes over the race periods of those who either cannot afford, or choose not to stay in, conventional accommodation.

Until the late 1980s competitors rode their racing bikes through the streets of Douglas and up to the Start area before every MGP, in what was known as a 'Grand Parade'. Having weighed-in their bikes on the afternoon before the race, competitors would leave them overnight in Mylchreest's Garage in Westmoreland Road, Douglas. Then, an hour before the start of a race, bikes would be returned to the riders and the escorted 'Grand Parade' would take place. It was not uncommon for a bike to refuse to start, or for one to be found with a flat tyre. Whilst riders would start to panic, the organisers would bring their back-up van into service. This followed the Parade to the Start where any rider with a problem would have a small amount of time to rectify the fault before coming under Starters Orders. With the construction of brick-built scrutineering garages at the back of the Grandstand in the late 1980s, all pre-race weighing-in and scrutineering is now done in the three hours before a race.

Some TT races can have 90 or more competitors and whilst they all have to reach the requisite qualifying standard in terms of lap time and speed, they are not all at the top of the professional racing tree. This is sometimes to the annoyance of those who consider that they are in that lofty position and that slower runners are not fit to race with them. It is an unrealistic attitude if spectators are to have an interesting race, although it is one that does create occasional safety worries due to major speed differentials between riders on the Course. The term 'holiday racers' is sometimes used in a disparaging way to describe the not so quick riders, suggesting that they do not get in as much racing activity as the professionals. (Many would probably love to have the chance to do so.) But how much racing do you have to do to lose the 'holiday racer' tag. No one could doubt that multiple Sidecar TT winner Dave Molyneux was a serious racer, but when he arrived for the 2003 TT it was his first race since early October 2002, some eight months before, for he had been too busy constructing sidecar outfits for his rivals to find time to race.

The terms 'Bad practice, Good race' and 'Mist on the Mountain' are mentioned elsewhere in the book and both are ones that are particularly related to Island racing.

TT TIPPLES

At today's TT, riders can be subjected to random breathalyser tests and any trace of alcohol in the blood means no race. Back at the first event in 1907, attitudes were slightly more relaxed. The winner of the multi-cylinder class that year was Rem Fowler and he recalled in later years that he was physically run-down before the race and how *'twenty minutes before the start a friend of mine fetched me a glassful of neat brandy tempered with a little milk. This had the desired effect and I set off full of hope and Dutch courage'.*

One knock-on effect of the current no alcohol rule is that, if they are riding in another race on the same day, today's winners cannot take a celebratory drink from the bottle of champagne that they receive on the presentation rostrum. But there were no such restrictions to trouble a couple of earlier TT winners, Howard Davies (1925 Senior) and Freddie Dixon (1927 Junior). Both men had a taste for champagne - and both of them partook mid-race! At Howard Davies pit-stop during his 1925 winning ride, it was reported: *'he had a hurried drink of champagne and went off again feeling quite refreshed'*. Freddie Dixon used the same tactic in 1927, where at his stop: *'a swallow of champagne and Fred is off'*. Graham Walker retired from that same 1927 Junior race and, seated himself on a wall at the edge of the Course. Graham recalled that each time Freddie Dixon passed *'I tempted him every lap with a bottle of Bass but he refused to stop and have one'*. Perhaps Freddie did not like to mix beer with champagne.

Graham Walker liked a moderate tipple and revealed that his race-day breakfast recipe for each of the 23 TT races he contested was: *'two eggs beaten up in a pint of milk and laced with a double brandy, the delightful concoction being taken precisely two hours before starting time'*. What Graham had at his pit-stop he did not reveal, but in a report of the 1952 Senior race 'The Motor Cycle' indicated that the days of taking strong refreshment were not over. They wrote: *'The end of lap 3 is, of course, pit time, when riders pick up fuel, don clean goggles, and wash out their mouths with liquid or liquor as their taste moves them'.*

Jock West was feeling the effects of 'flu before the 1935 Junior race but, dosed overnight with plenty of whisky and aspirins, he felt better on race morning though still a bit shaky. In 'Racing Reminiscences' by Geoff Davison, Jock

Freddie Dixon's win in the 1927 Junior TT was commemorated by the issue of this Manx stamp in 1982. In the background is The Highlander Inn, but Fred was in too much of a hurry to stop on that occasion.

told how it was arranged that *'if I got as far as the petrol stop there would be a "short" waiting for me'*. He got to the petrol stop, refuelled the bike and downed what he later found was a treble brandy, with the result that *'I was taking some bends flat out that in the past had been treated with considerable respect and a noticeable drop in engine revs'*. He had to make a second stop but, sensibly, declined the further glass of brandy on offer.

A vastly experienced TT rider is Chester dealer, Bill Smith. In his long TT career Bill rates the 1959 Senior as the worst, weather-wise, that he competed in. Although the race started dry (having been postponed from Friday to Saturday) it soon began to rain in a manner few had seen before. Bill stopped several times to check if the race had been abandoned and each time he was told no. It seems that at each stop he was offered a tot of whisky to, literally, keep his spirits up. When he reached the finish, he was very wet, very cold - but very mellow.

It is no coincidence that many well known spots around the Course are known by the name of a nearby pub. The Highlander, The Hawthorn, The Ginger Hall, The Bungalow, are names that have gone down into TT history. At other famous spots: Quarter Bridge, Ballacraine, Ballaugh Bridge, Parliament Square and Creg ny Baa, there are similar places of refreshment. Marginally less well known are pubs that riders usually pass at speed: The Railway Inn at Union Mills, The Crosby Hotel, Halfway House, The Mitre at Kirk Michael and The Sulby Glen Hotel. They constitute a generous enough supply of 'watering-holes' for watching spectators, although several have surrendered their licensed status and been converted to private houses in recent years, whilst The Bungalow was demolished long ago.

The Bungalow at the foot of Snaefell was a well-known TT landmark that saw more than one rider clip the posts of its verandah when off-line. The tracks of the electric tramway going to the summit of Snaefell cross the road here.

The Travelling Marshals who have circulated the Course at speed with the racers since they were introduced to the organisation in 1935 are probably regarded as paragons of virtue by most spectators but, do not forget, they are all former racers. Nowadays they are governed by the no alcohol rule, but forty years ago some were known to enjoy a pint, or more, of beer. Jimmy Linskey was one who regularly stopped at The Ginger Hall between races, for he knew that a friend would have a pint of Okells ale ready for him in one of the upstairs rooms that overlooked the Course. Now, a Travelling Marshal stopping and disappearing into the pub was not the sort of thing to escape the notice of the large crowd of race-day spectators at somewhere like Ginger Hall. On one occasion after downing a pint, Jimmy made a hash of getting back on the bike and finished in a heap on the floor. This resulted in a huge cheer from the crowd, several of whom helped him to his feet, dusted him down, and sent him off on his official duties.

A journalist from 'The TT Special' also liked The Ginger Hall and wrote: *'Ginger Hall is a delightful spot for a pressman who wishes to combine speed with relaxation. He can sit on the steps of the hotel armed with a notebook, pencil and glass of ale'*. Journalists who nowadays prefer to report on the races from the Press room at the Grandstand find that it comes equipped with its own supply of free-flowing Okells Ale whilst, out on the track, experienced racers know just how to coax an ailing bike along as far as a pub, so that they also may partake of a similar free-flow of ale from generous spectators. The wily Charlie Williams did just that in the 1982 Senior. Plagued with a mysterious mis-fire, he brought the bike to a stop at the Sulby Glen Hotel. A quick look over it revealed nothing amiss, so Charlie accepted the offer of a consoling pint and resigned himself to signing a few autographs and settling down to watch the race. However, in the restless way of a rider hyped up by the speedy race miles he had already completed, Charlie continued to prowl around the bike, pint in hand. Suddenly he spotted a kinked fuel line that was the work of a moment to straighten. Less than a minute later he was back in the race but, unfortunately, he had lost too much time to threaten the leaders. Did Charlie sup of his pint at his enforced stop? He is not saying, but such was his pace when he rejoined the race that he set a new lap record of 115.08 mph.

It was just over 50 years earlier that Jimmy Simpson had a similar experience to Charlie Williams, but up on the Mountain. He had his engine cut near Brandywell, so he knocked it out of gear and coasted. As he approached Windy Corner a spectator held a bottle of beer out to him. In his words: *'I just could not pass it'.* Jimmy stopped, drank the beer, then looked over his 'works' Norton. He changed the plug, checked compression and sparks and petrol - all OK, and then eventually found a blocked main-jet. Getting back into the race he finished eighth.

Francois and Sylvie LeBlond helped to finance their ride in the 2004 Sidecar TT by selling this French red wine whose label shows them leaping Ballaugh Bridge.

The long-established Okells Ales are probably the beers that most older TT fans associate with their Island visits, whilst others may relate to the newer Bushy's beers.

How the local Okell ales were advertised in the TT Programme of the 1960s. Forty years later a special Okell Blade Brew was produced to commemorate the 10th anniversary of the Honda Fireblade.

TT WILDLIFE

The fact that the TT Course consists of roads that are normally in general use by the local population means that it is extremely difficult to seal them off completely from the influences of everyday life. In particular, it took many years (and a few scary moments for riders) to convince the Manx people to keep their livestock secure and off the Course during practice and racing. Even today, undaunted by racing motorcycles, ducks from Ballacraine Farm seek to maintain their right to cross the Course, something that marshals have had to look out for at the spot since 1911.

Jimmy Simpson recalled how he came third in the Junior race of 1927 even after a mid-race collision with a dog in Kirk Michael. In his words: *'Right in the middle of the village there was a woman on one side of the road and a greyhound on the other. And just as I approached, the daft creature called the dog across to her'.* Cats and dogs remained a problem in urban areas and sheep were a common hazard on the Mountain stretch until the mid-1930s when most of the Mountain road was fenced. Thereafter, there would be an occasional few that found gaps in the fence and it would be the job of marshals to clear them from the Course before the first rider appeared. Veteran of 22 TT races and twice a winner, Charlie Dodson claimed that one of his most exciting Island moments was riding through a flock of sheep at speed during the 1933 Lightweight race.

Island livestock generally seems to be untroubled by the passage of race machinery. Cows and sheep continue to graze on the other side of the fencing edging the Course and pre-war TT man Noel Pope recalled: *'Just outside Ramsey, a large white horse looked over the hedge every day watching the practices and racing. I cannot remember when I first noticed him, but certainly by the mid-30's, he was quite one of our regular friends. I would very much like to know what his thoughts were as calmly, year after year, he looked over the hedge as though taking in all the finer points of racing'.* Similarly untroubled by the passage of the racers were two bulls (each with a harem of about 30 cows) who occupied fields on opposite sides of the Course during the 2004 MGP. The flagman there (who had to stand inside one of the fields with the cattle) recalls: *'During Wednesday evening's practice one of the bulls was lying in the middle of the field for the first hour. Eventually he got up and began to walk towards the fence at the edge of the course, making a loud*

This dog was keen to join the racers at the entrance to Parliament Square, Ramsey.

roaring noise in his throat. I then saw and heard another bull in the field on the opposite side of the course doing the same thing. They arrived at their fences together. Then 'my' bull, standing less than 5 yards from me, began butting the fence and pawing the ground, ripping up divots as he did so. It was beginning to look a bit serious. Both bulls then put their heads over the fences and bellowed across the course at each other for several minutes on end. It was an unreal sensation. I was trying to concentrate on a stream of bikes passing between the bulls at 140 mph - that they totally ignored - and I was also wondering what I was going to do if they broke through the fences. A waved yellow would hardly have been adequate to control riders or bulls in that situation, but I had serious doubts about the wisdom of producing the red flag within sight of those two beefy fellows!'

Rabbits were far more common than they are today and when the Course inspection car returned to the Grandstand at 4.25 a.m. on a TT practice morning in 1936, the first rider waiting to set off, Jack Williams (HRD), was told: *'good visibility, lots of wind and millions of rabbits'*. In the 1930s, Bray Hill was not the built-up area that it is today, and Eric Briggs told how on two consecutive practice mornings at the 1938 MGP, a hare tried to race his Manx Norton at the bottom of the hill.

Although rabbits were regarded as an obstruction to racing when they appeared on the Course, for one man the proliferation of rabbits in the local fields provided a major contribution to the cost of racing. After competing in the 1964 MGP, Manxman Bob Kewley set his sights on buying a new Manx Norton to progress his racing career. To supplement his normal wages with the £500 required for a new Manx, Bob spent countless night-time hours over the winter of 1964-65 trapping rabbits; a task followed by gutting, cleaning, packing into tea-chests and getting them onto the morning's boat for Liverpool where they fetched 2/6 (12½p) each. Come the Spring of 1965 and Bob had his new Manx, paid for largely by the proceeds of his rabbit-trapping activities.

Bigger four-footed obstacles were to be found, and in his first year of Island racing with MV Agusta, John Surtees describes how: *'I had taken out the race machine for the final morning's practice, to settle it for the big event, and was pulling away up the steep climb out of Glen Helen, and round the right-hander at the top. I was just about ready to snick from second to third gear when a cow jumped over the bank in front of me. I hit the cow full amidships. It, however, actually got up, lumbered away and, I am told, made a full recovery'*. John's MV Agusta was rather more badly damaged than the cow. Some years later Dave Croxford encountered a pig on the Course which he avoided, due, he said, *'to my Norton having the edge over the pig on acceleration'*.

Doing what most do when they arrive on the Island, a first-time visitor in 1952 set out on an early lap of the Course, an experience which he described with: *'Immediate trip around the Course at 6.30 am, passing a peacock, geese, two lots of cows and - on the Mountain - a Clubman's competitor on unofficial practice with a broken knee, a Norton and two dead sheep'*.

Dogs and cats still occasionally stray and the notorious 'Barney', a spaniel from Kirk Michael, caused over an hour's delay to the start of the 2003 Senior MGP, while he wandered in the vicinity of the Course. There have yet to be any race sightings of wallabies, although, surely, it is only a matter of time, for they are known to live wild in the Ballaugh area.

There has been more than one report of peacocks strutting across the road as riders thunder past, plus there are many truly wild birds that they have to cope with. Travelling Marshal Mike Kneen was hit in the face by a dove in the mid-80s that, in his words: 'felt like a brick'. Sidecar driver Steve Sinnott was similarly struck by a jackdaw and there have been many others, including Tommy Robb who estimated the impact speed of his meeting with an oncoming seagull as 160 mph.

This seagull is not the sort of thing a rider wants to hit at speed.

In each of the above bird-strikes the rider was able to keep control of his machine, but the crash that ended the racing career of Pat Hennen at Bishops Court whilst leading the 1978 Senior race has never been fully explained, although it is strongly suspected that he lost control after being struck by a bird.

Even worse was the incident that took Gene McDonnell's life during the 1986 TT at Ballaugh. It was one that, through dreadful irony, was indirectly caused by what is normally a life-saver, the rescue-helicopter. The 'chopper' had been called to an accident at Ballaugh, and as it took-off with an injured rider, the noise frightened a horse which broke out of its field onto the Course and into the path of Gene McDonnell.

TWO, THREE & FOUR WHEELS

A select few TT riders have been able to show racing prowess on more than two wheels. When the Sidecar TT was run from 1923-25, well-known solo runners of the time like Freddie Dixon, Graham Walker, Clarrie Wood, Harry Reed and Len Parker turned their attention to the three-wheel races as well as the two. They did it very successfully, for all took top three places, with Dixon, Walker and Parker winning the event for the three years that it was run. Dixon went on to win the 1927 Junior TT and his later win in a car TT (not on the Island), made him the only person to achieve TT victories on 2, 3 & 4 wheels.

Other motorcycle TT winners of the time who also raced cars with success were Charlie Dodson, Wal Handley and Syd Crabtree. Amongst the four-wheeled events that they contested were the round-the-houses Mannin Mooar and Mannin Beg races held in Douglas in the early 1930s.

Many good riders on the 'blackstuff' have also starred in off-road events. Winner of the 1939 Senior TT was George Meier on only his second visit to the Island. He was actually contracted to race on four-wheels for Auto Union in 1939 but was permitted to race on two just at the TT. A couple of years earlier he had brought his flat-twin BMW to the International Six Days Trial held in Llandrindod Wells and rode to a Gold Medal, as did previous Norton TT teamster Vic Brittain and AJS man George Rowley.

Graham Walker and passenger Tommy Mahon round Ramsey Hairpin in the 1923 Sidecar TT when they finished second to Freddie Dixon.

George O'Dell (Triumph) flies Ballaugh Bridge in practice for the 1971 Production TT. Injuries sustained during practice on his sidecar outfit prevented him from racing the Triumph.

After the Sidecar TT returned in 1954 it seemed to be sidecar racers who occasionally turned out on solos (rather than solo runners turning to sidecars as in earlier years). The exception to this was one of Britain's best ever sidecar drivers, Eric Oliver, for he rode in eleven solo TT races before turning to sidecars and taking a TT win and a World Championship. At least three other winners of post-war Sidecar TTs have ridden in solo TT races: Florian Camathias, Chris Vincent and Mick Boddice, while George O'Dell practised on a solo but did not race due to injuries sustained in sidecar practice.

Having achieved much success on two-wheels, some well known post-war solo TT winners went on to race cars, including Geoff Duke, John Surtees, Gary Hocking, Mike Hailwood, Stuart Graham and Bill Ivy. Other riders tried cars, including sidecar man Rolf Biland, whilst Steve Parrish made a big name for himself racing trucks after being a 'works' rider for Suzuki. It was John Surtees who added the world championship on four-wheels to his several two-wheeled crowns, so becoming the only man to do the double.

The degree of specialisation in today's world of circuit motorcycle racing means that the top men barely have the opportunity to look outside their chosen capacity class, let alone think of adding another wheel or two to their efforts. This same specialisation (definitely not so pronounced amongst TT runners) probably accounts for the fact that 'all-rounders' are much rarer than they were in the past.

On two-wheels Geoff Duke was a 'works' rider in Trials and Scrambles, as a well as a TT winner and World Champion road racer. He also did his share of car-racing with success.

Whilst men like Stanley Woods, Vic Brittain, Geoff Duke and Sammy Miller rode, and won, in various forms of motorcycle competition, both on and off-road, today's top men tend to stay 'focused' on a narrow field of activity. Are there any prospective all-rounders amongst them? Quite probably, but we are unlikely to get the chance to see them demonstrate their skills, even though some practice on moto-cross machines to develop their sliding skills, and triple TT winner in 2004 John McGuinness, rides Super Moto in the winter to keep fit.

WEIGHTS AND MEASURES

From the TT's earliest days the organisers had a preoccupation with weights and measures of both men and motorcycles. Initially the purpose of weighing their machines was to ensure that they were of a touring nature and not out-and-out lightweight racers. As to why they also weighed the riders is not known, although the organisation of early motorcycle racing was modelled on horse racing, with talk of runners, riders, mounts, the payment of retainers, plus the weighing-in process, owner/manufacturers riding colours and, in the 1920s, the presence of bookmakers behind the Grandstand. Weighing procedures for the first race took place at St Johns railway station a couple of hundred yards from the starting point at Tynwald Hill. Amongst the weights quoted in 1907, the lightest was a single-cylinder Triumph at 140 lbs (63.5 kg) and the heaviest the Roc at 237 lbs (107.5 kg). Riders varied in weight from 126 lbs (57 kg) to 183 lbs (83 kg).

The organisers eventually stopped weighing riders, but the weighing of machines continued to ensure compliance with regulation weight limits.

When 'weighing-in' had the true meaning! The two-stroke Velocette is weighed and noted in this early 1920s shot. The 'rider' on the scales is adjusting the balance beam.

An Ultra-Lightweight 175cc TT was introduced in 1924 for which a maximum machine weight of 150 lbs was set. Some riders found it difficult to get their race machinery down to this figure and various dodges were employed to shed excess weight. As well as the customary liberal drilling of components, several riders removed the substantial rubber knee-grips fitted to each side of their petrol tanks and fixed them to the inside of the legs of their leathers at knee-height. So artificially low was the figure imposed in 1924 for the 175 cc race that it dissuaded people from entering and the organisers could only muster 7 riders. Charlie Dodson described the DOT that he rode as *'an enlarged bicycle'.*

Weight limits for machines fell out of favour, but at the 1958 TT the race organisers enforced an FIM rule that specified a minimum weight of 9 stones 6 lbs (60kg) for riders. Anyone beneath this weight had to make it up by adding weight to their bikes. The diminutive Gary Dickinson had to load his 125 MV Agusta with 23 lbs (10½ kg) of lead, and 6 other riders of 125cc machines also had to add weight, including top-runner Luigi Taveri who added 21 lbs. During the well recorded falling out between Yamaha teamsters Phil Read and Bill Ivy in the mid-1960s, Read threatened to submit a protest after one race on the basis that 'Little Bill' had not declared that his personal weight was below the official limit.

Team-mates at Yamaha when this photograph was taken in 1966, Phil Read (rightt) and Bill Ivy.

Today, pre-race measuring is part of the scrutineering process to ensure that wheels, tyres, streamlining, handlebars, ground-clearance and other dimensions meet the specifications contained in the race regulations, and minimum weight limits are back in force.

WHAT IF?

Racing is full of 'what ifs' and a few TT-related ones are worth looking at, just to see how the history of the event might have read.

The rider who finished second in the single-cylinder class of the 1907 TT and thus missed being the first name inscribed on the Tourist Trophy was Jack Marshall. Jack rode for the Triumph Company and suffered a time-consuming puncture during the race. With an unsaid 'what if', Triumph hinted in their post-TT advertising at the result that might have been in a puncture-free race, by claiming: *'The Triumph made faster time than any machine in the race after deducting time lost for repairing punctures'.*

TT-winner Jack Marshall (Triumph). This is what the well-dressed racer of 1908 wore; a flying helmet, corduroy breeches and riding boots. A spare drive-belt is coiled up on the carrier. The toolbox held tools to change valves, prone to break and tyre levers to repair the inevitable punctures caused by horsehoe nails.

In the 1921 Senior race, veteran Freddy Edmonds was denied a much sought-after victory. Starting as though he was going to win, he was 48 seconds in the lead at the end of the second lap, but then a petrol-pipe broke. He repaired it, got his head down, shattered the lap record as he pulled up through the field, but then suffered three engine seizures on the last lap. Losing all his hard-earned time, Freddy eventually finished 7th and so allowed TT history to be made by Howard Davies (AJS) who went on to win that same Senior (500cc) race on a Junior (350cc) machine.

Geoff Duke takes a careful line around Governor's Bridge on his four-cylinder Gilera as he nears the end of his 99.97 mph lap in the 1955 Senior TT.

History might have read differently if Freddy Edmonds had won in 1921, but although the 1925 Senior TT gave another well-earned victory to Howard Davies, there was another 'what if' involved. On his own HRD product, a virtually new machine built largely to his own design, Davies beat all the established makes of the day in 1925. However, HRD employee Albert Clarke noticed whilst the bike was being measured after the race that the bolt retaining the rear brake plate was on the point of dropping out. What if it had done so?

In the early 1950s there was much speculation as to whether a 100 mph lap could be achieved at the TT. With the increases in performance and improvements in handling of the Italian four-cylinder MV Agusta and Gilera machines during the period it soon became a question of when, not if, the 'ton' barrier would be broken. Geoff Duke (Gilera) threatened it in practice in 1955 and on race-day his many fans were delighted to hear that he had circulated in 22 minutes 39 seconds, a time that was announced as giving him an average lap speed of 100 mph. Some 40 minutes later the time-keepers, who operated with hand-held watches, declared that 22:39 was actually 99.97 mph, not 100. It was an action for which they were roundly booed by spectators in the Grandstand, but it was also one wherein if the individual timekeeper had pressed his button a mere fraction of a second earlier than he did, TT history would read so very differently.

In what turned out to be an extremely expensive case of 'what if', Robert Dunlop sued his sponsor when he sustained serious injuries in a crash at Ballaugh in 1994 due to his rear-wheel disintegrating. The Court was asked to consider 'what if' Robert had not crashed, and judged that he would have gone on to a racing career at world championship level. Accordingly, the substantial damages that he was awarded had regard to what might have been.

There are countless other 'what ifs' in TT history, such as would Stanley Woods have continued his pre-war winning ways if he had returned to racing after the war. Would Barry Sheene have made a great TT rider if he had persevered with the event instead of jumping on the anti-TT bandwagon of the early 1970s. And to close, what if Joey Dunlop had been spared in Estonia and was still riding the TT - would he still be winning?

WHOOPS!

The first motoring event over closed roads on the Island was for cars in 1904 with motorcycles following in 1905. Those events were classed as eliminating trials from which teams were chosen to represent Britain in competition for the Gordon Bennett Cup (cars) and the International Cup (bikes). The Island's Lieutenant Governor of the time, Lord Raglan, was a keen motorist and was instrumental in getting Manx legislation changed to allow the closing of roads for competition and thus paving the way for the first motorcycle TT in 1907. Just prior to the 1908 TT his Lordship was driving his Daimler away from Glen Helen when, in the words of the local newspaper: *'accidentally on the wrong side of the road'*, he collided with a (non-racing) motorcyclist. No great damage was done to man or machine and, unsurprisingly, nothing more was heard of the matter.

*

One man who proved, in unwanted fashion, that the drum brakes of the early 1930s could be quite effective was winner of the 1931 Senior MGP, J. Malcolm Muir. Crossing the finishing line with 10 minutes to spare over the next man, he slammed his brakes on so hard that he took an embarrassing tumble in front of the crowded Grandstand.

*

By 1933 the TT races were run on tried and tested lines and the organisers were rarely found seriously wanting. However, during the Lightweight race of that year, the organisation did falter when it opened the roads to the public at Creg ny Baa before several competitors had been through on their last lap. Fortunately, no great harm was done, and the riders affected were given a credit for the additional time that it took them to get to the finish riding at reduced speed.

Premature celebrations by Norton personnel after Jimmy Guthrie was wrongly announced to have won the 1935 Senior TT.

*

The close battle for victory between Stanley Woods (Moto Guzzi) and Jimmy Guthrie (Norton) in the 1935 Senior TT is told elsewhere in this book. Suffice to say here that Jimmy started 14½ minutes ahead of Stanley on the road and, going into the last lap, had a good lead on corrected time. When Jimmy finished his race there were many people who assumed that he had won, including the BBC commentator who announced his assumption to the world. Coming from such a usually reliable source, people naturally believed him, including photographers and even members of the race organisation. Jimmy was lined up to be treated as the winner, handshakes and congratulations were exchanged, photographs were taken and interviews carried out. It was only some 14 minutes and 26 seconds later when Stanley Woods and the Moto Guzzi flashed over the finishing line, that the time-keepers conveyed the embarrassing fact that it was Stanley who was in first place, having beaten Jimmy by four seconds over a race distance of 264 miles.

*

A similar situation occurred sixty years later in the Ultra-Lightweight race at the 1995 TT. Mick Lofthouse went into the last lap looking the likely winner and was still leading at Ramsey. So, when he arrived at the finish some people assumed that the race victory was his. Unfortunately for Mick, a storming last lap by Mark Baldwin (in which he broke the lap record on a rented Honda), saw him snatch victory by 0.6 of a second.

*

Jim Redman made his debut at the 1958 TT and went on to take many wins. But the man from Rhodesia learnt in his first year that the bottom of Bray Hill was not the place to check your rev counter reading when, momentarily taking his eyes off the road to do so, he looked up to find himself on a brief but spectacular two-wheeled excursion along the pavement.

*

It is not unknown for riders to strike machine trouble in a race, such as a loose exhaust or oil leak, and be unaware of the problem even though it may well have been noticed by course-side marshals. It is at such times that the organisers employ the black flag procedure. At selected points the marshals are equipped with a blackboard on which, upon receipt of telephoned instructions from Race Control, they chalk the rider's number. As he approaches, the blackboard is displayed and the black flag (with orange centre) is shown to attract his attention and indicate that he must stop. Black-flagging is invariably done at a point where a Travelling Marshal is stationed and it is he who carries out the machine inspection and determines whether a rider can continue or whether he must retire. Equipped with a stopwatch, he also records the time that the rider is actually stationary. In the 1979 Senior TT young hot-shot Steve Ward, winner of the 1978 Junior MGP, was black-flagged at Ramsey but, after inspection, no problem was found and he was allowed to continue the race. The business of slowing, stopping and accelerating away again had obviously cost him time and the timekeepers carried out their standard practice of crediting him with the time they estimated he had lost (backed up by the Travelling Marshal's stopwatch figures). Then a problem arose, for after his time credit was taken into account Steve was shown as having broken the lap record. A hasty adjustment was made to his time credit and Steve eventually finished in a fine fourth place.

*

In another black-flagging incident a Travelling Marshal who was new to the job carried out the instructions he had received from Race Control to stop number 14. This he duly did, only to realise after he had stopped the rider that he had no idea of why he had done so. Race Control had not told him and he had not asked them.

*

The TT is always happy to show aspects of its long tradition and, as part of their 75th anniversary celebrations, Moto-Guzzi were represented in the TT Classic Parade of 1996 by sixteen of their former race machines. The Parade was headed by an original version of one of the fabulous V-eight bikes (ridden by original rider Bill Lomas) and a replica V-eight ridden by its builder Giuseppe Todero. Veteran Bill rode the full lap whilst young Giuseppe threw his highly-expensive machine down the road at Braddan Bridge less than two miles from the Start. Fortunately, it was only the bike's fairing and Giuseppe's pride that were damaged.

*

Travelling Marshals are always held in high regard for their ability to ride the TT Course in close company with the fastest racers, but Dick Cassidy, who took over as Chief Travelling Marshal from the retiring Des Evans in 2003, managed to demonstrate how things should not be done when he dropped his 'M'-plated Honda at Braddan Bridge early in practice during his first year in charge. Whoops!

'WORKS' RIDERS

Most riders start their racing careers on the bottom rung of the ladder. Putting every penny of their hard-earned cash into the sport, frequently getting into debt with hire-purchase, making do with well used and sometimes abused race bikes, working every night of the week to prepare for the next race; that is the normal route into racing. But from the outset of their racing careers, almost all dream of going on to achieve success that will see them being snapped up by a factory team, paid huge retainers and bonuses, travel the world living in luxury hotels, and never again get their hands dirty - they will just turn up and ride. That dream becomes reality for relatively few, but they are the ones who truly bear the elusive title of 'works' riders.

As with most things there are varying degrees of 'works' support. At the first TT of 1907 a surprising 20 of the 27 entries were made in the name of motorcycle manufacturers or firms in the motorcycle trade, giving only 7 private entrants. It is unlikely that many of those factory and trade-supported riders received much in the way of hard cash for their riding efforts, the level of help probably being limited to the provision of a machine to ride and, perhaps, some assistance with expenses; but it was a sign of the keen interest in racing displayed by manufacturers of the time. This was the manner in which racing and rider support developed until the mid-1920s when teams like Norton realised that to ensure victory they had to have the best machines and that those machines needed to be purpose-designed for racing - tuned roadsters were no longer good enough. It took time for Norton to improve their race machinery with new designs, but when they did, they made doubly sure of TT success by also employing the very best riders. It was an expensive business, but one that resulted in them dominating the Senior and Junior TT races for much of the 1930s, and the riders they appointed to their 'works' teams, like Stanley Woods, Jimmy Guthrie and Freddie Frith, shared the world-wide publicity that came with Norton race victories. They were real 'works' riders, staying in the Island's best hotels, turning out to practice on ready-prepared machines, handing them back to the Norton mechanics after practice, and spending the rest of the time playing golf and socialising. By contrast, the mid 1930s also saw small factories like Vincent HRD making 'works' entries with good riders like Jack Williams and Arthur Tyler who, in return for basic expenses and use of a machine, returned to the team's garage after practice and helped to work on their race bikes ready for the next session. Arthur Tyler visited the Island for veteran car rallies many years after his riding career was over and recalled that he saw far more of it when participating in cars than he ever did when racing motorcycles.

Rider expectations were rather less in the 1950s than they are today. Geoff Duke was double World Champion at the end of 1951 and here he is taking delivery of his race transport set-up for 1952.

Manufacturer support for the TT continued in the post-war period, although the early 1950s saw the race fortunes of Norton and Velocette fading and those of Italian firms like MV Agusta and Gilera start to rise. This resulted in former Norton riders like John Surtees and Geoff Duke entering into 'works' contracts with MV and Gilera for considerably higher retainers than the British company paid. John moved on to racing cars at the beginning of the 1960s, just at the time that the Japanese factories entered racing with open cheque-books and provided even more substantial earnings for many new 'works' riders.

Most race teams of the time had an acknowledged team leader and he would often be asked to nominate new or replacement members to race with him. John Surtees did it with MV (bringing in John Hartle), Phil Read with Yamaha (bringing in Bill Ivy) and Jim Redman with Honda (bringing in several others). It was a tricky job, for whilst the team leader would be expected to make the best choice on behalf of the company, he would also be trying to pick the rider that best suited (and protected) his own position in the team. He would want someone who could ride to team orders and who would not outshine him on and off the track. John Surtee's approach in respect of bringing John Hartle into the MV Agusta team was an interesting one. Rating the other John highly as a rider, Surtees felt that there was a danger that Hartle might be snapped up by Gilera and, as Surtees regarded the Gilera as a better bike than the MV, he decided that it would be prudent to get Hartle into the MV team where he would ride to orders, rather than have him riding in opposition for Gilera.

John Hartle provided just the right level of support as number two rider in the MV team, for when he finished in a race that included Surtees he finished second, but he was unlucky to suffer a number of retirements at the TT, one of which saw his MV consumed by flames when leaking petrol ignited as he left Governor's Bridge. He was also usefully on hand to take victory for MV in the 1960 Junior, when Surtees retired with mechanical problems. John did later race Gileras when they made a TT comeback in 1963, but he was up against the formidable Mike Hailwood riding the MV and, again, had to settle for two second places. At the 1967 TT he took victory on a Triumph in the Production 750 class, but in 1968 he had two heavy crashes out on the Course. John was a man with a sense of humour and when someone said that he had chosen to fall-off in two out of the way places, he responded: *'For only £15 start money I wasn't going to do it in front of the Grandstand'.* Tragically, he was killed whilst racing at Scarborough, later the same year.

John Hartle riding a Triumph to victory in the 750cc Production class at the 1967 TT.

To non-works riders, those in receipt of full factory support would seem to have raced with somewhat unfair advantage, for not only were 'works' riders chosen from amongst those with the greatest talent, but they were then presented with the fastest and best handling machinery to ride - no wonder they won. And win they had to (unless riding to team orders) for there were always plenty of other young hopefuls ready to step into their shoes.

The Honda 'works' team at the 1966 TT with riders in T-shirts and mechanics in overalls. Riders are (from left) Jim Redman, Mike Hailwood, Stuart Graham, Luigi Taveri and Ralph Bryans.

A proper 'works' contract with Honda was as high up the racing ladder as a rider could get in the 1990s, yet the autobiographies of men like Steve Hislop and Phillip McCallen who signed to ride for that top Japanese company reveal that they were not totally satisfied that Honda's commitment to the TT quite matched theirs as riders. The suggestion comes through that Honda did enough to win, but no more. Certainly there were times when riders claimed that they did not have the latest forks, brake assemblies, etc, (although there were no indications that anyone else in the race had anything better). Jim Moodie had on/off relationships with Honda but he claims that a fortnight after riding Honda's best TT bike on the Island in 1999, he rode a 24 hour endurance race for them on one that had 45 bhp more than his TT machine. That seemed a strange way for Honda to contest the power and speed-hungry Mountain Course but, after 40 years experience of Island racing, they probably knew what they had to do to win - and win they continued to do through the 1990s.

Whilst Joey Dunlop was a 'works' rider for Honda for most of his TT career, there were several unusual aspects to their arrangement. Long-time Honda boss Bob MacMillan is on record as saying that Joey was rarely under a written contract to Honda, everything being done on the basis of a handshake and gentlemen's agreement. In addition, although the 'works' Hondas came race-prepared from their workshops, Joey was allowed to take his bikes away and do some work on them himself - a most unusual concession. Racing Hondas in most solo classes at the TT was another area in which Joey got his own way, for there were many years when the company would have preferred him to limit his Island racing to the Formula 1, Senior and Junior (600) races. But Joey was also determined to race 125s and 250s and if Honda did not supply him with a bike then he rode his own (or privately sponsored) bikes. As Honda well knew, this added pressure to Joey at the TT, and there were occasions when the limited amount of practice time available made it difficult for him to get both his 'works' and 'private' machines up to full race trim.

The level of manufacturer commitment to all forms of motorcycle racing tends to go in cycles, being influenced mostly by economic factors. These fluctuations in support sometimes leave spectators unclear who a rider is actually racing for. The present trend at the TT is for the makers to hand their 'works' machines to others to run on their behalf, so, instead of victory in the early 2000s going to Yamaha, Suzuki and Triumph, they went to V & M Yamaha, TAS Suzuki and V & M Triumph, with the riders of those 'works' bikes being contracted to the team rather than the manufacturer. But, whoever they are contracted to, the riders of those pseudo-works bikes still aim to match the long-established rewards of genuine works riders, seeking generous retainers and bonuses, the best hotels, plenty of time for socialising and little need to get their hands dirty.

In support of those lucky few are the lesser riders - essential to any race meeting - plus the army of officials, marshals, sponsors and spectators, who, with the backing of the Manx authorities, provide the combined effort, enthusiasm, and finance required to run the century-old Isle of Man Tourist Trophy races, and thus continue to generate tales of interest from 'The Road Racing Capital of the World'.

Joey Dunlop enjoyed support as a 'works' Honda rider for many years.

Index